How Madness Shaped History

An Eccentric Array of Maniacal Rulers, Raving Narcissists, and Psychotic Visionaries

Christopher J. Ferguson

Prometheus Books
Guilford, Connecticut

 Prometheus Books

An imprint of The Rowman & Littlefield Publishing Group, Inc.
4501 Forbes Blvd., Ste. 200
Lanham, MD 20706
www.rowman.com

Distributed by NATIONAL BOOK NETWORK

British Library Cataloguing in Publication Information available

Library of Congress Control Number: 2019955276
ISBN 978163388574 (cloth)
ISBN 9781633885752 (ebook)

♾™ The paper used in this publication meets the minimum requirements of
American National Standard for Information Sciences—Permanence of Paper
for Printed Library Materials, ANSI/NISO Z39.48-1992.

To my dad,
Edwin Stuart Ferguson,
who is, himself, now part of history.

CONTENTS

INTRODUCTION: MAD AS A HATTER

S ometimes it takes only one mad hatter to change the course of history. Undoubtedly societies are sometimes riven by invaders or lain low by droughts, famines, and plagues beyond their control. But occasionally there are times when the fate of societies teeters at the crossroads between victory and ruin, glory and shame. Into these breaches a crucial individual can step, guiding society down the road to grandeur or decay. Societies hope for an individual with a firm but steady hand to steer their people through the occasional rapids. Sometimes instead they get madness: individuals with severe cognitive or mental problems or limitations.

Under more mundane circumstances, these souls might be pitied and cared for in therapy or institutions, but when thrust into these critical times they become the agents of disaster. What if, during 1860, the United States had elected not Abraham Lincoln, who himself suffered from major depressive disorder,[1] but rather the ineffectual Franklin Pierce, who some scholars claim was debilitated by depression and anxiety after witnessing his eleven-year-old son being crushed to death by a train? If Jesus of Nazareth or Muhammad ibn Abdullah were born in modern society, would they be treated as religious visionaries or instead forced to take antipsychotic medications? The right or wrong person at a particular period in history can have considerable influence on the course of events. And their mental well-being, of course, can guide their path.

In modern Western society, mental illness—any mental illness—is commonly (and unfortunately) viewed as a liability. In 1972 Senator

Thomas Eagleton was replaced as a Democratic vice presidential nominee after his considerable mental health problems were publicly revealed.[2] Granted, this may or may not have been a reasonable move. After all, a central premise of this book is that the mental status of a leader *can* have a major effect on the society he or she leads. Having the power of nuclear weapons at the fingertips of a suicidal or psychotic individual may not be entirely wise (just look at North Korea). Nonetheless, stigma and perceptions about mental illness tend to wax and wane and change over time. Consider, however, that one study of U.S. presidents published by psychiatrists in 2006 concluded that almost half of U.S. presidents have experienced mental health problems, with issues such as depression, anxiety, and substance abuse being most common.[3] The authors further concluded that these problems were present during term in office for about a quarter of presidents, most often impairing their performance. That might explain some things.

Then again, madness does not always impair a political leader. Alexander III of Macedon, better known to history as Alexander the Great, took a second-rate power on the fringes of the Hellenic world and built one of the mightiest empires of all time.[4] Undoubtedly Alexander changed the course of Western civilization, and his influence may have been greater still had he not died unexpectedly at the age of thirty-two, perhaps the result of either poisoning or illness exacerbated by his chronic heavy drinking. Undeniably, Alexander was a man of considerable tactical talents. Yet it is worth considering the degree to which the peculiarities of his mental condition might have propelled him to become both the man of the hour as well as drawn him irreversibly toward his untimely death.

Alexander is a remarkable case example of how extreme psychological traits can lead to both great accomplishments and a great fall. Despite great intelligence and charisma, Alexander is unlikely to have been the sort of individual one would be confident about inviting over for a calm family holiday celebration. With his overweening and perhaps delusional narcissism, impulsive rages, and compulsive consumption of alcohol, he appears to have been a difficult man to get along with or to understand under the best of circumstances. After all, Alexander murdered his general and friend Cleitus at one gathering, as I discuss in detail later. It's only because of Alexander and his father Philip II that we hear much about Macedonia at all. Until the fourth century BCE, Macedonia was something of a backwater second-rate power in the Hellenic world. Its inhabitants spoke Greek and considered themselves part of the Greek world, although the main Greek city-states (Athens, Thebes, and such) were less enthused about the association.

Things changed during the mid-fourth century BCE. Alexander's father, Philip II of Macedonia, was the driving force of this change and the brains behind Alexander's future military operation. Philip modernized the Macedonian army and diligently organized Macedonia's political world. With Philip poised to unleash his professional army on Persia, Macedonia was on the cusp of world (or at least Western world) domination.

Then Philip was assassinated during his daughter's wedding. The reasons for this remain historically murky but it threw Macedonia into crisis. Without Philip, things quickly went pear-shaped. The Greek city-states, which naturally had been less than thrilled about being ruled by the upstart Macedonians, immediately rebelled. The Macedonian Empire, such as it was, required a firm hand to hold it together. Without Philip, that hand was lost.

Thus, there was a moment of crisis. A moment wherein a society could either rise to greatness or spiral into ignominy. In this case, the Macedonians had Alexander, whom they promptly declared king and who immediately smashed all resistance to Macedonian rule in Greece (with the exception of the Spartans, who the Macedonians apparently figured weren't worth the trouble).

It's interesting to consider the origins of Alexander's personality, both brilliant and troubled. We generally think of the personality as arising from an interaction of genetic predispositions shaped by developmental environment, the familiar nature/nurture interactions. Sometimes we overestimate the impact of nurture (genetic influences are quite powerful, it turns out), and we might also allow that humans have some degree of choice or free will in their actions. But it's worth taking a look at Alexander's upbringing.

Whether genetic or environmental, there's little doubt Alexander was the product of ambitious parents. Philip's designs on ruling the Aegean world are already clear. His mother, Olympias, was no slouch, either.

Most of history has been firmly patriarchal, limiting women, with rare exceptions, to secondary roles in governance. But it would be wrong to assume that women were necessarily passive supplicants; many worked furiously, even ruthlessly, to maneuver male allies, sons in particular, to positions of power. Olympias was intelligent and ambitious and dedicated to seeing Alexander's rise. She was also mysterious to the point that Plutarch claimed she sometimes slept with snakes, although this is likely an embellishment.[5] She was certainly willing to kill on Alexander's behalf, but I'll get to that in a bit.

Alexander lived in what we'd now call a broken home (it didn't help that Olympias was only one of Philip's wives.) Philip and Olympias were often in conflict. Alexander's relationship with his father appears to have been complex. However, Alexander certainly earned his father's confidence and played an important role in his father's military campaigns. One advantage Alexander had in his subsequent career was that his father had already done much to lay the groundwork for considerable success. Perhaps for this reason, Alexander seems to have felt the shadow of his father on him. This may be one factor that drove Alexander through his unbelievable conquests, which continued beyond all rational reason. Freud might have explained Alexander's entire rage through Persia as history's most consequential Oedipal complex.

Family conflict did come to a head toward the end of Philip's life. Philip married yet again, a woman named Cleopatra (not the famous one from Egypt), which potentially jeopardized Alexander's claim to the throne. Things got so heated that Olympias and Alexander actually went into exile following a quarrel during which Philip nearly murdered Alexander. Alexander and Philip soon reconciled, but rumors persisted that Olympias had a hand in Philip's assassination (though these are probably untrue).

Rocky familial relationships such as these were not uncommon among despotic monarchies. Males and sometimes females (the more famous Cleopatra of Egypt killed several siblings in her bid to remain pharaoh) competed bloodily for power. Individuals raised in such environments may have basked in luxury, but they also lived with constant fear and uncertainty that could be countered only by one's own ruthlessness. It's difficult to imagine such a thing now with our own twenty-first-century ideal of loving, extended families, but many early monarchical families must have been terrifying, vicious environments in which to be raised—hardly incubators for empathy or emotional stability.

Histories of Alexander's youth tend to focus on the positive: being tutored by Aristotle, enjoying the affection of Philip, or his physical and intellectual prowess. But it's not difficult to imagine that his early life must have been shrouded in a kind of stress and potential threat we'd now recognize as traumatizing. The combination of genetic inheritance of ruthless personality traits from both mother and father, the strained and competitive relationship with his father, and threats to his own legitimacy and life combined to create an overwhelming and burning ambition that cast its gaze far beyond merely uniting Greece under Macedonian rule.

So, with Greece secure, Alexander turned on the mighty Persian Empire to the East. At that time the Persian Empire was the regional superpower. The notion that the backward Macedonians would ride out of the north and conquer not only Athens but the entire Persian Empire and beyond was simply absurd. Historical analogies are often fraught with imperfections, but it would be something akin to imagining Canada suddenly going on the attack and conquering not only the United States but the entire western hemisphere.

Yet that is exactly what Alexander and his Macedonians did.

The Persians were surprised by the ferocity of the Macedonian invasion. The Persian king, Darius III, initially seemed to think Alexander's campaign a minor crisis, much to his error. Despite the Persians fielding massive armies funded by mountains of gold, Alexander cut through the Persians like a knife through butter. Again and again their king Darius III

Mosaic, circa 100 BCE, Alexander at the Battle of Issus. *Source: The Guardian.*

raised mighty armies, only to see them fall. Contemporary sources frame Darius in a bad light: a coward who flees from battle, but it's possible this might be unfair, history being told by the victors and such. Darius ultimately left behind his family including his wife, mother, and daughters while fleeing the Battle of Issus.[6] Alexander reportedly treated them cordially, eventually marrying one of the daughters (what a gentleman).

The downfall of Darius III can be contrasted with the rise of Alexander. The Persians obviously were having their own crisis moment wherein the decisions of a ruler could turn a society's fortunes. Instead of getting an Alexander, they got Darius III. Darius comes down through history as fairly even-handed and well-intentioned, as Middle Eastern despots go. In fact, that was half the problem: Darius seems to have been a rather average fellow. He wasn't mad. He even had some moxie, at one point forcing an assassin to drink poison meant for him.[7] During a time of stability and peace, he may have made for a perfectly effective bureaucrat. This was not that time, however. Darius ultimately was murdered by one of his own associates. Alexander—the precedent of folks murdering kings not lost on him—had Darius's killer executed and assumed the throne of Persia. He had Darius buried in the royal tombs in honor.

Alexander certainly was driven. Some have speculated that Alexander's drive, coupled with his rages and drinking, might have indicated bipolar disorder, but I don't find this likely. Individuals with bipolar disorder typically are impaired to such a degree that building an empire such as Alexander did would not be possible. Rather, I suspect Alexander had what we would now call narcissistic personality disorder (NPD) coupled with alcohol dependence. Individuals with NPD have a grandiose sense of their own self-importance. Such individuals are usually driven by fantasies of fabulous success or power and experience a sense of entitlement and need for admiration. They typically come across as arrogant and lacking empathy toward the concerns of others.

The origins of this, again, are both genetic and environmental. Both of his parents were supremely ambitious and neither come down through history as the most modest of individuals. As noted earlier, Alexander's upbringing was a mix of privilege and horror. It's little wonder if he emerged less than entirely stable.

Many of Alexander's actions speak to his narcissism. Upon assuming the throne of Persia, he adopted some of the local customs including proskynesis, or demonstrative subservience through laying prostrate before the king, or engaging in ritual kissing. He ultimately didn't insist on it for his Greek companions, who naturally scoffed at the practice. This prudence in backing off such worshipful gestures, at least among his Greek companions, was probably a bit of pragmatism rather than true empathy on Alexander's part (and such pragmatism also argues against bipolar disorder). Along his travels, he founded numerous cities in his own name (approximately seventy), including the magnificent city of Alexandria in Egypt. At least one city he named after his horse.

One of the incidents that most illuminates the darker side of Alexander's image was the murder of his friend Cleitus (or Clitus) in what amounted to an intoxicated pique of rage over exchanged insults. Apparently Cleitus, amid a drunken argument, publicly suggested that Alexander's victories were due to his father's careful planning. Cleitus's words were, to say the least, impolitic. Friends who were present during the altercation attempted to separate the quarreling men to no avail. Not one to take insults lightly, Alexander, after some scuffling, killed Cleitus with a spear.

Alexander's narcissism influenced not only his relations with peers and supplicants but also fueled his lust for war. Alexander's primary motivation for war seems to have been naked glory. By and large, he made war simply for the sake of doing so—and because he was very good at it. Granted, he took the same risks his soldiers did, but he pushed them on past Persia and into India with relatively little regard for the best interests of his troops. Only upon facing near mutiny did he relent and return to Persia.

To Macedonia's great fortune, Alexander combined his narcissism with incredible tactical talent and leadership. He was the right guy at the right time to meet a crisis moment for the Macedonians. After his unexpected death at thirty-two, likely due to infection exacerbated by his alcoholism and multiple war injuries, the Macedonian Empire fractured into multiple pieces (the Egyptian bit would end with the famous Cleopatra, who was ethnically Greek, not Egyptian). With no Alexander, there was no Macedonian/Persian Empire. It had been held together by the force of his will alone.

One interesting question to ponder is what Alexander might have achieved had he survived past thirty-two. Could he have held his own empire together? Alexander was an awesome vanquisher but could he have been a good *ruler*?

Alexander doesn't come across as a talented politician in the vein of Thomas Jefferson or Franklin Delano Roosevelt.[8] However, he had the sense to appoint gifted bureaucrats, and the force of his personality was enormous. Had he been able to settle down and rest on his accomplishments, it's possible he might have held his empire together, aside from some rebellions on the fringes. But nothing in his history suggests that Alexander was capable of peaceful rule. He was a man of war, impulsive and dedicated to action. Even his legend was that of a conqueror, and the awe that comes with victory can die fast without new achievements. A gambler, Alexander probably couldn't have stopped rolling the dice. And, as Sophocles claimed, only the dice of Zeus always fall luckily.

Much has been written about the circumstances that bring both societies and individuals to the point of great success or great failure, and despite numerous books that try to boil it down to one or two things, it's more complex than that. Sometimes a stable government such as the early Roman Empire or the United States or United Kingdom can survive the government of a succession of madmen and -women. In essence, the unsung work of the average bureaucrat keeps the society functioning so long as crisis is not imminent. At other times, the presence of a single person on the scene can make or break things. For a steady course, a society is best off with a George Washington, Mahatma Gandhi, or a Nelson Mandela, reasonably well-adjusted fellows who guided their societies through crisis moments with rational thought and compassion.

On the other hand, society can roll the dice on someone who has perhaps a few more mental health peccadilloes. It's gambling on a grand order. Sometimes you get Alexander the Great. Sometimes you get someone like Caligula, the Roman Emperor who launched an infamous reign of terror before being assassinated.

History Isn't All in the Past

Looking back at a figure such as Alexander, we can see the power that a single personality can wield over the world around him. But the distant historical past was a wild time before the rule of law, before we believed

in the intrinsic value of human life, when might made right. But human societies have evolved, developed codified laws, accepted that kings
and queens are not above them, and developed bureaucratic checks and
balances to prevent power from being centralized on any one mad personality. What can Alexander tell us about today? Have we entered a
post-madness world?

Some might argue that we live in a more reasonable time now, where
the rule of law is sacrosanct and governments have moved toward pragmatic democracies fueled by reasoned debate and enshrined human rights.
To be certain, the early part of the twentieth century is well known for
its madmen and -women, particularly the Hitlers, Stalins, Mussolinis, and
Maos who so brutally shaped our recent history. But wasn't even the Cold
War something of a more rational animal, wherein both sides managed to
step back from the brink? And hasn't the world since emerged into a kind
of Pax Americana and a new hopeful future?

Whether we can divide history so neatly into present and past is
unclear. In fairness, evidence does suggest that things have gotten better.
We tend to think that we're always living in the worst historical period
ever, with violence proliferating and society disintegrating. But a wealth of
evidence suggests that, quite to the contrary, we are living during the most
peaceful epoch in human history.[9] Men are less likely to be murdered,
women less likely to be raped, soldiers and civilians alike least likely to
die in war than at any period prior. Contrary to the common myth that
humans once existed in a utopian, egalitarian, primitive past, violence in
premodern societies appears to have been ubiquitous.[10] Is it possible that
human societies are evolving toward a state of relatively peaceful, rational
democracy?[11] Alexander undoubtedly wouldn't know what to make of the
comparative powerlessness of the U.S. presidency and might wonder why
the president didn't simply unleash the army on his detractors or impale
them with javelins (undoubtedly there have been some U.S. presidents
who would have seen his point).

Thus, by many metrics, whether violence, poverty, or education,[12] the
world has come a long way since the U.S. experiment with democracy
in the eighteenth century, with democratic reforms having swept across
much of the world. But these advances aren't guaranteed, and recent
reports suggest that human rights and democratic institutions may be
eroding in much of the world.[13] These reforms are founded on their own

fragile psychology, particular the belief that we have entered a social contract with government, exchanging taxes and some freedoms for the belief that government will act benevolently on our behalf.

Generally, the welfare of the average person around the world has improved over past decades. World hunger is dropping, poverty is dropping, access to health care is rising, as are living conditions and life expectancy.[14] At the same time, much of the world seems to have increased in distress. For example, in the United States at the time of this writing, suicide rates have increased in almost all age categories.[15] Contrary to the belief that adolescents are particularly prone to suicide, middle-aged adults appear to be experiencing some of the most significant rises in suicide. Why this is happening and its effects on society and history I'll discuss in chapter 10. But the impact of madness on the course of history didn't end with the twentieth century.

Even if the twentieth century has brought an unprecedented rise in good fortune and human rights to much of the world, it is important to realize that, even in modern times, much of the world labors under madness. This madness can develop in two main forms. First, the psychological perception of a social contract can erode then shatter when citizens or minority groups no longer believe a government is acting on their behalf. The result can be violence, riots, terrorism, or even civil war. We'll look at this form of madness in chapter 7.

However, in some parts of the world, the perception of a social contract never developed. Law still depends on the whims of the despot, and our perceptions of human rights have not yet fully taken hold. In such parts of the world we still see military strongmen (and occasionally women) whom even Alexander might have found extreme. A nontrivial portion of the world's population still struggles under egomaniacal dictators, paranoid religious faith leaders, or bloodthirsty military juntas. Consider the case of poor Uganda, which, from 1971 to 1978, was ruled by one of the most bizarre characters in modern history.

Madness in Uganda

Idi Amin rose through the British colonial army in Africa and then the military of Uganda once that country became independent of the United Kingdom. In 1971, Amin led a coup d'état against the president of

Uganda, Milton Obote. The reasons for the coup aren't entirely clear but have been suggested to be related to the possibility Obote was considering having Amin arrested, to the Ugandan military's perceived loss of privilege under a socialist system run by party bureaucrats rather than the army.[16]

Amin set himself up with dictatorial powers, which provided sweeping authority over the military. He instituted a program of torture and execution of political opponents, including supporters of Obote and minority ethnic groups. All told, his regime is believed to have killed between one hundred and three hundred thousand Ugandans.[17] His use of violence and military suppression against his own citizens has led modern historians to regard Amin's Uganda as a terrorist regime.[18]

As with Alexander, it can be illustrative to look at Amin's early life. His background appears to have been modest, raised in a country colonized by the United Kingdom and divided ethnically and religiously. Like Alexander, he had a mercurial relationship with his father who, at one point, rejected him as potentially illegitimate. (Whether father-son—or mother-daughter—conflicts are a common thread among

Amin, left, in 1966 with Israeli Prime Minister Levy Eshkol. *Source:* National Photo Collection of Israel.

megalomaniacal despots is a topic I return to in chapter 3.) Uganda, like Hellenistic Macedonia, emerged from its colonial period without the traditions of rule of law and humanitarian social contracts. Violence was power and ever threatening. For a man with ambition and lacking empathy, this was an environment in which to make a mark.

Amin adopted a grandiose style that crossed over to buffoonery. He loudly insulted world leaders and bestowed himself with titles, honors, and a doctorate degree. He expelled British Asians from Uganda in 1972, a move that damaged Uganda's economy.[19] He seems to have had a taste for exotic titles including "lord of all the beasts of the earth and fishes of the seas" and "conqueror of the British Empire in Africa in general and Uganda in particular." He also appears to have offered to become king of Scotland and lead the Celtic peoples in rebellion against the United Kingdom. Some reputed that he cannibalized some of the victims of his regime, although this claim appears to be largely apocryphal.

One of the most memorable moments of his reign was the July 1976 raid by the Israelis on the airport in the Ugandan city Entebbe.[20] An Air France jet had been hijacked by terrorists seeking the release of Palestinian and other militants from jails in exchange for the release of the hostages on the plane. Amin sided with the hijackers, perhaps hoping to lord it over Israel and put himself in the role of heroic negotiator. The hijackers threatened to kill the Israeli citizens on board the plane unless their demands were met.

The Israelis were having none of it and launched a daring raid, transporting commandos thousands of miles to Entebbe. Their commandos managed to kill the terrorists and free the majority of the hostages (several died during the raid), and they also killed Ugandan soldiers who tried to prevent their escape. A number of Ugandan jet planes also were destroyed to prevent interference with the Israeli escape.[21]

The Entebbe raid was a humiliation for Amin. He retaliated against innocents. Unfortunately, this included one hostage, Dora Bloch, who had been taken to a hospital for some medical issues. She reportedly was dragged from her bed and shot by Ugandan soldiers, possibly along with some Ugandan medical professionals who attempted to intervene on her behalf. He also retaliated against Kenyans living in Uganda (Kenya had supported Israel) and Entebbe airport workers, one of whom was killed by having nails driven through his skull.[22]

This episode highlights not only Amin's cruelty but also the fragility of his ego, typical of narcissists. What made him position himself as negotiator between the hijackers and Israelis, apparently oblivious to Israel's considerable reluctance to dialogue? Likely he saw himself as the "man of the hour" and the hijacking as an opportunity to boost his international esteem and to emerge a hero. Thinking himself smarter than either the hijackers or Israelis, he positioned himself to control the crisis. The Entebbe raid smashed that illusion and cast him as a fool. His megalomaniacal personality could not adjust to the failure and he could only lash out with senseless violence at the helpless innocents he could control. In his rage, Amin undoubtedly had to release his frustrations on *someone*, however unfair or cruel. Alexander killed Cleitus over a foolish argument. Amin killed dozens to salve his wounded self-perception. Fragile egos do not deal well with humiliating failure.

Like Alexander, Amin was motivated not just to rule a great country, but to make that rule *entirely about himself.* Alexander was clearly the more talented of the two, but are there hints in Amin's downfall about what might have come of Alexander had he survived early adulthood?

Amin eventually overreached by attempting to invade neighboring Tanzania. The Tanzanian army proved stronger, initiating an invasion of Uganda that saw the overthrow of Amin, who died in exile in 2003. During a historical period rife with bizarre, cruel dictators, Amin nonetheless stands out. Living in a free, humane democracy, it is difficult to imagine what life for the average Ugandan must have been like in Amin's shadow.

History's Rapid Turns

During the last decade or two, much has been written about macro-level processes, or large, environmental forces that have influenced the rise and fall of cultures. Excellent books such as *Why the West Rules—For Now* by Ian Morris[23] and *Guns, Germs and Steel* by Jared Diamond[24] are two examples. In differing ways each author argues that the rise and fall of cultures have had much more to do with physical geography than with culture or biological differences between human populations or the actions of specific individuals.[25] To be clear, neither Morris nor Diamond rule out the importance of individuals or even culture as they highlight the importance of location. Arguments in favor of the influence of physical geography on history are persuasive, and I believe Morris and Diamond are correct to point to these elements. But at certain crisis points, individuals may matter more than geography. For instance, particular geographical advantages may have led to the general dominance of "the West" in recent years, yet there's nothing definitive to say that the revolution of 1776 need inevitably have led to the birth of the United States, that Britain definitively would have survived the summer and fall of 1940, that western Europe would have prevailed in the Cold War, or, for that matter, that China would be a potential beneficiary of the financial crisis of 2008. Although geography certainly plays a role in these events, so do the influence of culture and individual decision makers. England owes its victory in 1940 as much to Churchill and the fortitude of the British people as to the English Channel.

A society is perhaps best off with a little caution in its crisis moments, playing it safe with a steady hand like George Washington. Imagine if the United States had gotten Alexander instead of Washington. Would Alexander have been content with thirteen measly colonies (not to mention a nonhereditary and temporary presidency rather than a kingship)? Those steady hands such as Washington, Gandhi, or Mandela are effective at righting the ship, uniting the people, reaching for a tangible and realistic goal, and easing a culture out of its crisis moment and into moderate stability.

Or a culture can roll big. It might get a Lincoln, whose depression may have been oddly inspirational. Or even an Alexander, whose megalomania led the culture into historical greatness far beyond its obvious value. But, as in gambling, when cultures roll big, they more often seem to get snake eyes. In 1776 the United States could have passed up Washington and rolled big. Perhaps the country would have gotten Alexander and gone on to conquer Canada and Mexico in a few short years, likely renaming itself the United Kingdom of Alexander along the way. But more likely it would have gotten a Nixon or a Caligula, and the entire enterprise of rebellion could have gone down in flames and ignominy. One need only look at a sister rebellion in France in 1789, which brought France first Robespierre and the "Terror" and then Napoleon, dictatorship, and defeat. That's rolling big. Madness can be touched with a hint of brilliance, but it is always fragile and the culture that embraces it takes a great risk.

This book is about those crisis moments and the cultures that rolled big. Not surprisingly, most of the moments I discuss track the declines, defeats, and disgraces of the cultures in question. The characters I examine all left indelible marks on the societies they touched, sometimes good, more often bad.

What Does It Mean for Us?

Although historical anecdotes and psychological profiles can be fun, this book is not about that alone. As I write this, my own country and many others seem to stand at a precipice of crises small and large. Who do we want to lead us? A strong but mad authoritarian or the steady but bland bureaucrat? How does the madness of the masses influence our choices? Does, for instance, the U.S. primary system put too much influence into the hands of the most extreme—indeed, outright crazy—voters? Are there ways to restore sanity to our political processes or are we lost in a chaos of unbridled emotion and hatred for the foreseeable future?

Perhaps our culture of humanism, the belief that each person has intrinsic value, will prevent the worst excesses of madness in contemporary times. It's easy to lose this perspective in a partisan world in which those with different beliefs are not just wrong, but bad, evil, and impure. What would life look like if we gave up these values and counted on the firm hand of the strongman or -woman to protect us? We need only look to history.

Much of our bloody history can be blamed on men. History has been patriarchal, with women typically forced into secondary roles. This sometimes leads to the perception that madness runs in the male line and that a matriarchal world would avoid the violence, madness, and "toxic masculinity"[26] of the patriarchal one. Evidence generally belies such a claim and one need only to scratch the surface to find plentiful examples of madness among women and men both. Consider the case of the Blood Countess.

The Blood Countess, Elizabeth Bathory (Erzsébet Báthory in her native Hungarian), was a Hungarian noblewoman during the late sixteenth century with an awful temper and an insatiable lust for sadistic sex. As the story goes, Elizabeth's interest in sadism turned to murder in response to her own concerns about aging. One day, while upbraiding a young servant girl, she raked the poor thing with her fingernails and got blood on her own skin. Rubbing the blood away, she found the

Portrait of Elizabeth Bathory.

skin underneath to be soft, supple, and younger looking. This led her to conclude that human blood is, in effect, a natural moisturizer. She was quite right, of course; granted, many other moisturizers are available for the young women of modern times.

Bathory was able to torture, mutilate, and kill girls for years because she herself was a noblewoman and her victims were members of the peasant class.[27] The lower classes in medieval and early Renaissance society often had less access to the rule of law, and the concept of humanism was not yet widespread. As such, authorities were slow to respond to multiple homicides Bathory perpetrated.

Details of her crimes were supplied by witnesses as well as several accomplices who were questioned under torture, their testimony obviously tainted by those circumstances. Even if some of her crimes were embellished, it seems clear that she was one of history's most prolific serial killers.[28] She seems to have been creative in her torture, sticking pins into her victims' lips, cutting them with scissors or other blades, forcing them to eat their own flesh, or cannibalizing them herself. She is said to have had some girls dragged through snow and splashed with water in frigid weather until they froze solid. Others she coated with honey and exposed to insects.[29] In addition to a whole host of physical and often sexual horrors unleashed on her female employees, she also used their blood to keep herself youthful. Exactly how she did so remains a matter of some controversy, and claims that she bathed in blood are likely a later embellishment of her story.[30] Some accounts suggest she might have constructed an apparatus to slowly bleed women placed within it. Images that portray her as bathing in a tub of blood are likely inaccurate, given the amount of blood required and inability to keep it from coagulating. However, she may have washed herself in the blood of her victims using a cloth or, perhaps, drank it. Although estimates are sketchy, she is thought to have killed six hundred young girls before finally being caught and imprisoned in her own manor.

How did Elizabeth become a sadistic killer of legend? Alexander and Idi Amin displayed some similarities, exhibiting what we'd today call narcissistic personality disorder. That's not to say that they were identical in psychological profile: Amin may have been crueler but less strategic than Alexander. Then again, the world around Amin's Uganda may have been more prepared to push back against a tinpot dictator than

17

Alexander's Macedonia. Elizabeth appears somewhat different from the two men, however. Today she'd likely be diagnosed with a variant of antisocial personality disorder known as sadistic personality disorder.[31] This condition is more or less what it sounds like: individuals who take intrinsic pleasure in causing harm to or suffering in others. In Elizabeth's case, this involved sexual sadism.

So what happened with Elizabeth to bring out this sexual sadism in her? Details about Elizabeth's early life are murky to say the least. As with many noble families, inbreeding was common, and this may have exacerbated negative traits. Elizabeth's parents came from two branches of the same Bathory family. Accounts suggest her relationship with her parents, and her mother in particular, was strained at best, and her family certainly married her off at an early age. Given the ubiquity of corporal punishment of both adults and children, Elizabeth would have witnessed harsh treatment of peasants on her family's estate. Thus we see a similar pattern of biological risk coupled with a harsh environment that lacks opportunity for the development of empathy. I look at this pattern in more depth in chapter 3.

The world for most people in the late 1500s was a cruel one. Most societies had not yet adopted the belief that human life necessarily had intrinsic value. Cruel punishments for even minor transgressions remained the norm. Coupled with a predisposition toward aggression, Elizabeth had few opportunities for developing empathy, particularly toward those of lesser status. To be sure, Elizabeth's actions were extreme even for her time, but they can be understood in the context of a historical period that did not place high value on kindness and compassion.

Elizabeth also shared with Alexander and Amin an estrangement from parents. Alexander, at the very least, had his mother Olympias and perhaps that bond staved off the worst excesses seen in Amin or Bathory. But there's something to be said for the importance of the parental bond in blunting the worst excesses of those who might be predisposed to violence. Elizabeth provides a clear example of the horrors that can result when a biological predisposition toward violence is combined with a harsh and chaotic environment in which close attachment bonds are not fostered.

Bathory was certainly mad (indeed, her exploits are credited as having influenced vampire mythology along with those of another mad Hungarian, Vlad Tepes), but her madness had little influence beyond the hundreds of unfortunate victims of her vanity and sexual sadism. So it tends to go for women who have been largely excluded from the corridors of power, with some notable exceptions, until modern times.

In the chapters that follow I introduce a host of lunatics, sadists, poor unfortunates, visionaries, psychotics, and the demented. These people ruled governments, shaped cultures, guided religions, and held the destiny of countless others in their hands. With a subtle twist of fate, they might have joined the legions of the mad in asylums, madhouses, or even burned at the stake. Instead they were given power and influence. Sometimes the societies and cultures that embraced them benefited from rolling the dice. More often, they suffered. Some of them are in power today or have already begun a trajectory to bring them to power in our immediate future. As such, they may influence our own lives in profound ways.

I hope you enjoy the stories of these people's lives, and perhaps learn from them as well. As they say, if we don't learn from history, we are doomed to repeat it. And that would be just plain mad.

MADNESS, MENTAL ILLNESS, AND INSANITY

On April 7, 1978, the partially decomposed remains of a twelve-year-old girl, Kimberly Leach, were found discarded at a state park in Florida. Two months earlier, Kimberly had been abducted from her middle school, lured away by an adult man with enough charm to temporarily ease her natural inclinations to distrust strangers. Forensic evidence suggested she had been sexually assaulted and beaten. Evidence from her remains as well as eyewitness accounts would tie the death of Kimberly to notorious serial murderer Ted Bundy who, through the mid-1970s, killed dozens of young, pretty women.[1]

Bundy is one of the most famous serial murderers because he combined sexual sadism with considerable intelligence and great charm. He also was a handsome man, making him a photogenic subject for the press. In everyday interactions with those around him, he came across as personable and trustworthy.[2] He used these skills to set women at ease, sometimes posing as a security guard or an injured person in need of assistance.[3] Bundy raped and tortured his victims, often returning to locations where he dumped them to have sex with their bodies, dress them up, or apply makeup and relive his fantasies. The exact number of victims of his predatory urges isn't clear, although he is suspected of killing more than thirty women in multiple states across the Northwest. His spree ended in a final panicky run for Florida, concluding with the death of Kimberly Leach.

Few would disagree that Bundy was a madman. But what does that mean? Did he have some form of mental illness or personality disorder?

Colloquially, people might conclude Bundy must be insane, but legally he was found to be well aware of what he had done.[4] Was Bundy born this way, shaped through early experiences, or both? Obviously, if we're to discuss madness, we need to be as clear as we can in delineating what madness means in relation to associated terms such as mental illness and insanity. And with that issue, an obvious madman such as Bundy can help us. First, though, let's look at how madness has been viewed throughout history.

Madness in Early History

Three terms are often used interchangeably among the general public: madness, mental illness, and insanity. Obviously, there is both overlap and differences among them. It wasn't always this way: through much of history, madness and mental illness were considered synonymous. Even during the early twentieth century, the chronically mentally ill were looked upon as "degenerates" and "scum," the equivalent of criminals and scoundrels.[5] These unfortunates were exposed to all manner of torture and sham treatments. In some cases, these unfortunates desperately resisted their fates, in others, the mentally ill were trustingly led into damaging therapies by their psychiatrists and neurologists.

Throughout much of history, mental illness was treated with remarkable cruelty. To many early societies, mental illness was synonymous with demonic possession or communication with gods or spirits. Presumably those mentally ill who could still communicate effectively might be considered prophets or religious leaders. But those who became more confused and incomprehensible might be thought of as tortured by devils or evil spirits.

One possible outcome for the mentally ill in early cultures was a process called trepanning or trephination. This involved primitive surgery to remove pieces of the skull, undoubtedly under the influence of limited or no anesthesia. Such procedures were used for head injuries, epilepsy, as well as for mental illness.[6] The working theory at the time was that the procedure provided some incentive for evil spirits to leave the body.[7] Amazingly, some people actually survived trephining, as evidenced by regrown bone around the cut-away skull. Whether this procedure *worked* in the modern sense to relieve mental illness is doubtful. However, it may have had similar effects as the more modern lobotomy, which tended to

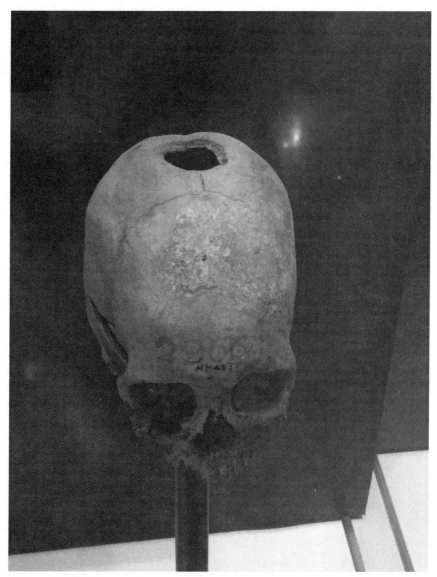

Skull showing trephination with some bone regrowth, National Museum of Health and Medicine. *Photo:* Author.

result in more compliant, less aggressive mentally ill individuals and may have been considered a relative success. Likewise, one presumes that individuals learned to be more circumspect about sharing their delusions with others after a hole was pounded through their skulls.

Equating mental illness with sorcery and evil spirts changed largely due to the efforts of the Greek physical Hippocrates, whose basic beliefs still influence the modern medical approach to mental illness.[8] Put simply, Hippocrates viewed mental illness as largely equivalent to physical illness, generally involving an imbalance of four fluids: blood, phlegm, yellow bile, and black bile.[9] This general view of mental illness as a result of a chemical imbalance should be familiar in concept to modern viewers. Hippocrates brought experimentation to medicine and mental illness and sought effective treatments. He also looked critically at overused harsh physical "cures" such as bleeding and purging.[10] This humane approach to mental illness survived through to the mid-200s ACE, eventually brought low by first Roman, then Christian, superstitious leanings.

Indeed, the massive interruption of the Hippocratic approach to medicine represents a considerable historical *what if.* What if Hippocratic medicine had been allowed to progress uninterrupted through to the present day?[11] Would modern medicine be even more advanced than how we experience it currently?

In the middle ages, physicians (such as they were, most surgery in those days was done by barbers)[12] were aware that mental illness was generally caused by physical disease. Attribution of mental illness to demonic possession, contrary to popular movies, was uncommon, although it did sometimes happen.[13] The publication *Malleus Maleficarum,*[14] or "Hammer of Witches," by two monks in 1487 likely did not help the matter, as it tended to identify symptoms of mental illness (not to mention being a woman) with evil and possession.[15] Some of the mentally ill underwent torture and were burned at the stake, but one supposes the thinking of the day assumed a few eggs must be broken to make an omelet. *Malleus Maleficarum,* it should be noted, is still available for purchase through many online retailers today.[16] Eventually, treatment moved into the age of confinement, wherein the mentally ill were warehoused in dank, disease-ridden asylums for which life expectancy was often rather short.[17] Out of sight, out of mind.

Mental Illness in Recent History

Only in the late eighteenth and early nineteenth centuries did treatment of the mentally ill take a truly humane turn since the days of Hippocrates.

Reformers such as Philippe Pinel, William Tuke, Benjamin Rush, and Dorothea Dix argued that the mentally ill should be treated as human beings, given humane treatments, and shielded from torturous interventions that did more harm than good.[18] Such gentle treatments may have worked to some degree in restoring at least a fair proportion of the mentally ill to relative functioning. Not much money to be made in that, though, so early modern psychiatry gradually fell back to crowded hospitals and vicious, painful interventions that didn't help.[19]

Mental patients, many only newly ill or with conditions they may have recovered from with time, experienced permanent brain damage due to the psychiatric interventions of modern medicine during the late nineteenth and early twentieth centuries. The brains of some were starved through insulin-induced comas or burned via electroshock. Toward the end of this period, many physicians simply carved away at their patients' brains with ice pick–like tools inserted into the eye socket, past the eyeball, then hammered into the brain. Egas Moniz, the pioneer of these surgical lobotomies of the frontal lobes of the brain, won a Nobel Prize in medicine for this brutal innovation in 1949.

Such horrid procedures proliferated during the twentieth century. The medical profession often seemed unconcerned with whether interventions *benefited* patients but rather whether the treatments rendered patients more docile, childlike, and easier to manage.[20] In a societal atmosphere of indifference or repugnance toward the mentally ill, few people seemed interested in speaking out for these unfortunates. Thousands of people were left incontinent, childlike, unable to make plans or form coherent memories, devoid of passion, stripped of intelligence—in a way, severed from their souls—all in order to make them less of an inconvenience for the rest of society. To say that the mentally ill have labored under enormous stigma doesn't even begin to touch the surface of the issue.

What is fascinating is the role of professional organizations such as the American Psychiatric Association and American Medical Association in promoting such barbaric practices. Such organizations often have been highly resistant to evidence suggesting that the mentally ill were being harmed.[21] As one lesson from this, we must understand that such professional guilds are not objective purveyors of scientific facts but exist to represent and market their professions. My own organization, the American Psychological Association (APA), is little different. Recently, the APA released clinical guidelines for post-traumatic stress disorder (PTSD) highlighting the value of the trendy cognitive behavioral therapy (CBT) over other treatments.[22] Ironically, at about the same time, several meta-analyses were published indicating that CBT actually offered few benefits over other treatments and may have had worse dropout rates in treating PTSD. Did this lead the APA to reconsider its clinical guidelines highlighting CBT?[23] Nope. Given that an internal investigation of the APA once found the organization to be complicit in changing its ethical guidelines to allow psychologists to be involved in the harsh interrogations of detainees in government detention sites,[24] a cynical perspective toward the APA and other professional guilds appears warranted.

What Is Madness After All?

Certainly, it is not the point of this book to increase the stigma many people feel toward the mentally ill. But what exactly is mental illness, and how does it relate to madness? Currently, in the United States, mental illness is defined by the American Psychiatric Association's *Diagnostic and Statistical Manual (DSM)*. This book lists everything from simple phobias of dogs and airplanes, through caffeine addiction, all the way through chronic mental illnesses such as schizophrenia.

At this point it is worth mentioning that mental illness is not a static concept the way that many medical illnesses are. Influenza is not defined differently whether one comes from the United States or Libya or China. By contrast, our concepts of mental illness are, at least in part, culturally defined. Diagnosis of mental illness has also been historically unreliable, with clinicians' judgments prone to subjectivity, mistakes, and over-pathologizing. Perhaps the most famous illustration of this was the experiment by psychology professor David Rosenhan. Rosenhan and several students, all free of mental illness, each went to psychiatric hospitals claiming to hear some vague voices no one else could hear but without other symptoms. All were admitted and prescribed neuroleptic medications (which they did not take). They were retained in the hospitals despite no longer complaining about their symptoms nor acting oddly once admitted. Only the actual patients in the wards correctly identified them as imposters.[25] This experiment highlights the prejudices of many psychiatric staff when interpreting behaviors as benign or pathological and accepting signs of improvement slowly. Although this study was published in 1973, arguably little has changed in the care of the mentally ill since this time.[26]

It has become common in recent decades to equate mental illnesses directly with medical illnesses (as did Hippocrates twenty-five hundred years ago) in a well-meaning attempt to reduce the stigma of mental illness. These messages may be popular because they appear to absolve the sufferers of mental illnesses from blame for their condition, though even many medical illnesses such as lung cancer or type II diabetes are often the product of choices we make. Barring mutations, the same microorganisms that caused syphilis or smallpox or cholera four centuries ago are the same critters that cause them today. Similarly, a cardiac arrest or a glioblastoma today is the same as it was ten—or ten thousand—years ago. Although nothing is universal, most medical illnesses have a factual basis in reality that is not influenced by history or culture or opinion. Either you have a brain tumor or you don't—and you still have a brain tumor whether you are in the United States, or in Japan, or on the moon (in which case, granted, a brain tumor may not be your most pressing worry).

Regarding the social construction of mental illness, consider the issue of homosexuality, which remained a diagnosable mental illness in the *DSM* in one form or another until 1987. Although homosexual individuals do sometimes experience psychological distress, we now are aware that this has much more to do with societal prejudice and lack of acceptance (including being labeled mentally ill) than with simply being homosexual.[27]

More recently the World Health Organization's (WHO) decision to include "gaming disorder" in its *International Classification of Diseases* (*ICD*) targeting video game players has provoked controversy. Critics contend that the research literature does not support that games are uniquely addictive, and if behavioral overuse is a concern, why not have a catchall category for all the behaviors people sometimes overdo: food, sex, exercise, religion, work—there are even research papers on dance addiction![28] The WHO largely responded to an ongoing moral panic regarding video games by creating a dubious diagnosis that actual data don't support. These concerns, for instance, led the media and technology divisions of the American Psychological Association and Psychological Society of Ireland to jointly author a public policy statement condemning the WHO diagnosis.[29] Other scholars have noted that the WHO acknowledged that political pressure "primarily from Asian Countries" was one factor in the decision to create the gaming disorder diagnosis.[30]

This isn't to say mental illness is entirely a social construction, but rather that its boundaries are often defined as much by societal beliefs and prejudices (particularly among old people), money, politics, and ideology as it is by good science. And over time, there's arguably a certain "mission creep" with the concept of mental illness in manuals such as the *DSM*, so that it's become easier and easier to be defined as "mentally ill" in recent decades. For instance, experiencing intense depression for more than two weeks—even after the death of a cherished loved one—is technically diagnosable in the latest edition of the *DSM*.[31]

So, to be clear, mental illness is a broad term and by no means are most mentally ill individuals "mad" in the way that term is used in this book. But efforts to reduce stigma can also miss the mark. For instance, I often hear advocates for the mentally ill claim that the mentally ill are no more likely—or even are less likely—than the average person to engage in violent behavior. Although such statements are obviously well meaning, they conflict with the wealth of psychological data that find mental illnesses such as schizophrenia, depression, and attention deficit hyperactivity disorder increase the risk of violent behavior.[32] In my own work with youth, I find that the strongest risk factors for violent and aggressive behavior have nothing to do with societal bogeymen like violent video games, but rather relate to a combination of depression and antisocial personality traits.[33] To be fair, some scholars such as Robert Whitaker in his book *Mad in America* suggest that for psychosis, violence risk may be increased by the brain incapacitation brought on by neuroleptic medications rather than by the psychosis itself. Either way, suggesting there is no increased risk at all is mistaken, however well intentioned.

Back to Mr. Bundy

So did Ted Bundy have a mental illness? In the sense that Bundy might have had a psychosis that rendered him unable to understand the wrongness of his compulsive actions, which robbed him of responsibility and free will, the answer is clearly no. Bundy was a cruel sexual sadist who lacked empathy for his victims and enjoyed violent rapes and murders and even sex with their corpses.[34] He was rational and his crimes premeditated. This can be seen even in the failed kidnapping of Carol DaRonch, the crime that effectively ended the most productive element of his crime spree. Dressed as a security guard, Bundy approached DaRonch in a shopping mall parking lot, claiming her car had been broken into and offering to take her to the police station for safety and to file a complaint. When she noticed he was not driving on the correct road to the station, a struggle ensued. Bundy attempted to handcuff DaRonch. Fortunately for DaRonch, Bundy accidently put both handcuff cuffs on the same wrist and she was able to flee the car. Later the same day, a high school student was kidnapped not far away. A handcuff key matching the cuffs on DaRonch's wrist was found at that scene. The student, Debra Jean Kent, was never found.

Bundy was purposeful and rational but lacked empathy or a sense of guilt for his actions. This condition, also accompanied by hedonistic or thrill-seeking behavior and difficulty learning from punishment, is typically diagnosed as antisocial personality disorder. The terms psychopathy and sociopathy are identical in terms of behavior, and henceforth I use the term "psychopathy" for ease.[35]

To say Bundy was a psychopath is undoubtedly true but still somewhat unsatisfying. First, not all psychopaths engage in such horrible sprees of violence. In fact, many psychopaths do not commit substantial crimes at all but find fairly productive roles in society in which lack of conscience is actually an asset (politics, business, or the law, for instance. One might also cast a suspicious eye at psychology professors). Further, psychopathy as an explanation is something of a tautology or circular logic. So we might ask, "Why did Bundy commit so many horrible murders?" To which the answer is, of course, he was a psychopath. But one might then reasonably ask, "How do you know Bundy was a psychopath?" To which the answer would be: well, he committed all those horrible murders. Obviously, we need to look a bit deeper.

One thing we know is that psychopathy and antisocial behavior have significant biological and genetic roots. This understanding often has been met with significant resistance. Perhaps the most notable is the 1986 Seville Statement on Violence, signed by twenty leading scholars of the time and endorsed by groups such as UNESCO and the American Psychological Association.[36] This position eschewed the belief that genetics or evolution contributed to human propensities toward violence.[37] This statement is now widely understood to be rubbish.[38] Genetics appear to account for about 50 percent of the variance in aggression, violence, and antisocial behavior.[39] To some extent, people like Bundy are indeed born bad.

But that doesn't leave out the potential for some environmental influences. Indeed, genes and environment interact with each other in complex and nuanced ways.[40] For instance, harsh childhood environment appears to exacerbate the inclinations of some who are predisposed toward psychopathy. Therefore, many individuals can experience remarkable abuse yet live full and productive prosocial lives, whereas others appear to live out a cyclical pattern of family violence. Genetic predisposition and environmental stress combine to produce antisocial outcomes.

Did Bundy experience the kind of harsh upbringing we might expect to interact negatively with a predisposition to violence? What we know about Bundy's childhood is, unfortunately, based mainly on his own interviews following his arrest. He was less than reliable, often contradicting himself. Some of these accounts note that he was initially raised to believe his unwed mother was in fact his sister (exactly when he found out the truth is unclear). Some accounts suggest his maternal grandfather may have been abusive, and his upbringing appears to have been chaotic at the very least.[41] However, none of this is terribly striking in the sense that literally hundreds of millions of people worldwide grow up with chaotic, potentially abusive families without becoming sadistic sex murderers. Even the bizarre bit about his mother pretending to be his sister is something he shares with musician Eric Clapton.[42] So perhaps being raised to believe one's mother is one's sister leads either to becoming a serial murderer or to the blues.

What about pornography? Prior to his execution, Bundy suggested that his fascination with pornography may have led to his interest in sexualized violence. Bundy had a habit of blaming anyone and anything for his actions other than himself, so why people might think he was speaking God's truth when discussing porn is anyone's guess. Nonetheless, his claims were catnip for anti-porn crusaders, quite common in the 1980s. The federal government, under the Meese Commission, had proclaimed pornography a leading cause of sexual violence, although scholars quickly pounced on methodological flaws and conflicts of interest among commission members in that analysis.[43]

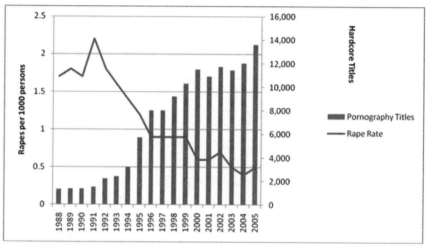

Pornography consumption and rape rates in the United States inversely correlate. Data on pornography titles after 2005 was not available.

Since then, evidence linking porn to rape or dating violence has been unconvincing. Colleague Rick Hartley and I conducted a review of research in 2009 and found the evidence to be underwhelming.[44] Research since then hasn't changed much. Some studies even find porn viewing to be associated with more positive attitudes toward women.[45] And increased pornography viewing over the past few decades has been associated with considerable cross-national declines in rape and domestic violence rates, including in the United States. So we can reject Bundy's claims of pornography leading to sexual violence.

Bundy's end came in Florida. Arrested and put on trial for the kidnapping of Carol DaRonch, he managed to escape twice. The first time, he acted as his own lawyer and was given unsupervised time in the courthouse library where he managed to jump out a window. Rearrested a few days later, Bundy escaped a second time by sawing his way into the prison ceiling crawl space, coming down into the chief jailer's apartment, and walking out with his clothes.

Bundy made his way to Tallahassee, Florida, where he assaulted five young women during a single night on the Florida State University campus. By this point, he had become more of a spree murderer than serial murderer, his identity known and behavior increasingly out of control. A month later, he killed his final victim, Kimberly Leach. He was arrested in a stolen car soon after.

Convicted in Florida, Bundy was sentenced to die in the electric chair. Fascinatingly, he managed to marry and conceive a daughter while on death row (presumably, he bribed a prison guard to allow a conjugal visit).[46] Bundy was executed in 1989.

Madness and Insanity

Mental illness, thus, involves a broad range of behaviors typically marked by maladjusted behaviors (i.e., persistence in behaviors despite their obvious negative cost) or distress (sadness, fear, or anger). Not all nor even the majority of mental illness is what I mean by madness. By madness, I refer specifically to behavior that persists despite its destructive nature either to oneself or to others. The notion of madness that I advance is similar to that of insanity, although in most Western cultures, insanity has taken on legal ramifications. To be insane in a legal sense involves a mental state that is so impaired that the individual can't understand reality and thus is not responsible for his or her actions. Not everyone with a mental illness is insane in the legal sense; in fact, the vast majority are not. So Andrea Yates, a Texas mother who drowned her five children in 2001 because she believed Satan had influenced them, fits within this definition of insanity. Obviously, Alexander the Great would not. He might have been out of control and even delusional at times, but he was not divorced from reality in the same sense as Andrea Yates. But he persisted both in his heavy drinking and ceaseless wars despite the massive damage that resulted to himself, his close colleagues, and the countless innocents ground under the wheels of his war machine. That's madness.

So we can think of madness as being a very small subset of mental illness, with insanity being even smaller still. Everyone who is *mad* is experiencing a mental condition of some sort, whether a traditional mental illness or personality disorder. But not everyone with a mental condition is *mad*. Many mental illnesses involve relatively minor problems (though some, such as suicidal depression or schizophrenia, are quite serious, of course). A teen girl who still feels sad six months after breaking up with a boyfriend could potentially qualify for an adjustment disorder, a mild mental illness, but no one (aside perhaps from a few crotchety old-timers) would claim she is mad.

There is one other group of disorders that bears mentioning as I introduce terms being used in this book. These are the personality disorders, which are lifelong patterns of deviant or maladaptive behavior that result from the individual's core personality rather than an illness per se. I mentioned already that Alexander the Great likely experienced narcissistic personality disorder. Narcissism essentially was who he was, not an illness that afflicted him. In this sense, personality disorders are different from traditional mental illnesses such as depression or schizophrenia. They may be just as disruptive but result from different processes. A mental illness might be cured or at least put into remission with the proper treatment. Personality disorders generally cannot be, as they reflect the individual's core identity. One disorder, borderline personality disorder, which is marked by severe instability, rapid mood swings, manipulative and aggressive behavior, and irrationality and impulsivity, gets the most attention of late. Yet there are several other personality disorders that similarly may be of great concern. Indeed, personality disorders are common among the individuals I discuss in this book.

When Societies Go Mad

That individuals have considerable opportunity to change the course of history is a central theme of this book. But, of course, the behavior of individuals does not occur in a vacuum but is inevitably a part of a societal structure that, intentionally or not, gives them the opportunity to exert power.

Societies are not independent entities that exist with wills or desires self-governing the individuals that make up those societies. Rather, they reflect a kind of summed view of the powerful within those cultures and collective agreements on motivations, interpretations, culture, and belief. As those centers of power change, beliefs and motivations of societies can change, sometimes toward the rational, sometimes away from it.

At times, a society can shift toward madness by, in essence, giving greater power and authority to members of that society who are, themselves, mad. For decades, considerable argument has persisted in social science regarding the degree to which individuals are merely malleable cogs in society's wheel or actively shape the societies in which they live.

Obviously, we shape our societies and are, in turn, shaped by them, but how interchangeable are we as individuals? Or, to bring it home with an example from one of the twentieth century's most notoriously mad societies, to what degree did individual Germans become complicit and accepting of the mad Nazi regime of the 1930s and 1940s?

During the mid-twentieth century, social science research seemed to suggest that most individuals are indeed little more than cogs in the machine. Of these, the most notable were the Milgram study and the Stanford Prison Experiment.

In the Milgram study, psychologist Stanley Milgram induced adult participants to deliver potentially dangerous electric shocks to another person as part of what was ostensibly a learning task. As the "learner" made mistakes, the participant would deliver increasing levels of shock as punishment. Higher levels of shock were labeled with warnings about the potential for severe shock, and the "learner" (actually someone who was in on the experiment—no one, in fact, was actually shocked) continually asked to be released, began complaining of his heart, and eventually went completely silent as if unconscious or dying. Although some participants refused to deliver the higher electric shocks, many went all the way through the highest shocks, particularly when assured that any consequences would be borne by the researcher, the authority. This experiment appeared to suggest that a great many ordinary citizens would willfully follow an authority figure (in this case the researcher) to the point of potentially causing great harm to another person.[47]

In the Stanford Prison Experiment, psychologist Phil Zimbardo randomly assigned students to be prisoners or guards in an experimental setting. Despite both groups knowing that they were randomly assigned, the guard participants began acting authoritarian and even brutally toward their fellow prisoner students. The experiment was called off after only one week. Once again, this study suggested that ordinary folks could become monsters under the right circumstances. Zimbardo went on to write a not-too-subtly titled book *The Lucifer Effect: Understanding How Good People Turn Evil.*[48]

Apparently mad societies can indeed turn ordinary folks evil. Not so fast—both of these studies have come under more recent scrutiny for, at very least, exaggerating their findings and perhaps for not being valid at all. Of the two, the Stanford Prison Experiment is most damaged. A follow-up study from 2006 conducted with the British Broadcasting Corporation was unable to replicate Zimbardo's findings and suggested that, to the degree tyranny develops, a sense of powerlessness often underlies it rather than authoritarian compliance. The leadership of individuals was also an important part of the development of tyranny.[49] More damning are accusations that the Stanford Prison Experiment isn't valid at all and that Zimbardo cajoled the prison guards into doing what he wanted them to do. They behaved the way they did not because it reflected the reality of authoritarianism in the real world, but rather to please the researcher in an artificial setting. In other words, everybody was acting, and Zimbardo molded (consciously or unconsciously) the experiment to be more a reflection of what he wanted to see than anything that happens in the real world.[50] On balance, I believe the evidence against the validity of the Stanford Prison Experiment is significant enough that it should not be used as a primary source to inform our discussions of human nature.

The Milgram study also has faced criticism, although it is not as damaged (yet!) as the Stanford Prison Experiment. For one thing, new evidence suggests participants in the Milgram study did not believe they were causing harm to anyone. Presumably being brought to a psychological laboratory then asked to engage in behavior that looks like it could cause someone a heart attack might make most participants suspicious that a game was afoot. That seems to have been the case based on interviews with participants in that study.[51] A 2012 exposé by psychologist Gina Perry suggested that Milgram may have fudged his numbers a bit to make them appear more dramatic and more applicable to events like the Nazi Holocaust.[52]

At any rate, it is now less clear that specific individuals shift in and out of tyrannical roles depending on the societies they find themselves in. It is, perhaps, more likely that most people tend to keep their heads down, protecting themselves and their own families. This may make them reluctant to defend complete strangers in the face of frightening authority (although there are cases of exactly that worldwide in authoritarian regimes), which may make the general populace of a brutal society appear complicit. This is not to give human nature a complete pass: we might like to hope that people would be more heroic in resisting despots, but the idea that the average person is a budding Nazi given the right conditions is probably wrong.

What can happen, though, is that circumstances can allow openings for the mad to assume power, thereby promoting the influence of other mad individuals. As I discuss in chapter 10, this can happen even in republics or democracies. Madness can accumulate via numerous small but poor political decisions culminating in a regime of madness, which happened with the transferal of power from the Weimar Republic to the Nazi regime in early twentieth-century Germany. The failure of the rational allows power to slip to the mad. At that point, the situation is less that most people join in the madness, but rather that society's mad find themselves newly empowered at all levels.

This can explain the rise of individuals such as Irma Grese, who was nicknamed the "Beautiful Beast" or "Hyena of Auschwitz." Grese had an austere upbringing and may have been bullied as a child. Her home life was a difficult one, involving conflict with her father and the suicide of her mother when Grese was thirteen. Grese appeared to be on the trajectory toward an unsatisfying and unaccomplished life until being "rescued" by the Nazi movement and achieving infamy as a female concentration camp guard during World War II.[53]

Most of what we know about Grese comes from her trial records after the war. She was stationed variously at the Auschwitz, Bergen-Belsen, and Ravensbrück camps. Witnesses describe her gleefully beating camp inmates and kicking them until bloody with her heavy boots. She shot some victims, sent dogs after others, and selected women to go to the gas chamber. By her own admission, she carried a whip to use on prisoners. Though not part of Grese's trial, later accounts by witnesses accused Grese of sexualizing some of the tortures against inmates, including tying together the legs of an inmate in labor and masturbating while watching surgery performed on the prisoners. Some accounts also suggest Grese made lampshades out of the skin of some victims. However, like the sexual accusations, these accounts are not as clearly sourced as Grese's more general violence and brutality presented at trial.[54] Grese was executed for her crimes in December 1945.

Nazi Germany did not make Grese a monster. As with most of our examples of madness, Grese was a product of both an unfortunate genetic inheritance coupled with a harsh early environment. Had the Weimar Republic persevered, Grese might have been relegated to petty crimes or eventually the prison system. Instead, Nazi Germany gave her a position of authority in which her viciousness could take full bloom. Grese thrived in a mad society because she, too, was mad. She was not merely a student in some professor's prison experiment.

Diagnosing across History

The challenge in assessing the impact of madness on history is an obvious one: it's difficult for clinicians to make a reliable diagnosis for a person for whom they've conducted a thorough analysis of in the present, let alone across millennia of time. The task is made more difficult when original sources are writing years or decades after a subject is deceased or with personal agendas rather than an accurate historical record in mind. Further, behaviors that may appear odd to us may be normative in other cultures. With that in mind, diagnosing historical "others" through our own lens can be a fraught and delicate process. For instance, declaring oneself descended from the gods might seem an obvious symptom of narcissism, but this may be common for the royalty of some cultures. Can we decide that such normative behavior is diagnostically useless for those people, or is it the case that the narcissists simply managed to seize power of some cultures?

That said, records both recent and ancient often do contain powerful hints and clues. With a bit of caution and humility I believe we can make some educated conclusions about how things transpired for history's madmen and -women. Let's try with one of history's most notorious madmen, Rome's third emperor, Caligula.

For those who have heard of him, most get a picture of a clear madman, one who had incestuous relationships with his sisters and named his horse a high-ranking court official. One might assume Caligula was psychotic, experiencing hallucinations and delusions—or at least seriously disconnected from reality. But the real story of Caligula is more complicated than that.

To be sure, his classical biographers such as contemporaries Philo and Seneca, as well as later Romans writing several generations after his death, Suetonius and Dio, all tell wild tales of his behavior and paint him in a most unfavorable light. But historians of that day could be something akin to

Bust of Caligula. *Photo:* Ed Uthman.

court gossips,[55] so some of their claims must be considered carefully, even if that does not change the larger picture of Caligula as an unhinged emperor.

Born Gaius Caesar (he was nicknamed Caligula, or "little boots," because he dressed in military uniform while accompanying his father, a general, on campaign), Caligula was raised in the cruel and murderous world of the early Roman Empire. His father, the popular general Germanicus, died while Caligula was young, and it was rumored he may have been poisoned. Caligula and his family came under the control of the second emperor Tiberius, a mediocre leader known for paranoia and bitterness who had been a better general than emperor. Caligula's mother, the acid-tongued Agrippina, and two older brothers would die while in Tiberius's custody, as he viewed them enemies of the state. Caligula proved exceptionally resilient, however, and ultimately was taken into the care of the elderly Tiberius.[56] Upon his death, Tiberius named Caligula and Tiberius's own grandson Gemellus as co-heirs.

Aided by Macro, the prefect of the Praetorian Guard,[57] Caligula nudged the somewhat simple-minded and harmless Gemellus out of the way and assumed the seat of the empire. Initially things went well and citizens at all levels of the empire were content with Caligula's rule, particularly coming after the tense reign of Tiberius.

This is not to say that all was necessarily well with Caligula, of course. Despite being an heir to the empire, Caligula was raised in an environment of heightened threat coupled with extreme opulence. His father died young, possibly poisoned, and his mother and older brothers all confined by Tiberius where they would all die. His own life hung in the balance, and if he learned remarkable survival skills for enduring the reign of Tiberius, it's not hard to see that those early years would have left significant scars. Further, there's little evidence to suggest Caligula received much tutelage in running an empire and less in restraining his own extravagant impulses. Nonetheless, Caligula, guided by Macro, seemed to get off to a relatively good start.

So what changed? The ancient sources provide some tantalizing clues. During the first year of his reign, Caligula contracted a serious illness from which many did not expect him to survive. The Jewish ambassador and scholar Philo says of this illness, "in the eighth month a severe disease attacked Gaius who had changed the manner of his living which was a little while before, while Tiberius was alive, very simple and on that account more wholesome than one of great sumptuousness and luxury; for he began to indulge in abundance of strong wine and eating of rich dishes, and in the abundant license of insatiable desires and great insolence, and in the unseasonable use of hot baths, and emetics, and then again in winebibbing and drunkenness, and returning gluttony, and in lust after boys and women, and in everything else which tends to destroy both soul and body, and all the bonds which unite and strengthen the two; for the rewards of temperance are health and strength, and the wages of intemperance are weakness and disease which bring a man near to death."[58] Philo isn't only discussing a moral issue, a change in behavior, but a protracted illness that threatened Caligula's life. It was bad enough that, according to Suetonius, some men vowed to fight in gladiatorial combats or commit suicide if only Caligula would recover (these fellows would come to regret their hastily made vows).

To be clear, some modern biographers see Caligula's behavior as entirely rational,[59] and undoubtedly the ancient sources were at least somewhat slanderous. But I'm not so sure this illness can be waved away as unimportant given that Caligula's behavior seems to have changed so radically following it.[60] Naturally, we can't be sure of the specific nature of the illness, but one that caused inflammation of the brain (encephalitis) or the meninges covering the brain (meningitis) also could have caused enough permanent damage to influence Caligula's behavior. Damage to the frontal lobes of the brain in particular can cause difficulties with impulse control, anger, violence, and despondency.[61] With the caveat that it is impossible to definitively diagnose an illness twenty-one hundred years in the past, the most likely explanation for Caligula's sudden turn is that an illness in the brain caused a permanent deficit in his ability to restrain his violent and paranoid instincts. Note one need not assume Caligula was an angel prior to his illness, merely that his illness and injuries removed from him all constraint.

The hapless Gemellus was among the first to die, with some sources suggesting he was so innocent as to need to be aided in committing suicide.[62] Caligula's mentor Macro, along with Macro's wife (with whom Caligula had once had an affair), were forced to commit suicide, possibly because Macro had made plans for succession during Caligula's illness. Being practical does not always win favor with the mad. Beginning to see conspiracies everywhere, Caligula began a period of arrests, tortures, and executions among Rome's elite class. Interestingly, Caligula kept his uncle Claudius alive because he found him to be an entertaining, stuttering fool. Claudius, it turned out, would become a reasonably successful emperor following Caligula's death.

The ancient sources agree that Caligula's violence turned not only paranoid but capricious. The historian Dio credits Caligula with throwing spectators at the gladiatorial games to die at the claws and fangs of wild animals when the supply of condemned criminals ran out.[63] Naturally, those poor fools who had offered to sacrifice their own lives should Caligula survive his illness were called upon to make good their promises. Dio claims Caligula bemoaned of the Roman people. "Would that you had but a single neck," and Suetonius has him repeat the famous line, "Let them hate, so long as they fear." Some of the murders he committed may have been designed to seize the assets of the wealthy victims. In addition to being a tyrant, Caligula spent profligately, burning through Rome's finances and unable to control his own excesses.

Thus, perhaps already scarred by a childhood marked by loss and constant threat, a brain illness pushed Caligula further into impulsivity, paranoia, and cruelty. But there is little evidence to suggest Caligula was psychotic or had an illness such a schizophrenia. In some cases, Caligula's behavior appears to have been intended to humiliate his foes and were not actions he himself took seriously. Two incidents stand out.

Suetonius and Dio both claim that Caligula lavished attention on his favorite horse, Incitatus, having him as a guest for dinner and proclaiming that he would make Incitatus a consul.[64] Sometimes this is interpreted as evidence of mental illness, as if Caligula seriously believed a horse might make a reasonable consul or simply was so mentally ill as to make almost random decisions. More likely, Caligula was having a great laugh, as if to say his horse would make a better consul than most of the senators and other elite of Rome.[65] In other words, Caligula was poking his finger at the powerful in Rome to humiliate them. Granted, this in and of itself may not have been the wisest of decisions, but it's a bit different from having faith that one's steed might make a good politician.[66]

The other incident is Caligula's celebrated "war with the ocean." Caligula drew up several legions to secure the German frontier and invade Britain (still in the hands of Celtic tribes at the time). The details aren't clear but somehow it was botched and the invasion was aborted. In a pique of anger, Caligula appears to have humiliated his legions by ordering them to gather seashells as war booty for having defeated the ocean itself. Again, this is sometimes interpreted as a sign of lunacy on Caligula's part, helped along in particular by the historian Dio, who portrays Caligula as something of a cackling nutcase while doing so. Dio was probably embellishing. The account by Suetonius portrays Caligula as frustrated without much to show in way of military victory and inclined to take some measure of vengeance on his troops. Again, perhaps not the wisest course of action, particularly for an empire largely dependent on the support of the army, but not exactly psychosis, either.

Caligula does seem to have tried to make a case for his own divinity. This was hardly unheard of in ancient times, but he might have been pushing things for the Romans, who weren't used to viewing their emperors as living gods, preferring to deify them after death. His behavior almost certainly threatened a rebellion in Judea when he sought to reconsecrate the Temple in Jerusalem for himself.[67]

Eventually, Caligula's antics caused consternation for too many people, including members of his own Praetorian Guard. The motives for his assassination are undoubtedly many. Certainly, his viciousness and the fear he instilled in the people of Rome played a central role. But the Romans may have feared he would move the capitol of the empire to Alexandria, which would have deprived Rome of its influence. Caligula taunted his chief murderer, Cassius Chaerea, with sexually humiliating derisions. In 41 ACE, Chaerea and his co-conspirators murdered Caligula along with Caligula's wife and infant daughter. An attempt to restore the Roman Republic was quashed and Caligula's stuttering uncle Claudius was elevated to imperial authority. Chaerea was executed for his role in the assassination of the emperor (the authorities, as usual, having little patience for such things).

The origins of Caligula's tyranny and downfall are many and complex. It would be too facile simply to say that all would have been right for Rome had Caligula only not caught that one fever. Undoubtedly genetics coupled with a chaotic and threatening, if privileged, early life shaped Caligula's motivations. The social circumstances of Rome's early empire made the accumulation of such power possible. But the injuries to his brain likely suffered during that crucial illness may have eliminated what restraint he otherwise might have possessed. The paths to madness are themselves, complex, confused, and maddening.

CHAPTER THREE
DEVIANCE OF THE PERSONALITY

The story of the mad emperor Caligula highlights the discrepancy between sensationalized madness and the realities of history. People delight in stories of Caligula that suggest he had sex with his sisters or truly believed himself to be fighting the god Neptune or actually thought his horse might make a reasonable consul. These salacious stories embellish a more sinister truth: although Caligula was deviant and cruel and may have struggled to restrain his impulses, he was not thoroughly cut off from reality. We tend to be attracted most to stories of lunacy, perhaps because it's unconsciously comforting to think of madness as a condition separate from humanity rather than a variant of normal human horribleness.

To be sure, there are some individuals whose deluded and psychotic illnesses made them incompetent to rule, and I discuss a few of those folks in this book. In some cases, rulers with psychological or intellectual impairments were propped up by supporters or lackeys or became the source of chaotic dynastic struggles to the chagrin of their realms. In these cases, the issue was not cruelty and destruction but impaired fitness to rule, which created power vacuums that inevitably led to infighting, national weakness, and chaos. Systematic and institutional cruelty takes a certain degree of basic competence and coherence to organize. Most of the madness I discuss in this book results less from traditional mental illnesses such as schizophrenia or bipolar disorder, but rather from deviations of the personality itself.

From chapter 2, recall that mental diagnoses are codified by the American Psychiatric Association (not without some significant controversy) in its *DSM*. The *DSM* classifies a certain set of disorders, personality disorders, apart from the others.[1] Personality disorders, as the name suggests, reflect essential deviance of core personality traits that influence a person's perception of the world, his or her interaction with others, and his or her behavior. Although there are seldom clear margins when it comes to mental health, the general difference can be conceived as the distinction between an illness that changes one's normal behavior and a deviant pathology of the core identity itself. So, for instance, an individual suffering the illnesses of depression or schizophrenia experiences a change from their normal behavior due to the illness.[2] By contrast, a disorder of the personality represents a pathology in the individual's core identity. In effect—and with no intent to be pejorative—the individual's entire psyche is deviant, not merely pathological due to a disease process.

Personality disorders are often extreme variants of normal human personality traits that overwhelm the rest of the personality and are rigidly applied to the disadvantage of the individual or others in their social environment. Not all personality disorders are prone to the sort of destructiveness we call "madness." Many are distressful to the individual, such as excessive shyness (avoidant personality disorder), desire to please others and unwillingness to make decisions (dependent personality disorder), or adherence to interests or beliefs that most people find unusual (schizotypal personality disorder). Some, by contrast, may be irritating to others but are unlikely to cause wholesale destructiveness, such as those who exhibit flirtatious self-centeredness (histrionic personality disorder), focus on order and control (obsessive-compulsive personality disorder),[3] or desire to be left alone (schizoid personality disorder). In most cases, treatment for such disorders tends to focus on helping individuals adjust maximally to their motivations and obligations rather than "curing" the disorder.[4]

This leaves a few personality disorders that are most relevant to our concept of madness. To be clear, not all individuals—nor even most—with these disorders would necessarily fit this book's conceptualization of madness. Indeed, most find reasonable avenues to fit into society. Rather, these personality disorders are best considered "risk factors" for the types of destructiveness we would consider mad.

Among these are antisocial personality disorder, or "psychopathy," which we mentioned in chapter 2. Marked by a lack of conscience coupled with thrill seeking and difficulty learning from punishment, its connection to destructive madness is straightforward. Again, this does not mean that every psychopath is "mad." Indeed, many find perfectly suitable professions in business, law, and politics.[5] But this condition is a nontrivial risk factor for madness. Psychopathy is seen more often in males than females but a relatively similar condition, borderline personality disorder, is seen more often in women.

Borderline personality disorder is more representative of pure chaos than is antisocial personality disorder, and symptoms include impulsiveness, extreme mood swings,[6] anger control problems, and issues such as self-mutilation and impulsive violence. Borderline personality disorder is marked by increased risk for domestic violence,[7] which, as a disorder more common among women, may explain why, unlike most violent crimes, women are about on par with men as perpetrators of domestic violence.[8] As with most personality disorders, borderline personality disorder both runs genetically through families and can be exacerbated by early childhood environments, particularly those marked by harshness and chaos.[9] Placed in a position of authority, someone with borderline personality disorder might appear to be normal enough day-to-day but would make decisions based on impulse, anger, capriciousness, and emotion—not a recipe for success.

Two other disorders bear mentioning. One is narcissistic personality disorder, which is marked by a grandiose sense of one's own self-importance.[10] Not surprisingly, narcissism is widespread among those who seek power and fame, including those in politics. The other is paranoid personality disorder, which, as the name subtly alludes, is marked by extreme suspiciousness of the motives of others. Individuals in this latter group may be particularly prone to drifting into extreme radical groups or those that promote racism or other forms of hate. Paranoids, not surprisingly, tend to blame others for their lives' misfortunes.

If the thought of a leader with one personality disorder weren't nerve-wracking enough, personality disorders can combine dangerously. For instance, some scholars have pointed to a "dark triad" of psychopathy, narcissism, and what they call Machiavellian personality traits. The latter involves cynical strategic decision making with little regard for ethics or morality. This dark triad is particular predictive of negative behaviors toward others.[11] Mixtures of psychopathy with paranoid personality traits can, likewise, produce vicious and cruel tyranny in world leaders.

The Curious Case of Herr Hitler

It is, of course, inevitable that a book on political madness would consider the singular case of Adolph Hitler, who led Germany to war in World War II. There are already copious books written about Hitler. Indeed, one cannot throw a rock in a library without hitting a biography of Hitler or a history of World War II. Hitler combined an enthusiastic devotion to destruction and violence as a prime instrument of nationalist survival with a bizarre paranoia about Jewish conspiracies. The capricious hand of fate also put him in charge of one of the mid-twentieth century's most powerful military nations. Even if we ignore military casualties, Hitler was directly responsible for the deaths of more than six million Jewish civilians as well as millions of other Russians, Ukrainians, Poles, Gypsies, and other "subhuman" (*Untermensch*) groups. Few in history can match this bloody tally, other than perhaps his contemporary and rival Joseph Stalin, who receives attention in chapter 6, or China's Chairman Mao. How does a person develop such that they set out to purposely create suffering in the world on an industrialized scale?

Presumably, most readers have at least a basic knowledge of who Hitler was: led Germany into World War II, funny mustache, responsible for the deaths of millions, leader of the National Socialist German Workers' (Nazi) Party. How a strange man of relatively ordinary origins managed to turn an extreme, violent, and bizarre group like the Nazis into the governing class for a major world power is a fascinating story. But first, let's look toward Hitler's personality and what we can say about it.

Hitler had a kind of mad genius. This is evidenced in the systematic, sadistic murder of millions, his strategic manipulations in achieving power over the German state and subsequent diplomacy (if the brute threats used by Hitler can be called such) with England and France leading to the 1938 Munich Agreement, which handed considerable parts of Czechoslovakia to Germany without a fight. Given these achievements, both amazing and horrifying, Hitler appears to fit the dark triad scheme of personality. He believed himself to be uniquely bestowed with the ability to restore

German power,[12] showed little remorse for the devastation he unleashed, and displayed remarkable cunning. Other elements of his personality add to the complex mixture; for instance, his paranoia about the Jews. It is not clear where and when this developed, and little evidence has emerged regarding negative experiences Hitler may have had with Jewish individuals that might explain such passionate hatred.[13] Of course, anti-Semitism was common throughout history, and "internal traitors" emerged as one way of rationalizing German's defeat in World War I.

Throughout his adult life, Hitler also displayed difficulty connecting with others and tended to remain a loner. He was capable of some intimate relationships, such as evidenced by his longtime mistress, Eva Braun, whom he married before his suicide at the end of World War II in April 1945.[14] Even this relationship was fraught, however, with Braun twice attempting suicide during their early relationship. Hitler's half-niece Geli Raubal did commit suicide in 1931. Hitler had been domineering and possessive of her and may have been in love with her. Kept as a virtual prisoner in Hitler's apartment, she committed suicide with his gun. Even during his service in World War I, which was otherwise considered meritorious, Hitler remained aloof from the other soldiers, which may have prevented his promotion up the ranks. This difficulty with social connections has no clear place in the taxonomy of the *DSM*. His mechanical facility with charisma and persuasion contraindicate most disorders of social impairment such as the autism spectrum or schizoid personality disorder. Nonetheless, this oddity regarding social involvement seems an important clue to Hitler's psyche.

So too was Hitler's fascination with death and destruction, which he saw as instrumental to human evolution and national power. Before World War I, Hitler lived a bohemian and directionless lifestyle, eking out a living as a painter, a practice he continued into his army days. The war gave Hitler purpose, and he took to it in ways most young men did not, his fervor for the war continuing past the point when most other soldiers became disillusioned. Thus, Germany's unexpected defeat in World War I shook him particularly hard.

Hints of mental illness are speculative. There is little evidence that Hitler had symptoms of a major mental illness such as schizophrenia or bipolar disorder and efforts to explain his behavior as largely delusional can be dismissed. Others have speculated that Hitler may have suffered from

Painting by Hitler, circa 1914.

neurosyphilis, a sexually transmitted infection that can target the nervous system, but evidence for this is thin. Hitler undoubtedly had periods of depression and anxiety, but these are hardly unusual for a person in his position. Hitler did suffer from a number of medical symptoms, particularly stomach distress and tremors, which could indicate some chronic illness, but the origin of his symptoms, whether medical or stress related, remains unknown. Hitler was prescribed considerable amounts of amphetamines, which may have increased the erratic nature of his decisions during World War II, although they do not explain his behavior and motivations.[15]

Thus, the best explanations of his behavior relate to a disorder of the personality, symptoms of which can be seen in his early life before his rise to power.[16] Though producing some limitations for Hitler, particularly related to social interactions, his personality traits also provided him with the drive, obsessiveness, and demagoguery that would allow him to master a unique moment in Germany history.

In Hitler's case we can see how a single individual can alter the course of history. Of course, Hitler's rise was dependent upon the desperate circumstances of Germany following World War I. For a decade, Hitler's Nazis were regarded as little more than a violent and despicable fringe group. But Germany's experiment with democracy following World War I, the Weimar Republic, failed to meet the needs of Germany's citizens. Burdened with heavy debts and reparations following defeat in World War I, humiliated by its unexpected loss of the war, and buffered by social confusion in transitioning from empire to republic, the Weimar Republic never managed to control Germany's well-being for more than a few years. Communists as well as right-wing nationalists gradually saw their fortunes rise as the common people hankered for a stronger hand to rule the country. In 1929, the Great Depression set in and people began to turn to the Nazis in greater numbers.

Hitler didn't create authoritarianism in post–World War I Germany. In fact, Germany's leaders, including President von Hindenburg, were already moving in the direction of autocracy, albeit without Hitler's anti-Semitic hostility. Here, Germany's leaders grossly miscalculated, underestimating Hitler and thinking he could be controlled even when named to the post of chancellor. In this, of course, they were tragically wrong. But the transformation of Germany from a republic to Nazi dictatorship involved an unlucky concordance of economic depression, lack of social cohesion, gross misjudgments by political leaders, and the unique set of skills of Hitler himself.

If a personality disorder explains Hitler's unique set of attributes, understanding the origin of this personality disorder may prove frustrating. Personality disorders are well known to result from genetic inheritance.[17] Hitler's father was a hard man, which could suggest similar traits in Hitler. But as for environmental factors, relatively little information is known. Hitler did not get along with his father and may have been abused by him, though he remained very close to his mother. Her death from cancer in 1907 was a devastating blow to Hitler. Ultimately, however, we arguably have more insights into the development of the mind of Caligula than we do Hitler.

It is tempting, in noting Hitler's conflicted relationship with his father, to see a pattern of fatherly absence in the cases of madness we have covered thus far. Perhaps, combined with the genetic risks toward personality deviance, conflicted relationships with father figures provide an environmental trigger for propelling minor deviances into terroristic and sadistic outcomes. Yet it should be noted that literally hundreds of millions of people experience the absence of or conflict with father figures yet lead normal, healthy lives. Further, development of such a theory can lead us to selectively interpret evidence in support of it. For instance, Caligula's father was the admirable Germanicus, who, despite dying relatively early in Caligula's life and often being away at war, appears to have treated his son well. We might speculate that, after Germanicus's death, the more ominous figure of Emperor Tiberius fulfills the role of errant father figure in our theory, but we must resist the temptation to give a theory of effects such flexibility. Thus, likely the best we can say is that Hitler's state of mind certainly originated from an unfortunate combination of genetic risk and environmental triggers, but the exact mechanism remains unknown.

Hitler's subsequent rise to power, manipulation of the Western powers, and involvement with World War II is the stuff of history. Regarding the prewar years, Hitler successfully reoccupied the Rhineland (forbidden by the Versailles Treaty, which ended World War I), incorporated Austria into the German homeland, and annexed areas of Czechoslovakia with large German-speaking populations with the acquiescence of England and France. By 1938, Hitler had greatly expanded the German state, secured alliances with Italy and Japan, and asserted considerable influence over other countries in Eastern Europe such as Bulgaria and Hungary,[18] all without resorting to war. It is less the case that Hitler pulled off a flawless string of diplomatic maneuvers than that the mistakes of his opponents in England and France (and the Soviet Union) were greater than his own.[19]

Probably few moments in history are the source of more counterfactuals, or alternative possible histories, than World War II. Germany, in many respects, seemed close to winning early in the war.[20] What might have happened if, after 1938, Hitler had exercised patience, forgoing war with the West and martialing Germany and Eastern European resources for an inevitable confrontation with the Soviet Union? Had he the inclination (which he clearly did not), Hitler might have forgiven Poland for being created from former German territories and nudged and bullied that country into the Anti-Comintern Pact. War with the Soviet Union was probably inevitable (Stalin almost certainly would have invaded, even had Hitler not invaded the Soviet Union in 1941).[21] An alliance of Eastern countries, potentially enlisting Ukrainians enraged by their treatment in the Soviet Union,[22] could have prevailed. With the Soviet Union out of the war, he might *then* have turned on France and England if he so desired.[23] The quality of German arms arguably increased as the war progressed, even as production became harder to manage under allied bombing. Germany's armies might have been far better equipped than its enemies if start of war could have been delayed to 1941, 1942, or even 1944.[24] Germany's early war successes owed more to innovative tactics than to first-rate equipment. Had Germany combined those innovative tactics with innovative war machinery, the results are frightening to consider.

The problem with counterfactuals, though, is that they by nature must assume circumstances that simply aren't true. Hitler was always intent on war and, by 1938, pushed desperately toward it, whatever the readiness of the German military. War itself revealed his weaknesses—his impetuousness, difficulty of character, obsessive control and focus on details—and these weaknesses contributed to his overall demise and that of the country he'd seduced and bullied into following him. These negative attributes became more pronounced as the stresses of war accumulated, undoubtedly exacerbated by his amphetamine use. An alternative ending to World War II is impossible because the very characteristics that made World War II possible in 1939 also led to its inevitable end in 1945. In April 1945, with Russian troops surrounding Berlin, a distraught Hitler, in weakened physical and mental health, shot himself. His new wife, Eva Braun, likewise killed herself.

The Roots of Evil

By defining the madness of Hitler as a facet of a personality disorder, the "dark triad" mixed with paranoia and a dash of social isolation, we arguably are medicalizing the concept of evil itself. Although this does help us to understand it, it runs the risk of converting evil itself into a banal circumstance of mental instability. This nonetheless brings us to two related, disturbing conclusions: First, that this evil is inextricably linked to our own genetic code, at least in some small way. And second, particularly if we regard Hitler's youth and abusive father as a fairly unimpressive etiological circumstance (given the commonality of child abuse, which, in most cases, does not result in incapacitating cruelty in the victim), that such evil can spring forth from the human genome both spontaneously and unpredictably.

Hitler didn't create the evil of the Holocaust himself, and like other mass slaughters, Hitler found himself at a confluence of social and political events. Germany found itself humiliated by its surrender in World War I, under economic and social strain, and devoid of strong leadership. A history of dehumanization and racism created the precedent for Nazism's virulent anti-Semitism and other racist views.[25] These circumstances provided an opening for a man like Hitler. Had the proverbial time traveler, as many a slightly intoxicated college student enjoys speculating on, traveled back to 1889 and killed baby Hitler, would World War II and the Holocaust still have happened?[26] I'd argue probably not, or at least not in the form in which it did. I don't mean to imply all would have been roses and ponies for Europe. A different sort of World War II might well have happened but likely in a different form. Hitler was not the only ingredient in that toxic mix, but he was a unique and required one.

Returning to the issue of evil, however, the question arises: if we accept that, to some degree at least, horribleness is a wired-in, perhaps even an evolutionarily adaptive element of the human genome, to what degree is a man like Hitler responsible for his actions? Are we all reducible to the biochemical actions of our brains? And if we were able to know and understand all those interactions and the environmental circumstances in which they would occur, could we fully predict our actions in the future? Or do we retain some element of control, agency of free will, and thus responsibility for our behaviors?

This question has puzzled philosophers for, quite literally, thousands of years. Most folks agree that, of course, biology and our environment play some role in determining our actions, but debate whether free will is compatible with this.[27] The criminal justice systems of the United States, United Kingdom, and many other countries are founded on the basic idea that we maintain some responsibility for our actions, aside from some limited circumstances of mental incapacitation. But is there evidence to support the concept of free will? Is human evil a real thing or merely the uncontrolled product of deviant brain dysfunction?

Providing research to support the concept of free will using scientific methods that are, by design, deterministic is fraught to say the least. Nonetheless there is interesting evidence that, for the most part, has mainly stoked further debate. Let's look at a few studies from both psychology and neuroscience and then see how they apply to the case of one of North America's most notorious female serial killers.

Until recently, considerable psychological research appeared to indicate that most human behaviors happened automatically. That is to say, our behaviors were being shaped unconsciously by events and stimuli around us, even when we thought we were making conscious choices. In a classic experiment, psychologists exposed some research participants to words that stereotypically evoke elderliness (gray, wrinkled, retired, knit), whereas others were exposed to neutral words. When the participants left the experiment, a research assistant timed how long it took them to walk down the hall. Those who read the "elderly" words were timed taking longer to walk down the hall, as if simply being exposed to concepts related to elderly people made them behave in a more elderly fashion (i.e., walking slowly).[28] Called *social priming*, hundreds of other studies seemed to confirm this basic result in various contexts. If humans are such easily manipulatable machines, this suggested some interesting possibilities. (Want your kids to eat more carrots? Leave some pictures of bunnies lying around.) Social priming also opened up the possibility for governments to use subtle cues to control human behavior, which could be either a really good or a really bad thing, depending on one's point of view.

Only it actually doesn't work. A follow-up study used infrared lasers rather than human research assistants to time the walkers as they left the lab. When timed this way, no differences were found. In fact, it was the *research assistants* who unwittingly hit the stopwatch earlier, causing false positive results.[29] Indeed, we've entered a period in psychological science called the *replication crisis* in which perhaps half to two-thirds of research results that we thought were absolutely true are now proving false under more rigorous testing conditions.[30] This collapse of previously held beliefs in psychological science has predictably triggered all manner of infighting, with some scholars claiming these replication failures are due to "methodological terrorists."[31] So much for psychology as the realm of disinterested scholars.

So it appears that humans are not merely dumb machines easily manipulated without their knowledge by every little stimulus in their environment. But this isn't necessarily evidence for free will. Finding evidence for free will using scientific principles that are inherently deterministic is an understandably difficult process. Nonetheless, belief in free will requires some form of empirical proof, else it be considered an unfalsifiable idea. The psychologist Joseph Rychlak is most famous for tackling this issue. Over a long career, Rychlak demonstrated that learning does not occur mechanically, but rather in line with individuals' goals, aspirations, and affective assessments, suggesting that the will is required for efficient learning.[32]

Likewise, evidence from neuroscience has been complex. Investigations attempt to assess which comes first: neurophysiological evidence for the intention to move, for instance, or the neurophysiological response involved in movement itself. So, if movement always precedes intent, free will is an illusion and our perception of intention merely a byproduct of automatic movements. The opposite indicates that intention does indeed cause later movements. Boiling down a lot of neuroscience to just a few observations, it turns out that variants happen. This makes sense. If someone tosses a ball at your head, you automatically duck without wasting precious milliseconds deciding "Hmm . . . I wonder if getting out of the way of the hard, round object is to my advantage?" Nonetheless, you may still have a sense of *wanting* to dodge the ball, even if the behavior was automatic. But it turns out that we also can form the intention to move, with movement coming later.[33] Not exactly slam dunks for free will but tantalizing clues at least. Scientific theories of free will posit that such actions are evolutionarily determined, giving creatures both greater power for problem solving and less predictability, which increases survivability. Free will can be thought of as a continuum, waxing and waning depending upon the circumstances.[34]

Thus, we can say that reasonably scientific foundations, both empirical and theoretical, indicate that free will is plausible. I might add the observation of Renouvier's wager, which suggests that it is best to believe in free will.[35] Here's why. If free will exists and you believe in it, you are correct! If free will does not exist, you're wrong, but it's not your fault since you were determined to believe in free will. If you don't believe in free will and are correct about that, so what? You were always determined *not* to believe in free will. However, if you don't believe in free will and are wrong, well that's entirely on you, as that was your choice. So, best to believe in free will since you get credit for being right and no blame for being wrong!

Our beliefs in the free will of others are circumstance dependent. We acknowledge, for instance, that individuals with severe mental incapacitation may lose some degree of their free will such that they should not be held accountable for their crimes. But we often apply this in lopsided ways, such that our stereotypes and prejudices about certain groups may cause us to evaluate their free will differently. For instance, we have stereotypes about women as inherently moral, nurturing, cooperative, and caring. As such, when women engage in evil behaviors, we may consider this de facto proof that they are mentally incapacitated, for no woman would willingly choose to engage in violently evil behavior (a patronizing perspective that, ironically, removes free will from women's decisions, reducing them to biological determinism). Indeed, laws in the United Kingdom presume that women who kill their infants may suffer from "lactational insanity," often reducing penalties for maternal infanticide.[36]

The Diabolical Christmas Present

In 1993 police in Toronto were presented with a most unexpected development. Through her lawyer, a young woman by the name of Karla Homolka sought a plea deal wherein she would provide evidence that her estranged husband had murdered three girls. In exchange for her testimony and pleading guilty to manslaughter, Homolka sought immunity from further charges. Her husband, Paul Bernardo, was suspected not only of battering Karla herself, but in a series of vicious rapes in which a sample of his DNA was found. Homolka now could connect him to several sadistic murders as well.

What followed was a textbook case illustrating the difficulty our society has had in applying a template for evil to women.[37] To be sure, folktales are filled with evil stepmothers and wicked witches, and actual witch burnings targeted women through the seventeenth century. But in the modern era, women are likely to receive shorter sentences than men for committing the same crimes.[38] This reversal of the harshness with which women were treated in earlier times arguably reflects residual benevolent sexism from the Victorian era, wherein women were thought both of greater virtue (prostitutes presumably being the exception) and in need of male protection. Are women capable of evil in the same sense that men are? Or, if women commit destructive acts, does this inherently provide evidence for severe mental illness as the only explanation for why some women may diverge from our stereotypes of women as nurturing and caring?

With the ink dry on her plea bargain, Homolka told investigators a fascinating and disturbing tale. Under coercion and fearing abuse from her husband, Homolka assisted him in the murder of three young girls. The first was her own sister, Tammy, age fifteen. Homolka had allowed Bernardo to intoxicate and sexually assault Tammy once before (unconscious at the time, Tammy apparently did not remember it), and she offered Tammy as a "Christmas present" to her husband. Only this time, things went horribly wrong. Tammy had a bad reaction to the animal sedatives Homolka had slipped her and choked on her own vomit while being assaulted. Homolka and Bernardo managed to disguise the incident as an accidental overdose on alcohol, believed by both investigators and Homolka's family at the time.

According to Homolka, this gave Bernardo a further edge over her, and she was coerced into assisting him rape and murder two other teen girls. The first was fourteen-year-old Leslie Mahaffy, who was kidnapped near her home, tortured, raped, and murdered. Her body was dismembered—possibly the day Homolka and Bernardo entertained her parents in their home—encased in cement, and dumped. Despite their efforts, her body was later found.

The next victim was fifteen-year-old Kristen French. As with Mahaffy, French was tortured, raped, and murdered. Her body was shorn of hair and dumped nude but intact in a ditch.

Key to Homolka's version of events was her role as victim. Assaulted and coerced by Bernardo, Homolka participated in Bernardo's crimes out of fear. This did not excuse her involvement but did mitigate it in the eyes of the Canadian authorities. They felt comfortable exchanging her testimony for slightly more than a decade of incarceration for her role in three murders. After all, it was widely believed at the time that women were incapable of sadistic predatory sexual abuse. Women were not *mad* in the way that men often are. Indeed, such beliefs are not entirely out of order. The vast majority of sexual crimes is committed by men, as are 85 percent or so of violent crimes more generally (mostly by men against other men). But our brains tend to deal in generalities rather than subtleties. *Most* very quickly becomes *all* in our minds, and exceptions become difficult to accept.

Unbeknownst to investigators when making the plea deal with Homolka, the couple had filmed their torture sessions with their victims. Far from documenting Homolka's role as coerced victim, the tapes suggested Homolka was a willing and engaged partner in the tortures and rapes of the three young girls. They failed to document any evidence of victimization, but rather reportedly showed an assertive, excited women, often egging her husband on during their assaults on the three victims. The murders themselves were not included on the tapes, so which partner actually killed the girls remains unknown (both Homolka and Bernardo blame the other). Canadian authorities maintained that Homolka's vivaciousness and assertiveness on the videos themselves were the scripted performance of an unwilling and frightened accomplice. Psychological evaluators were themselves left puzzled in trying to explain her behavior. They based their evaluations largely on her testimony, without knowing the contents of the videos.[39] Those conducted before her husband's trial largely explained her behavior as due to trauma from spousal abuse.[40] However, psychological evaluations conducted after the videos were revealed were less supportive of Homolka, suggesting a kind of "moral vacuity" in her.[41] In other words, before the videos were known, she was a victim, afterward, a creature of evil, a *mad* destructive force. A later evaluation conducted in 2000 also revealed her to be quite intelligent, in the "very superior" range (what we more colloquially would call a "genius").[42]

Ultimately, it may be possible to make an argument both for and against the role of battering in Homolka's motive; that is to say, whether she was a victim of her husband's abuse or a willing participant in multiple murders. Certainly, a significant assault ended their relationship and there's little reason to believe he would have been incapable of prior assaults. However, evidence for such is based largely on her own accounts. The recovered videos cast doubt on the story of Homolka as passive victim, and her superior intellect suggests considerable resources. Though Bernardo had certainly raped other women without Homolka's involvement, he only killed women when partnered with Homolka. Ultimately, I agree with other scholars[43] that Homolka benefited from gender stereotypes and our culture's reluctance to see mad, violent evil in women. In fairness to Homolka, since her release from prison in 2005, she has largely stayed out of trouble and the public eye. She has remarried and has children.[44] Nonetheless, her case and other high-profile cases of violent women have provoked some reassessment of the role of women in destructive violence.

Madness against Women

Homolka's case is fascinating because witnessing a woman participating in such horrible violence against other women conflicts with our modern stereotypes of women as the more virtuous and nurturing gender. Her case causes us to reevaluate how we must consider behaviors of destructive madness in women as well as men. It also puts a chink in the common belief that more women in world governance would reduce societal violence more generally. Though women personally participate in far less physical violence than men, many male world leaders who led their countries to war were not physically violent themselves (Hitler included).

Then again, women have generally been excluded from national leadership throughout history, minus some notable exceptions. One analysis suggests that women monarchs, at least, were *more likely* to lead their countries to war.[45] There may be many reasons for this other than assuming women are more aggressive upon assuming power, such as greater need to assert power in a male-dominated political world. Nonetheless, we can say that women leaders don't appear inclined to shrink away from using military force any more than male leaders.

Throughout much of history, however, women have been generally on the losing edge of politicized violence. Burned at the stake as witches, raped and murdered during times of war, traded as political pawns in marriage by their fathers, women's history is indisputably one of widespread victimization at the hands of men—and often at the hands of other women as well. Political madness unleashed always has had the power to disproportionally impact women.

Let's have a look at one particular madman known rather fittingly as Ibrahim the Mad. Ibrahim ruled the powerful Ottoman Empire for a brief and unpleasant period between 1640 and 1648. Like Caligula some fifteen

Ibrahim the Mad of the Ottoman Empire.

hundred years earlier, Ibrahim was eventually cast from power due to his own irrationality and destructiveness.

If Hitler and Homolka, in different ways, presented a conundrum for our assumptions that early trauma is a key element to madness among rulers (neither's early life was particularly traumatic), Ibrahim represents a comforting return to that narrative. Ibrahim's early life was

59

almost certainly a terror. The Ottomans, Turkish-speaking people from central Asia named after Osman, the founder of their empire, noted a problem in the succession of sultans. When a sultan died, his sons often competed for rule, causing destructive civil wars that frittered away the power of the empire. Succession of the sultan was reserved for sons, thus preserving the Osman family line, but aside from that, succession could be chaotic. Whichever son managed to ascend to rule the empire often would have his brothers strangled so that they could not become rallying points for revolts. This cruel practice had pragmatic purpose, but it also deprived the empire of replacements should a sultan die prematurely without sons of his own.[46]

By the time that Ibrahim's brother Murad IV ascended the throne, the practice of killing one's brothers was no longer quite so routine. Nonetheless it remained common and Murad practiced it, sparing Ibrahim possibly because Ibrahim already had shown signs of madness and, Murad figured, posed little threat. On Murad's deathbed, dying from natural causes at a young age (liver disease is thought to have been the cause), he is said to have ordered the death of Ibrahim, which was not carried out. Ibrahim had spent most of his life living in the Kafes, a kind of gilded prison on the palace grounds. Ibrahim apparently lived in terror that his own death was always imminent. When Ibrahim became sultan upon the death of his brother, he initially thought it a cruel joke, his suspicions dispelled by his powerful mother, Kösem Sultan, and viewing his brother's corpse.

Ibrahim's mental state had not been improved by his years of confinement and worries that any day might bring strangulation. The early years of his rule were stable, but the Ottoman Empire ultimately plunged into a long and financially difficult war with Venice.[47] Much of Ibrahim's efforts were spent making up for lost time, spending lavishly, and accumulating a massive harem of hundreds of girls.

In modern imagination, the purpose of a harem is a kind of sexual slavery of female playthings by Middle Eastern monarchs. There's an element of truth to that, although harems were more complex, functioning as a kind of protected space for all the women (and children) of the royal household and often a center of significant political power and intrigue. The status of concubines, or unmarried sexual partners of the ruler, likewise varied over time and culture from near slavery to voluntary positions of potential power and influence. Ibrahim, however, comports a bit more closely to the stereotypical image, amassing an unusually high number of concubines who, as we see, were largely disempowered.

One day, one of his concubines with whom he was particularly close informed Ibrahim of a rumor that another girl had carried out an affair. Unfortunately, she didn't know which of the other concubines was responsible for this breach in protocol. Enraged, Ibrahim had all of his concubines, save a couple of favorites, sewn into weighted bags and thrown into the sea to drown.[48] Only one girl managed to escape from the bag and survive. Estimates for the number of dead range in excess of two hundred.[49] Like many of the most lurid tales of madness, documentation of this episode is sketchy, and some suggest that it might reflect slander aimed at a disliked ruler. Either way, even the possibility that this event may have occurred points toward the perceived value of women's lives at this time.

Ibrahim's wild spending, cruel ways, and irrationality proved too much for the Ottomans. In 1648, Ibrahim was removed from office, possibly with the agreement of his mother. He was replaced on the throne by his son Mehmet IV. Soon after his overthrow, Ibrahim was strangled, the fate that had terrorized him for years.

Raised in such a cruel environment, perhaps Ibrahim never had a chance. But other sultans managed to survive fraught childhoods to become, at very least, competent rulers. And there isn't a clear line between exposure to cruelty and adoption of cruelty oneself. Madness had afflicted other members of Ibrahim's family, thus, like others in this book, he may have experienced an unfortunate combination of biological risk and harsh environment that propelled his personality to unimaginable selfishness and cruelty. Handed the levers of power, such a twisted personality inevitably caused suffering among many and eventually his own downfall.

CHAPTER FOUR
MADNESS OF THE MONARCH

In October 2018 when I visited the Melbourne Zoo in Australia, I had a chance to see hamadryas baboons at their worst. Like many primate species, humans included, baboons have an enormous capacity for cruelty toward one another. Males compete, often violently, for status. Males also can be aggressive toward females, and females likewise form dominance hierarchies among themselves, if with less physical violence.

On this particular day, the baboons were being fed carrots for lunch. A primped and sleek alpha male set about hoarding many of the carrots for himself. One ragged-looking baboon managed to find a morsel and started eating it. Enraged, the alpha male immediately attacked this interloper, slamming him into the edge of the containment area and biting him. The alpha male, of course, swiped that carrot for himself, despite already having an outsized stash of goodies. The victim of this aggression was left hungry and wounded with significant bite marks and scratches on his side.[1]

Aggression among males to assert dominance is common among animals from insects to humans. These sorts of vicious dominance behaviors are quite common among male primates. They establish who has access to mates, who can claim the lion's share (which also literally happens among lions) of resources, and how individuals in a social group relate to one another. They also can cause significant stress since alpha males continually come under physical challenge from other males who understandably want to usurp the throne.[2] It's tough to be the king.

The spoils of war: the great baboon carrot conflict of 2018.

Among chimpanzees, males establish complex patterns of alliance and union with different individuals in order to establish a particular male as alpha with that male's supporters also enjoying comparatively high rank.[3] This can stabilize dominance hierarchies, albeit imperfectly, and can lead to alpha males who are adept socially rather than physically the strongest.

"I see where you're going with this," you now say, dear reader. "You're about to compare monarchy with the dominance structures of chimpanzees." Why, yes, I am. Given the behavior of kings and queens over the past few millennia, does this seem remotely surprising?

Let's remember that the philosopher Thomas Hobbes described the basic state of humankind as "No arts; no letters; no society; and which is worst of all, continual fear, and danger of violent death: and the life of man, solitary, poor, nasty, brutish and short."[4] Here Hobbes is basically describing the state of humankind as essentially violent and chaotic. Archaeological records more or less back up Hobbes's somewhat cynical view, with evidence for violent injuries common among prehistoric humans.[5] Physical violence and aggression are more common among males, naturally, but far from being cooperative and egalitarian, females tend to develop their own dominance hierarchies, often using indirect aggression.[6] Through a process of deterrence, modern societies reduce interpersonal violence.[7] This may explain why, contrary to what many adults waving their fists at TV news shows seem to think, we currently are living in the least violent epoch in human history.[8]

As humans settled into organized tribes, violent competition among males for leadership likely remained high. Such a system could result in high mortality rates and expenditure of resources on within-group conflict, weakening the overall social unit, particularly when this involved multiple alliances of males. This form of alliance-focused violence within groups coupled with genocidal violence between groups as seen in modern chimpanzees[9] probably remained the dominant form of social hierarchy formation among most prehistoric hunter-gatherer human societies. Put more simply, early male tribal leaders tended to fight it out to see who was boss. To be sure, there may have been some tribes of pacifist, egalitarian humans, but unless they were geographically isolated, they likely were annihilated by their more aggressive neighbors. In other words, the *noble savage* was never particularly noble.

With the development of agriculture, larger groups of humans could coalesce, and this system of repeated violent overthrows understandably made less sense. Across the globe, the alliance dominance systems evolved further into an early version of monarchy, in which chief dominance was held as a position for life by a particular male independent of physical prowess or much else to recommend him in terms of qualifications. This system ostensibly offered greater within-culture stability. That this system arguably evolved out of dominance hierarchies of males among primates also helps us to understand why, for so long, females were largely excluded from this process.[10] What's more, monarchies offered even more promise of stability by conferring succession from one monarch to another, typically a son of the deceased king or emperor, in a reasonably predictable manner.

I don't wish to oversell the point, of course, as monarchies hardly produced a world of peace and virtue. Between-culture violence remained very high, and coups, rebellions, and struggles between brothers[11] remained a problem intra-culturally for many societies. But monarchies set the bar higher for usurpers to assume the throne by mixing early religions with dominance. A common theme of early monarchies, cross-culturally, was the "divine right of kings" or "mandate of heaven," which, in one form or another, spread from the Middle East through Europe, Asia, and into the Americas. Whether the divine right of rulers developed independently in different cultures or spread between cultures is up for debate.

The divinity of the king hardly eliminated rebellions and discord, but it did set a higher bar for would-be usurpers to overthrow the king. Just because you were strong, intelligent, and virtuous didn't give you much right in most people's eyes to replace the divine ruler, even if that fellow was a drooling schlub. The benefit for such a system in creating stability is straightforward. As, of course, is its main drawback, namely, that if a culture *did* have a drooling schlub, there were rarely clear paths for removing him, particularly given that those closest to the king (the alliance beta males in the parlance of chimpanzees) were often invested in keeping him there and ruling through him or simply lining their own pockets. Thus, cultures stuck with a mad king could be stuck with him for a long time, weakening that society to both internal and external pressures.

Particularly hard hit were monarchies that never developed a clear system of succession. The Roman Empire was one of these. After the initial line of Julio-Claudian emperors ended with the suicide of Nero (as mad a ruler as ever there was), the Roman empire vacillated between family-based dynasties and something more akin to the types of alliance-based chaos we might expect from chimps. Particularly during the third century ACE, emperors were more likely to die violently than in their own beds, unless that's where they happened to be murdered. Consequently, the empire oftentimes found itself in the hands of a mad emperor, the solution for which was only more violence. Let's consider the case of the Emperor Elagabalus, who ruled Rome for a whopping three years between 218 and 222 ACE.

What we know of Elagabalus, we mainly know from Roman historians Cassius Dio[12] (who also helped us with Caligula, as we may recall from chapter 2) and Herodian.[13] The accounts largely agree on the circumstances of Elagabalus's reign. To be sure, historians then (as now) sometimes distorted history for political purposes and we might understand that there are some embellishments in the story, but overall Elagabalus appears to have been a singularly ill-suited emperor at a time when the empire desperately needed stability.

It is a testament to the Roman Empire's strength that it survived the third century ACE at all. Most of this century saw considerable chaos

Silver denarius of Elagabalus.

within the corridors of power, with violent deaths of emperors more common than not, often after only a short period of reign. Elagabalus was part of the highly chaotic and murderous Severan dynasty of the Roman Empire. He rose to power following the execution of the usurper (i.e., non-Severan) emperor Macrinus, mainly due to the schemes of Elagabalus's powerful grandmother Julia Maesa.

Elagabalus proved to be an odd choice and, arguably, an unusual misstep for the shrewd Julia Maesa. Elagabalus was young at the time of his ascension, about fourteen or fifteen, and proved to be rather weird. He devoutly revered an unfamiliar sun-worshipping religion and aggressively sought to foist it on the conservative Romans. He indulged in strange public displays, including an odd ritual in which he ran backward before a chariot holding an image of his sun god. During these rites he is reputed to have thrown coins and other valuables to the crowds, causing stampedes in which many lost their lives. Herodian accuses Elagabalus of executing some Romans who ridiculed his new religion.[14] Perhaps to insult the religion of the Romans, he married one of the vestal virgins who, as the title implies, was expected to remain chaste and unmarried. This caused considerable scandal, particularly since he divorced her soon after.[15]

Probably the most controversial aspect of Elagabalus's behavior was his sexuality, however. The Romans could be a bit odd by modern standards when it came to sexuality. The Roman Empire was hardly the heartland of sexual virtue, filled as it was with brothels and pornographic art, not to mention its acceptance of a wide range of sexual acts, particularly by men. But the Romans also could be prudish and particularly valued masculinity in men.

One issue for Elagabalus was his gender identity. Historical sources report that Elagabalus engaged in numerous behaviors that suggest he may have had gender dysphoria. Gender dysphoria as defined by the American Psychiatric Association's *DSM-5* essentially refers to a condition in which a person's identified gender differs from their biological sex and this causes distress. In this case, Elagabalus was born male with male genitalia but apparently identified himself, at least to some degree, as a woman. Although he married several women during his time as emperor, he also took male lovers, referred to one as his husband, and is reputed to have taken the more submissive—or, we might say, ahem—*receptive* role in these relationships, generally frowned upon in Roman culture and certainly scandalous for an emperor. More crucial, the historical sources reference Elagabalus's desire to remove his male genitalia and find a surgeon who could fashion a vagina for him. This remarkable hope is only more astounding given the physical arduousness of such a surgery even in modern times, let alone for Roman medicine. However, such desires are common among individuals with gender dysphoria. The sources also suggested that Elagabalus prostituted himself, although it's possible this may be an embellishment on his having taken many male lovers.

Even today, gender dysphoria is the source of considerable controversy. Part of this is due to poor understanding regarding the origins of gender itself. As in Roman times, the issue is a very political one. Some individuals express little compassion and empathy for people with gender dysphoria, as this condition may conflict with conventional notions of gender. However, activists attempting to defend those with gender dysphoria or gender nonconformity more broadly have also created a false dichotomy between biological sex, as indicated either chromosomally or by the presence of a penis or vagina, and gender, which is sometimes falsely cast as a social construct. Indeed, the mantra "gender is a social construct" is a common belief among progressives. But this notion is false.

Gender is basically one's own sense of being male or female. Although a small number of individuals may not clearly identify as either male or female, the vast majority of people, even transsexual people, do.[16] Unlike biological sex, which is clearly indicated either by chromosomes or genitalia, gender exists within the brain. However, contrary to claims about gender being a social construct, considerable evidence points to gender residing within the brain, particularly an area called the hypothalamus.[17]

It appears that our brains start in a female position as a fetus. That is to say, initial brain development in fetuses is uniform and will progress along the lines of a female brain unless altered by testosterone. For males, Y chromosomes result in the development of testes, which in turn produce higher levels of testosterone. This changes the hypothalamus from a female structure to a male structure. For most people, these processes sync up, so that they have a male hypothalamus in a male body or female hypothalamus in a female body. But for a small number of individuals, the brain is either under- or overexposed to testosterone. In effect, these individuals develop with, quite literally, a woman's brain in a man's body or vice versa.[18] Evidence had made clear that, rather than parenting styles predicting gender-specific behavior, fetal testosterone exposure predicts masculine behavior in both biologically male and female children.[19] Further, autopsy studies of transsexual individuals reveal that their hypothalamic regions are similar to their identified gender, rather than biological sex. Thus, gender resides very clearly in the hypothalamus, not as some kind of social construct. To be sure, parenting or societal pressures can influence gender role behaviors to some degree, but not nearly as powerfully as biological processes, which are largely resistant to social influences. In one famous case, a boy whose penis was accidently burned off during circumcision was raised as a girl. Despite the best efforts of socialization, he nonetheless identified as male upon reaching puberty.[20] The psychological damage done to this individual by being made a guinea pig of the "gender is socialized" ideology was likely a contributing factor to his eventual suicide.[21]

Gender, like sex, is largely a biological rather than social construct. Of course, the behaviors we use to advertise our gender—our gender roles—are much more socially determined. For instance, in much of the Western industrialized world, it would be considered ridiculous for a man to wear a miniskirt. However, this behavior is perfectly acceptable in Scotland, where they dodge the issue by calling the outfit a kilt.[22]

People with gender dysphoria are obviously deserving of our compassion. It is difficult to imagine the psychological impact of being born one biological sex but having the brain of the opposite. The Romans had no such compassion for Elagabalus and found his behavior repulsive. As his popularity plummeted, Elagabalus became aware that the masses found his cousin Severus Alexander to be more palatable. Elagabalus attempted to have his cousin assassinated but failed. This was the last straw for the Praetorian Guard and they murdered Elagabalus as well as his mother, who defended him until the end. His grandmother, Julia Maesa, who had helped elevate him to the position of emperor, was likely complicit in his downfall.

During Elagabalus's time, the Roman Empire was sliding toward the chaos and violence that would mark most of the third century ACE. The Roman Empire was in desperate need of a steady hand, someone who met the empire's personal ideals, whether fair or not, and could devote his resources to steady management of the empire's many problems. Unfortunately, the empire found itself with Elagabalus, whose eccentricities and personal failings made him ill-suited for the role. Aside from potential gender dysphoria, Elagabalus likely had significant personality dysfunctions leading to his non-gender-related eccentricities, rigidity, and failure to understand the social ramifications of his behavior, such as attempting to assassinate his cousin.

Elagabalus thus represents a missed opportunity to right the ship of the Roman Empire. His cousin, Severus Alexander, who succeeded him, fared only slightly better. Unable to resolve the empire's many problems and failing as a military commander, he, too, was murdered, bringing an end to the Severan dynasty and ushering in almost a century of discord from which the empire arguably never fully recovered.

The Roman Empire's difficulties were obviously many. But these included unclear rules of succession, which allowed for considerable political machinations as well as the constant threat of assassination and civil war. This was, naturally, a recipe for madness on a social scale and invited the rule of the mad on an individual level. The solution to the social chaos was an increased bureaucratization of the rules of succession, leading to a clear and unalterable line of succession. Until recently, most kingdoms adopted some variant of male primogeniture, or preference for the oldest and closest surviving male relative of the monarch (typically the oldest son or, if there was no son, oldest brother). Only in recent years among surviving constitutional monarchies in the West have the rules been changed to eliminate male preference in succession.

Primogeniture became increasingly formalized in the later Middle Ages, with additional rules sometimes included to clear up confusion or other issues (usually at the expense of female relatives). This system did help to clear up many of the chaotic issues associated with the succession of monarchs that plagued the Roman Empire and other early monarchies. But what if the succession rules led directly to someone who was either clearly mad already or developed madness while on the throne?

Bookending the Spanish Empire: Joanna the Mad

Visitors to modern Spain will find a lovely country with a rich history, welcoming people, and beautiful architecture. Nonetheless it is a wonder that Spain became the world's first modern-era superpower (along with the Ottoman Empire) in the sixteenth and seventeenth centuries. Spain's population is not particularly large, nor is Spain overabundant in natural resources. But Isabella, the first queen of a united Spain,[23] rolled the dice on one Christopher Columbus,[24] ushering in an era of profitable colonial ventures that made Spain unfathomably rich.

Isabella and her husband, Ferdinand of Aragon, had several children, but when the two eldest died, the thrones of Castile and Aragon (and thus united Spain) fell to their daughter Joanna (or Juana). The only problem was that Joanna was mad.

So here Spain (technically still Castile and Aragon) has a perfectly good bureaucratic system of succession pointing clearly to the next monarch in line. Unfortunately, that individual is entirely unsuited for the throne. This situation created a crisis for the newly emerging empire of Spain.

Joanna's mental illness appears to have set in around the time of her marriage to the Habsburg Archduke Philip. Many chronic mental illnesses ranging from depression to psychosis can develop during the teen or early adult years. These years marked the onset of serious mental difficulties for Joanna. She became depressed, obsessive, and increasingly paranoid.

She also became highly attached to her husband. During long separations, she stalked the grounds of her family's palace, looking for him, not eating and raving to those who came across her. Once, Joanna attacked a court maid with scissors to disfigure her so that Philip would not be tempted by the poor girl. Her mother Isabella, convinced that Joanna's madness (and the deaths of her other children) was punishment for the family's sins, did her best to nurse Joanna back to sanity. Her efforts came to no avail, however, and Isabella herself soon died.

Joanna's Habsburg husband, Philip, died soon after, still a young adult. He likely died of an infection, common at the time, but Joanna suspected assassination. Night after night after his death, she visited his crypt and ordered his coffin opened so that she could embrace him. Only with her father's encouragement did she finally allow Philip to be buried.[25]

With her mother's death, Joanna became queen of Castile, and after her father's, queen of Aragon, effectively uniting the two kingdoms into Spain. The law did not allow her to be stripped of her titles, but while he was still alive, her father convinced her to retire to private life in a tower and allow him to rule as regent. Upon her father's death, Joanna's son Charles took over the rule of Spain as well as lands in the Netherlands and Austria he'd acquired from his father. Charles thus inherited a massive and powerful empire. Joanna lived out her days in isolation, accompanied for a time by her daughter Catherine, until Catherine married and became queen of Portugal.

Joanna's is a sad story of a potentially powerful woman with undoubted intellect whose life path was thwarted by mental illness. Her family members, first her father then son Charles, used her illness to secure and strengthen their own political positions. But these political machinations also functioned to preserve the welfare of the state and keep it in steady hands. Yet if Joanna had clear defenders or those who would prop her up for their own personal gain against Ferdinand and Charles, the outcome for Spain could have been far different.

Joanna's reign did have two fateful consequences. The first was the unification of Spain under her rule, which continued with her descendants. The second was the introduction of Habsburg blood into the family line, which would have unfortunate consequences for Spain when the Habsburg family ultimately doubled down on near-incestuous marriages.

Bookending the Spanish Empire: Charles II

Repugnance toward incestuous relationships has origins that go far beyond one's sibling being the most annoying creature ever. Many diseases have genetic origins. Incest increases the frequency of these diseases, whereas expanding the gene pool dilutes the frequency of genetic illness, making them less common. This is why many purebred dogs, often the result of restricted gene pools and incestuous or near-incestuous couplings, tend to have more genetic health problems than mixed breeds or mutts. It is thought that humans evolved a kind of incest-avoidance device in the brain by which we tend to find our identified genetic relatives to be sexually unappealing.[26] Or at least one hopes. It appears that association in early childhood is a key element by which siblings develop familial association, which appears to be mutually exclusive to sexual affiliation.

Nonetheless, as we know, familial sexual affiliation to varying degrees was not uncommon among monarchs, even as they remained largely taboo among the populations they ruled. Curiously, and perhaps small comfort to some, we may tend to exaggerate the overall risks of marital incest[27] on genetic disorders. Good numbers are surprisingly hard to come by, but marriages between reasonably healthy first cousins (or half siblings) may roughly double the rate of genetic abnormalities.[28] This admittedly sounds terrible until one considers that genetic conditions are actually quite rare (for a woman to have a child over the age of forty also increases the risk of some congenital conditions, for instance), meaning most children resulting from marriages of first cousins turn out just fine, even if the thought gives us the heebie-jeebies. However, in the case of an identified genetic illness within a family, the risks can be greater.

Remember, however, that the whole argument for monarchies to avoid continual coups was the concept of divine right to rule. This in turn was typically cast as hereditary. Thus, if divine right to rule ran in the blood, it stood to reason that one would not want to water down royal blood with nonroyal blood. This rationale provided a powerful incentive for overriding incest taboos and biological incest-avoidance mechanisms. Given that royal families were seldom model nuclear families in which parents and siblings sat around the dinner table telling each other about their day, royal siblings may not have had enough contact for filial affiliation to kick in and bring about incest repugnance. Then again, the wishes and desires of the siblings in question were rarely considered anyway. Some cultures accepted sibling marriages among royals and, more commonly, cousin marriages. By the last centuries of absolute monarchies in Europe (the seventeenth, eighteenth, and nineteenth centuries) the genetic pool of noble families had become rather restricted, cousin intermarriage was common, and many countries' royal families shared familial ties.[29]

After Queen Joanna was confined, Spain reached its apogee of power over the next century. Her son Charles I and his son Philip II ruled over a massive empire upon which, as the saying went, the sun never set. They turned back Ottoman threats to dominate the Mediterranean Sea, conquered South and Central America, and bullied their neighbors throughout Europe. Spain spread its empire into the Pacific with the occupation of the Philippines. Austria split formally from Spain but remained an allied power under a different branch of the Habsburgs.[30] At the same time, Spain remained embroiled in costly wars with France, England (Philip II being the architect of the infamous armada sent to teach Elizabeth I a lesson), and the rebellious Dutch. By the seventeenth century, Spain faced new threats from an increasingly ambitious England and the Netherlands. Unfortunately, Spain's Habsburg monarchy was also headed for a crash.

The Habsburgs had a clear genetic mutation exemplified by the Habsburg jaw. This disfigurement involved the unnatural protrusion of the mandible, or lower jaw, over the upper jaw, or maxilla. In mild cases this might be mainly cosmetic,[31] but in more serious cases it caused misalignment of the teeth with resultant speaking and eating difficulties. Evidence of the Habsburg jaw can be seen in paintings of the Spanish monarchs from Charles I on. Despite this, the Habsburgs continued to intermarry. Likely this disfigurement of the jaw was only the most visible sign of problematic genetic mutations affecting other aspects of the Habsburgs family's health.[32]

By 1665 Spain's empire was clearly on the decline with numerous financial, diplomatic, and military problems. Spain still had enormous resources to rely on but had been upstaged by ambitious powers in England, France, and the Netherlands. Spain needed a vibrant, energetic, and capable ruler to set things straight. Unfortunately, Spain instead found itself in 1665 with Charles II.

Charles II of Spain showing the pronounced Habsburg jaw.

To be fair, Charles II doesn't seem to have been a bad guy on the order of Caligula or Idi Amin. To the contrary, he tends to come across as a simple, passive individual not remotely suited to the role of leading a country. That he became king while a child certainly didn't help, but even as an adult he was unable to effectively rule in his own name, creating power struggles among courtiers and family that further damaged Spain.

The genetic impact of inbreeding on Charles II was enormous.[33] He did not talk until age four and struggled to walk through age eight. His misshapen jaw made both eating and talking difficult for him. Physically, he was short of stature and sickly, frequently experiencing physical maladies. His personality was uninquisitive and passive, and he often seemed disinterested and disconnected from events around him.[34]

Naturally, a leader with such qualities was ill-suited to maintaining or restoring Spain's position as a great power in European diplomacy. He had neither particular knowledge of nor interest in the complexities of politics. To what degree his intellect was impacted by his illnesses was a matter of some contention, but whether he experienced an intellectual disability in modern parlance or not, he showed little ability to put his intellect to work for the benefit of Spain.

One of the duties of the monarch was to secure a royal heir in order to ensure a smooth succession. Here, too, Charles was not up to the task. He married twice. To her credit, Charles fell in love with his first wife, the French Marie Louise. She was said to have described his experiencing premature ejaculation and, at any event, she never conceived a child. Upon her death, Charles was distraught but later remarried. Given that by this time he was entirely impotent, she did not conceive, either.

Charles aged prematurely, suffered significant gastrointestinal complaints like diarrhea, and experienced swelling in his legs, abdomen, and face. During his last years, he had difficulty standing and experienced hallucinations and seizures. He finally died at age thirty-nine. Autopsy revealed significant disease in multiple organ systems, including his reproductive system (a single, atrophied testicle likely explained his impotence).

This failure to produce an heir effectively ended the line of Spanish Habsburgs upon Charles's death in 1700. The War of the Spanish Succession, which followed Charles's death, plunged most of Europe—including England, France, the Netherlands, and Austria, as well as Spain—into a thirteen-year war. Charles's will favored passing the throne to his distant relative Philip V, from the Bourbon family in France. But the other European powers naturally did not a support a potential union of France and Spain. In the end, Philip V was confirmed as king of Spain but only upon renouncing his rights to the throne in France. The war effectively ended any pretension of Spain's continued great-power status, instead marking England's rise as the preeminent maritime power in Europe.

Some scholars[35] have speculated as to the specific origins of Charles II's inherited disease. Specifically, these scholars argue that inbreeding brought out pituitary disease, resulting in his body's failure to develop properly, as well as kidney disease, likewise resulting in his short, thin stature and pain and bone problems. These are merely speculative diagnoses, of course, but whatever the specific processes, it is clear that Habsburg inbreeding brought on Charles's infirmaries and premature death.

Spain ended up being stuck with him, however. Monarchies had become bureaucratic enough that simply assassinating the king (as with Elagabalus) was no longer an option, and the absence of any viable alternatives (as with Joanna's father and son) made it difficult for Spain to shift responsibility to another royal. Spain, in effect, simply had to wait for Charles II to die. Unfortunately, this merely lurched Spain into yet another unnecessary war, which left it in a permanently weakened state from which it never recovered. Spain continued to limp along as other European countries picked at the carcass of her empire until the United States finally put the Spanish Empire out of its misery in a brief 1898 war.

The Madness of King George III

Probably few cases of monarchical madness have been as popularized as that of England's third Hanoverian king, George III, who descended into an acute period of delirium late in his reign, nearly sparking a political crisis. Exactly what happened to George is worth considering, particularly as his madness is of an altogether different kind. Most of the individuals in this book either had deep-rooted disturbances of the personality or were chronically ill from at least their teenage years. By contrast, George first experienced madness in later adulthood, when he was fifty.

It's worth briefly looking at how the Hanoverians became kings of England as well as at George's upbringing. In 1714, the last of the acceptable Stuart monarchs, Queen Anne, died without any surviving children.[36]

I say *acceptable* because there were plenty of Stuarts running about, but most of them were Catholic and after kicking out the Catholic Stuart king James II in 1688, the English made it officially illegal for Catholics to assume the throne.[37]

The Electors of Hanover, a small German region in the chaotic Holy Roman Empire, were related to the Stuarts distantly but (to British sympathies) had the sense to remain Protestant, which made them good enough for the job of king of Great Britain. The very German George I became king of Great Britain in 1714, a situation that neither he nor the people of Great Britain found themselves as enthused about as one might have hoped.

The early Hanoverian kings, particularly George I and George II (yes, there are a lot of Georges in our near future, be prepared)[38] were through-and-through Germans who didn't speak English very well and kind of hated England. They were also—not to put too fine a point on it—jerks. Their family lives were chaotic, marked by dysfunctional marriages (George I imprisoned his adulterous former wife for decades, possibly after having her lover murdered) and incredibly hostile father-son relationships.

George III, to his credit, tried to break this horrible cycle. He was the grandson of George II and became the third Hanoverian king (and third George) after the premature death of his father, Frederick, who never became king.[39] It must be said that, whatever his faults, George III tried very hard to be a decent fellow, remaining faithful to his wife and, unlike the previous two Hanoverian kings, trying to be a good father to his children, albeit with mixed success. If George III had a fault, it is a common one among highly moral and self-restricting people, namely sanctimoniousness and lack of generosity toward the moral failings of others, particularly his sons.

George III's reign was marked by three notable international conflicts: the Seven Years' War (or French and Indian War in North America), which ended in 1763, the American War of Independence, and the Napoleonic Wars, which ended in 1815. All of these were fought largely against France. Although the first and last were successes for the United Kingdom, the American War of Independence obviously was not. George III's reign is probably known and blamed for this more than anything else.

One thing we can say about George III's madness is that it was not responsible for the loss of the American colonies. George's mental illness did not begin until years after the conflict was over in 1788. George was within his right mind (at least as much as any of the British kings) during the struggle. However, he is blamed for being obstinate and inflexible both due to his lack of sympathy for the grievances of the American colonists and in failing to support ministers who could competently navigate the conflict.[40] George III's stubbornness may have contributed to the loss of the colonies, but he certainly doesn't deserve all the blame. Indeed most, though not all, politicians in the United Kingdom as well as the general public initially supported the war. The American colonists were primarily aggrieved with the U.K. Parliament, not with George III, but his failure to see their side and his full support of Parliament made the Americans come to see him (probably a bit unfairly, to be honest) as a tyrant. But with the Revolutionary War, the American rebels stumbled into remarkably good luck regarding Britain's massive political and military incompetence, which handed the Americans eventual victory. The United Kingdom's best chance at winning the Revolutionary War would have been to avoid it in the first place, but this would have required deft leadership and flexibility in negotiating with the colonists, both in short supply at the time.[41] Had the British Parliament not been so heavy-handed or had George interceded on behalf of the colonists, the American colonies might have remained part of the United Kingdom, at least for a while longer. Alas, the path not chosen.

George III's mental health problems began in 1788. Initial symptoms were physical, particularly fever and gastrointestinal distress, but quickly became neurological. These primarily took the form of delirium manifested by confusion, loss of impulse control, and mania. He would talk quickly and at great length, often about fantastical topics and in a manner not entirely coherent. He rarely slept, and his behavior was erratic and often purposeless. He made sexual advances toward women who were not his wife (particularly one Lady Pembroke), something entirely uncharacteristic of him when in good health. As for his wife, Queen Charlotte, with whom he had shared a long and affectionate marriage, he now had harsh words, effectively casting her off as his wife.

Despite his evident madness, Charlotte was particularly wounded by those comments toward her. Did he really mean them? Probably not to the extent that she took them to heart. But most people's brains are full of positive and negative thoughts and we rely on our frontal lobes as a kind of filter, consciously choosing to express the good (at least one hopes) and filter out the bad. But during moments of incapacitation, that frontal lobe filter can break down, allowing more of the bad to escape. Did the faithful George sometimes harbor thoughts of other women? Probably, but they likely reflected only a small part of his thoughts that he chose not to express. Upon going mad, they broke free into the light of the sun, where they wounded Charlotte. One can only hope that she could see that they did not reflect the totality of who he was.[42]

Although George's problems were now mainly neurological, other health problems remained. Along with the gastrointestinal problems and pain, George sometimes developed purple-colored urine, perhaps a key clue to his diagnosis. With his behavior worsening, George, largely against his will, was secluded in a royal estate away from the public.

Here George was subjected to all manner of ill treatment. None of this was in bad faith, but medical treatments of the day were quite harsh, focused on drawing out or moving "humors" throughout the body. George's physicians gave him potions to make him vomit and blistered his legs with heated glass vials to try to draw the humors from his brain back to his legs (swelling of his legs had been one of the early symptoms of George's disease but had gone away). This latter treatment was dangerous because blisters could become infected and infections were serious business in the late eighteenth century.[43]

Not surprisingly, none of this worked and the queen brought in an unconventional physician, Francis Willis. Willis applied a kind of harsh behavioral therapy, threatening the king with straightjackets and other restraints whenever he acted up. To some degree, this had the effect of calming some of the king's behavior, much as brandishing a whip might subdue a caged animal, though it probably had little actual impact on George III's mental illness.[44] It's doubtful that the behavioral interventions helped George's mental illness any more than the blisterings or purgings did. What Willis did bring about was significant discord and contention among the physicians treating George who fought over the wording of updates regarding the king's health.

The king's illness also precipitated a governmental crisis. By the time of George III, the power of the monarch was greatly diminished but not irrelevant. George had the power to support government ministers and his assent was required for some legislation. As the king's illness stretched on for several months, this began to gum up some of the workings of government and reduced public confidence. Now George III's poor relationship with his son who was named—wait for it—George (he became George IV, so we'll call him that from now on to try to reduce confusion) came into play.

As noted, George III lived a highly moral lifestyle. His son, George IV,[45] did not. George IV loved drink, food, spending money on silly things, and women, particularly women who were older than him and already married. George IV caused no small amount of embarrassment for his upright father, and in return George III let his son know how he felt. So when George III was in a position of weakness, his son George IV pounced, seeking a regency that would take power away from his father.

In fairness to George IV, this wasn't entirely unreasonable; he simply was following in the footsteps of Joanna's father and son from centuries before. George III *was* mad, after all, and a functioning head of state was necessary for effective government. But it wasn't hard for many to read a power grab into the already-unpopular George IV's motivations.

George III thwarted his son's ambitions by suddenly recovering and resuming his duties. His behavior and speech returned to normal. Repairing the relationship with his son took longer, and the wounds between George III and Charlotte never fully healed. His marital relations only worsened during subsequent bouts of illness in the early 1800s, when he returned to his harsh treatment of her and obsession with Lady Pembroke. Ultimately, by 1810, George III's madness set in permanently, probably accompanied by dementia at this point. He lost his ability to understand events in the larger world, lost most of his sight, and rambled incoherently. He saw people who were not there and had difficulty identifying his own family, characteristic of senile dementia. Nonetheless, he survived until 1820, passing the throne to his son George IV.[46]

What, exactly, caused the madness of King George III? Several theories predominate. The most popular is that of the metabolic disease porphyria, a genetic disease in which the buildup of proteins can cause gastrointestinal problems, blistering when exposed to sunlight,[47] purple-tinted urine, and manic and psychotic psychiatric symptoms. Since it also can reoccur and remit, this appears to be a good fit for George III's symptoms.[48] However, it is merely a speculative theory.

Other sources have rejected the porphyria diagnosis, suggesting that George III had a more classic case of bipolar disorder.[49] The recurrent manic episodes of 1788, 1801, 1804, and the final illness beginning in 1810 are seen as significant fits characteristic of bipolar disorder. Certainly, the king's behavior during these moments is consistent with mania, and this hypothesis is not unreasonable. However, I find it unsatisfying for several reasons. First, it does not explain well the characteristic onset of George III's illnesses, which began with fever and gastrointestinal complaints then progressed to neuropsychiatric disorder in each case. Second, the presence of the purplish urine is difficult to wave away as an insignificant symptom. Presumably were you or I to pee purple, we might think to mention it to our physicians with some alarm.[50] Third, although it's not impossible for mania to begin so late in life, bipolar disorder more commonly begins in early adulthood.[51] Finally, the implication that manic episodes may have been brought on by stressful historical events[52] is certainly as speculative and selective as the arguments for porphyria and neglect the fact that George III was lucid during the entire Revolutionary War, probably one of the periods of his greatest stress. Although I do believe bipolar disorder is a reasonable differential diagnosis, overall, I don't find the weight of evidence supports it as the most likely explanation.

The porphyria diagnosis remains unpopular with many psychiatrists, however. Nonetheless, some historical evidence has emerged to suggest symptoms of porphyria in some of George III's descendants.[53] Recent analysis has revealed high concentrations of arsenic in the king's hair, arsenic that likely was administered as part of the treatments he received.[54] The presence of arsenic in medicines administered during early stages of George III's illnesses (such as the early fever and gastrointestinal distress) may have caused the metabolic disturbances that exacerbated what otherwise might have been relatively mild symptoms of porphyria. In other words, George III's madness was brought on by a combination of a genetic disorder, probably porphyria, combined with accidental poisoning by arsenic. Though certainly still speculative, this appears the most reasonable explanation.

Nonetheless, the diagnosis of George III remains controversial. However, it is certainly too simple to declare the case for porphyria to have been "thoroughly discredited" as some scholars have.[55] Nor should it be accepted without any doubt at all. It is easy to select evidence to support a beloved theory and ignore that which does not. We may never truly know the cause of George III's madness beyond a reasonable doubt.

The United Kingdom handled George III's madness not unlike Spain did with Joanna, seeking a regency of a capable male relative. From 1788 to 1789, this was thwarted by George III's recovery, and further bouts in 1801 and 1804 likewise did not necessitate a regency. By 1810, however, it was clear that George III was incapable of performing the functions of king on a permanent basis, and his son, the soon-to-be George IV, was given the responsibility of the regency. Unfortunately, George IV was concerned more for his own chaotic finances than he was the economic troubles of the masses during the early industrialized age and his popularity continued to decline. For good reason, one historical writer referred to the House of Hanover as "rubbish kings."[56] The bad luck of the Hanover monarchs ended with George III's granddaughter, Victoria. Ironically, she could not rule Hanover because she was a woman, and ultimately Hanover split from the United Kingdom.[57]

Fortunately for the United Kingdom, by 1788 the role of the king, while not insubstantial, was greatly diminished, and the mechanisms of state could grind on even during his periods of incoherence. Increasingly the United Kingdom, not unlike its wayward American colonies, was drifting perhaps unconsciously toward republicanism, though this wasn't entirely a recipe for avoiding madness as we see in chapter 10. Nonetheless, this insulated the United Kingdom from the worst of the potential catastrophes when a monarchy inherited an unstable monarch.

By the twentieth century, the majority of the world figured out that monarchy is mostly good for tourist pictures, fancy weddings, and elevating the occasional American divorcée into the royal family, such that little girls everywhere believe that they really *can* become princesses. A few spots, mainly in the Middle East, have maintained absolute monarchies. Depending on how one defines them, a few other states such as North Korea or even the Principality of Liechtenstein could be considered de facto absolute monarchies. But mostly the institution is on the outs and good riddance.

Potentially, the pope might be considered the absolute monarch of Vatican City. But madness as it pertains to religion is best considered separately, and to this we next turn.

WHEN GOD SPEAKS: MADNESS AND FAITH

In 1844, the Communist philosopher Karl Marx wrote, "religion is the sigh of the oppressed creature, the heart of a heartless world, and the soul of soulless conditions. It is the *opium* of the people." By this he meant that religion often serves to reduce people's pain in a world filled with suffering and injustice by giving them some hope for a post-now forever. Marx was not a fan of such beliefs and faith, which, he figured, prevented the working class from demanding more from the present life. Then again, given that Marx's own philosophies led directly to the deaths of tens of millions, perhaps he's not one to go wagging fingers.

There can be little doubt, examining Marx's quote a bit more optimistically, that faith has brought considerable insight, comfort, community, and grace to billions of humans who have lived since religions began to develop somewhere in our Stone Age history. At the same time, religion has often been at the heart of considerable darkness, war, murder, prejudice, and hatred as well. Many people who descend into mental illness become wracked by paranoid fantasies of gods and demons or think themselves prophets or magical healers. Religion can be a force for good but, in its darkest form, also a catalyst for madness. It is worth taking time to consider the roots of faith in a higher power and why this is so often turned to madness.

The Roots of Faith

To the best of our knowledge, humans are among the only critters on the planet to have shown definitive ritualistic or religious interest. One fascinating exception are elephants; though hardly attending mass regularly or genuflecting with their trunks, they do show particular interest in the bones of their dead when they come across them.[1] Biologists who study elephants suggest they show agitation upon finding these bones without showing such concern over the bones of other creatures. This awareness of and discomfort with death, apparently rare in most animals, is one precursor element of religion, as we soon see.

Most anthropologists and archaeologists look for the presence of "grave goods," that is, valuable objects buried with the dead that presumably they'd use in the afterlife as the indication of something like religious beliefs. That standard would pretty much limit religion to our own species and suggest that religiosity began no earlier than one hundred thousand years ago and perhaps closer to forty thousand years ago.[2] We'll leave aside for the moment the possibility that some form of higher intelligence might actually exist. It might—but there's only one certain way to find out and we'll each get our chance! Until then, the existence of god or gods is scientifically unfalsifiable[3] and, as such, beyond this book. It is nonetheless worth considering how the capacity to have faith evolved and what that means for how it can be so badly used at times.

Generally, evolutionary theories of religion suggest one of two things: religiosity evolved because it conveyed selective advantages, or religiosity is a kind of genetic goof that is the product of other evolved strategies such as culture or theory of mind. Regarding the first, that religiosity is a positive, evolved trait, it has been pointed out that the purity rituals of religion create a disease resistance strategy[4] or conveyed benefits involving cooperative behavior and social cohesion[5] with the individual benefit of increasing social status of the observant.[6] The alternate explanation for the evolution of religion is that religion evolved as a byproduct of other important traits, such as a tendency to investigate cause and effect or theory of mind, an ability by which we attribute reasoning capacity to others.[7] In that sense, we may find cause and effect when ritualistic behaviors appear to bring positive outcomes, even if by chance, and attribute reasoning ability to not just other humans, but also the weather, the ocean, and so forth. Thus, we erroneously attribute reasoned action (i.e., "acts of God") to random climate, geological, or even medical events. These two approaches aren't necessarily mutually exclusive, and accidental traits might subsequently be selected for. For instance, fear of punishment for religious transgressions might actually convey selective advantages such as less risk taking.[8]

Another piece of the pie is the fact that, unlike most critters, we have evolved to understand the inevitability of our own death. A potato, jellyfish, or even a dog doesn't necessarily comprehend that death is *inevitable* whatever we do with our lives. This can give rise to "death terror," which, like any anxiety, we seek to reduce. One theory called terror management theory suggests that we reduce death terror by creating culture and religion with attendant rituals as a means of convincing ourselves that our souls continue permanently after our physical demise, thereby reducing anxiety regarding death.[9] So, for instance, by faithfully not eating chickens, painting our skin purple every Thursday, and bowing to the great Pink Unicorn in the Sky, our souls can be selected to exist permanently after the deaths of our bodies. The trouble arises when we Pink Unicorn worshippers meet Fairy Princess disciples who must eat only candy canes for breakfast and stop whatever they're doing at noon every day to smile broadly for twenty minutes. Both sets of rituals and beliefs can't be right. So, either we admit that both sets of beliefs must be wrong and return to death terror or violently wipe out the Fairy Princess worshippers. Usually, we pick the latter.

In defense of religion, it's not like humans would have been pacific, interculturally cooperative critters but for organized religion. Humans are by nature rather violent.[10] And religion is often used as a pretext for violence motivated by other issues such as territory, cultural dominance, or hatred. Interestingly, when overdone, religion can become a focus for self-destruction as well as for war and murder. It is to an example of self-destruction that we first turn.

God's Diet Plan

At its best, religion can drive individuals to seek enlightenment and better themselves. However, this often comes with the perception that purification of the soul is at the expense of the body. The infliction of pain, suffering, and neglect (sometimes willing, sometimes not) for the purpose of purification is common across many faiths. This may involve minor sacrifices, such as Catholics avoiding tasty meat during Lenten Fridays; more serious sacrifices, such as the perpetual celibacy of the vestal virgins;

Participant in the Phuket Nine Emperor Gods Festival. *Photo:* Alan Chow, Creative Commons License.

or the extremes of purposeful self-mutilation. Perhaps one of the most famous of the later is the Nine Emperor Gods Festival from the Thai Island of Phuket, wherein many celebrants impale their faces with all manner of needles, rods, and other larger objects. This is all done without anesthetic, but with participants entering a trance-like state.

None of this is necessarily bad so long as it is healthy and rewarding for the participants (even the face-piercing Thais apparently suffer few ill effects). But at times religious zeal can be overdone, resulting in significant mental or physical harm to the participant.

As one example, extreme denial of the flesh, or asceticism, can result in dietary health issues or even anorexia nervosa (AN). As defined by the American Psychiatric Association's *DSM*, AN involves the willful restriction of one's body weight well below a person's recommended minimum weight for health.[11] Contrary to public misconception, AN does not necessarily involve restriction of weight to meet beauty ideals. Indeed, the restriction of weight typically does *not* match beauty ideals even for industrialized nations where thinner, more athletic figures are preferred. Likewise, evidence that AN is caused by viewing attractive actresses in mass media remains weak.[12] AN is rare in the general population, with less than one third of 1 percent of women ever experiencing the disorder (the numbers for men are too few to be calculated). AN does tend to be more prevalent in careers in which weight is a practical issue reducing job performance. For instance, symptoms of AN are far more common among male jockeys than other men.[13] However, this is to enable horses to run faster and obviously has little do to with ideal standards of physical attractiveness.[14]

During the Middle Ages, a pattern of extreme fasting to promote spiritualism in the Catholic community became recognized as symbolic of holiness. The patterns of weight restriction, self-neglect, lack of menstruation for women, and even preparing food for others are recognizable among individuals experiencing AN today.[15] One of the most famous such women was Saint Catherine of Siena, who lived and died in the mid-fourteenth century ACE.

Catherine was born in 1347 ACE as a twin, the twenty-third child in the family. Catherine began experiencing visions of Christ from an early age, reputedly about age six, and made a vow of chastity, avoiding a potential marriage by fasting. Instead, Catherine became a nun, much against the wishes of her parents, who ultimately gave in to her teenage stubbornness on the matter.[16] She matured into a prolific writer and political figure, using her influence as a living holy relic to influence the papacy and local politics. She is credited with aiding in the process by which the papacy returned from an exile in Avignon, France, to Rome. She wrote considerable other letters and prayers as well.[17]

As part of her ritual observations, Catherine adhered to strict regulations for eating as well as other physical punishments. She whipped herself and slept on only a hard board. She restricted herself mainly to eating vegetables and water, as well as the daily Eucharist. Eventually, she ate only inedible herbs, chewing them to extract the juice and spitting out the rest. At times she is reported to have induced vomiting in herself. She claimed to be made sick by any sweet foods and at one point gave up drinking even water. This, of course, quickly led to significant health complications and she briefly reversed course. By contrast, she gave away food and clothing to others, asking nothing in return. In 1380, she became paralyzed and died shortly afterward at the age of thirty-three, her body greatly weakened by starvation and dehydration.

What led to her extreme emotional state has been a matter of some speculation. Some have argued that her periodic religious visions suggest temporal lobe epilepsy, given that she otherwise was coherent and lucid.[18] Her visions were, indeed, quite strong and included a vision of marrying Christ himself. She commented to another woman in one of her letters, "Well seest thou that thou art a bride, and that He has wedded thee and every creature, not with a ring of silver, but with the ring of His Flesh," which is sometimes interpreted as Christ's foreskin, although one might generously interpret her meaning as more symbolic than that. She also had visions of stigmata, although apparently only she could see these, at least until after her death.[19]

Catherine also suffered from depression and experienced visions of the Catholic Church in ruins. Restricting what she ate appears to have been a means for her to assert some control and sense of power, a feeling (if less religious) shared with many modern individuals suffering from AN.[20] Indeed, AN is not typically a dysfunction of appetite, but rather the purposeful suppression of appetite as a means of asserting a sense of control. However, other scholars have suggested that deficits in taste perception may have played some role in Catherine's eating disorder, particularly involving her aversion to sweet tastes.[21]

Contemporary descriptions of Catherine suggest she was generally lucid and a powerful and persuasive persona, given her authority in the Catholic Church during her lifetime, which was relatively rare among women of that age. As such, her behavior cannot be attributed merely to psychosis. Indeed, her case is a classic one of AN, perhaps exacerbated by physiological issues, whether epilepsy or other nervous system dysfunctions. Cases such as hers help inform us that AN is a complex illness and that the familiar narrative that it is an unfortunate byproduct of beauty culture may be less true than typically thought. To a large degree, AN appears similar to obsessive-compulsive disorder, wherein ritualistic behaviors (such as weight reduction) are used to diminish anxiety-provoking intrusive thoughts (in this case about eating or the loss of some "perfectionist" state[22]). In this sense, the causal roots of AN may be far more internalized than externalized, though significant impacts from family environment is also likely.

Catherine of Siena Besieged by Demons (none of whom thought to bring her a cupcake*). Anony-mous, circa 1500.

* I jest, but of course AN is not a laughing matter for those experiencing it. The following resource provides a listing of treatment centers in each of the 50 U.S. states: www.eatingdisorderhope.com/treatment-centers. Be sure to research centers carefully, as some are better than others.

Catherine of Siena was sainted for her authority in the church as well as for reported miracles both during her lifetime and after her death. Without the "madness" of her AN, she might not have achieved such high status. Yet she also provides an example of the power of religion to become self-destructive. Religiosity, when combined with madness, need not be self-destructive, but it can bring on considerable sorrow in the world. It is to several such examples that we now turn.

The Fires of Waco

Religion is a common focal point for people with mental illness. Our university at Stetson has an open campus and occasionally mentally ill individuals from the local community wander through. Inevitably, whomever they happen to find sends them to the psychology department as if we were some kind of university clinic. Most of the religious psychosis I've seen has been in clinical settings, but I've had one or two unfortunate community members in my office, and I also get the occasional letter in the mail that somehow manages to discourse on video games, Jesus, and the Nazis, all in thick handwritten print. Unfortunately, mental health services in the United States remain rather threadbare and there are too few resources for long-term care.

Psychosis is a condition in which an individual experiences hallucinations, or perceptual experiences that aren't real, and delusions, or beliefs about the world that are false but resistant to reality testing. Most religion, of course, is not psychotic. But a search for spiritual meaning is common among humans, combined with the distorted perceptual experiences of hallucinations, psychosis commonly gives rise to distorted beliefs about spirituality.[23]

Most people experiencing psychosis also have difficulties with communication, social skills, organization, and even hygiene. Therefore it is difficult for these individuals to effectively pass along their religious beliefs to others, to attract followers, and such. But the *DSM* lists a condition, delusional disorder, which is marked mainly by the presence of delusions, but in which communication abilities remain intact. In other words, the person appears to be entirely lucid other than when talking about the content of his or her delusions. Even here, such individuals may be coherent and convincing enough to convince others that they are prophets, visionaries, and faith leaders. And voilà, a new religion is born.

Most new faiths don't get very far because attracting adherents is a challenge. What influences some individuals to abandon more traditional faiths and commit to a new cult is a complex process. It typically involves some degree of disaffection with the individual's society, a promise of inclusion or acceptance into the cult, and identification with a charismatic leader.[24] As such, some individuals may be particularly vulnerable to recruitment by cults, finding social belonging that had been denied them in more conventional outlets. Cults themselves likely vary from those that are of reasonably good faith in seeking spiritual enlightenment to those that are intentionally predatory on the finances, sexual consent, or health of their members. At the extreme, some cults have ended with the mass suicide of members, such as the 1997 deaths of thirty-nine members of the Heaven's Gate cult who believed an alien ship disguised in the Hale-Bopp comet had come to take them to heaven[25] and the more infamous mass suicide/murder at Jonestown in 1978 wherein more than nine hundred people died.

Another cult marked by senseless violence was the Branch Davidians, who came to infamy in 1993. The group that came to be called the Branch Davidians were a splinter from the Seventh Day Adventist Church with strict religious and millennialism views. For most of the group's history, members conformed to harsh rules regarding behavior and watched for signs of the end of times. When the end times did not arrive when expected, leadership of the group frayed and came to a head by the mid-1980s when rival factions of the group fought it out, sometimes at gunpoint. At this critical juncture a man named David Koresh[26] managed to assume violent control of the group, located near Waco, Texas. Koresh reinforced the typical elements of a predatory cult, including authoritarian rule, isolation from society, and particular advantages for himself. Specifically, he took multiple women in the community as wives and sired perhaps thirteen children among them while enforcing strict rules of sexual conduct and chastity on other members of the group.[27] His second-in-command, Steve Schneider, reportedly turned his own legal wife over to Koresh. Nonetheless, Schneider remained fiercely loyal to Koresh until the end. Koresh controlled his members' behavior rigidly, ridiculing those who misbehaved and subjecting members to hours of his sermons without food or bathroom breaks. Under his guise, the Branch Davidians began to stockpile weaponry and increasingly focus on the end of times, with Koresh the chosen leader who, as the Lamb of God, would lead the group through the apocalypse he himself was initiating by opening the seven seals of a book in God's hand.[28]

Thus Koresh seduced his members with visions of a fiery Revelation-inspired future, not to mention conflict with authorities in the U.S. government. Koresh claimed to experience holy visions, which assigned him leadership status as well as special rights to procreate with multiple women. In return, he offered the promise of safe passage for his followers through Armageddon and into the welcome embrace of God if only they followed him. An interesting question to consider is whether Koresh himself believed any of this. One possibility is that Koresh fabricated the entire thing in order to assume power and control over a group of others. The cynical use of religion for personal gain has a long and storied history, from the sale of indulgences in the Renaissance Catholic Church to the ultra-rich pastors of today's megachurches. Undoubtedly, the vast majority of religious leaders are sincere in seeking to guide their members toward enlightenment, but religion also can be good business for the clever and shameless.

The other possibility is that Koresh really believed most of what he was saying, even if it was rather self-glorifying. This would indicate that Koresh had a psychotic condition but was coherent enough to communicate it to others and convince them of its validity. This is precisely the combination we'd expect with delusional disorder, and it is possible that Koresh had this condition. Koresh appears to have had vivid beliefs and claimed to have visions related to his role in the end of times. He remained consistent to these throughout the ensuing standoff with the federal government and eventually died for them. Throughout, he repeated his religious beliefs, claimed to be astounded by a "guitar nebula," and looked for signs from God regarding what to do. This doesn't mean that Koresh might not also have had antisocial personality traits, but it does argue that he may indeed have been delusional as well. Ultimately, a definitive answer is impossible given Koresh's death and opinions still differ, but I suspect this second explanation is most likely.

Exactly how the Branch Davidians came to the attention of federal law enforcement and who is responsible for the way events unfolded is a matter of considerable contention to the present day. In its official report, the U.S. Department of Justice claimed that the federal government, through the Bureau of Alcohol, Tobacco, and Firearms (ATF), executed a search warrant on the Branch Davidian compound for the possession of illegal weapons and explosives as well as concern that some of the females that Koresh was having sex with were underaged.[29] This occurred on February 28, 1993. The raid went poorly, with gunfire exchanged between the Branch Davidians and the ATF agents raiding the compound. Four ATF agents died, along with five members of the Branch Davidians. Another Branch Davidian who had been away from the compound at the time of the assault died following an attempt to shoot his way back into the compound. Following the failed raid, the FBI took over negotiations with the Branch Davidians,[30] negotiations that would continue for almost two months, until April 19, 1993. This stalemate continued to the great embarrassment of the U.S. government, which seemed impotent to resolve the conflict. The Branch Davidian compound was surrounded by federal agents including armored vehicles.

Koresh informed the negotiating officers that he himself had been wounded in the raid but refused medical treatment for his own wounds or those of other Branch Davidians. He demanded and was granted permission to broadcast his religious views on local radio and allowed several children to leave the compound a day later. However, he did not exit the compound peacefully with his followers as he initially had promised in exchange for the broadcast. During the negotiations, Koresh repeated the belief that he needed time to finish opening the seven seals and this justified his delays. He also became agitated at times and, according to government accounts, threatened the deaths of the children and others within the compound.

Koresh did continue to allow a trickle of children to leave the compound. One of these children had what appeared to be a suicide note from one of the adults (the child's mother) in the compound, raising concern that the Branch Davidians intended mass suicide. Federal agents tried to increase pressure on the Branch Davidians by cutting electricity and blasting loud music to cause sleep deprivation while also negotiating for a peaceful end to the standoff. Along with the children, several adults, mainly women, also left the compound.

By March 22, the federal agents began considering nonlethal means to force an end to the standoff. The vague outlines of the plan involved the heavy use of tear gas to force the Branch Davidians out of their buildings. It was also becoming apparent that attempts to stress the Branch Davidians with loud music, including Tibetan chants, were not working. Several days later a man who belonged to the cult managed to breach the perimeter, joining the Branch Davidians in their compound.

Koresh claimed to be working on a manifesto regarding his vision of the seven seals, but by April 19, the federal authorities had lost patience. They enacted their tear gas plan, using armored vehicles to clear obstructions and to begin inserting the tear gas into the compound. In its report, the Department of Justice reported concerns that the children within the compound were being abused during the standoff, but it is likely that the impasse had also become a governmental embarrassment.

Poor weather and strong winds hampered the effort, and the Branch Davidians themselves began firing on the armored vehicles. Nine Branch Davidians escaped the compound during this time and were rescued. However, a fire soon started in the Branch Davidian compound. Seventy-five other Branch Davidians, including multiple children, died during the fire. Koresh died sometime during the conflagration, apparently of a gunshot wound to the head. Many other Branch Davidians had been shot, as well, including multiple children. One child died of a stab wound to the chest. Others suffocated or died from burns.

Government investigations determined that the Branch Davidians had set the fire themselves, possibly at three different points within the compound. The Department of Justice stated that the tear gas used was nonflammable, although damage to the compound caused by the armored vehicles might have helped ventilate the fire. Nonetheless the compound was poorly constructed and strong winds likely fed the fire. An investigation by Congress in 2000, however, suggested that several gas rounds may have included pyrotechnic means of discharging the tear gas, although little evidence emerged that these caused the fire. The report concluded that the FBI had not inadvertently set the fires.[31]

Exactly who is to blame for the original shoot-out remains a matter of contention. Some surviving Branch Davidians claim the ATF began

Branch Davidian Compound. *Photo:* U.S. Government.

shooting first, whereas the official government reports claim ATF agents were ambushed by the Branch Davidians. A more credible criticism is a breakdown in communication between FBI negotiators and the Branch Davidians, with the FBI failing to understand the religious perspective of the Branch Davidians and to make a clear argument to them why surrender was a desired outcome.[32] The congressional report of 2000 accused federal authorities of botching the initial raid on the Branch Davidian compound, as well as the final tear-gas attack, but cleared the federal authorities from discharging firearms or setting the final fire. Other accounts have been more sympathetic to the Branch Davidians, casting the federal authorities as bad guys in the narrative and claims of wrongdoing by the Branch Davidians as false or exaggerated, with federal incompetence leading to unnecessary deaths.[33]

It's difficult to escape the observation that David Koresh had become like a god to his adherents, who were willing to follow him into a situation where they and their children reasonably could expect to die. The available evidence suggests it is highly likely Koresh did believe his religious views, while also demonstrating an incredible need for control and power over his congregation and disregard for their well-being. Even the final blaze may have reflected his need to control his followers, burning them rather than setting them free.[34]

Sincere in his religious beliefs or not, Koresh was a madman who led himself and his followers to a mass murder-suicide. But as authorities feared, after their demise, the Branch Davidians became martyrs for the cause of far-right antigovernment groups, even those with fewer fringe religious pretensions. The Branch Davidians did not single-handedly cause the increased vociferousness and influence of far-right, neofascist, racist, and paranoid groups. But their story did contribute to a steady flow of anger seeping in that direction that continues to provide an existential threat to liberalism in the United States as of this writing.

Violent fringe religions are not uniquely the territory of the United States by any means. Next we turn to the example of a murderous cult from Japan.

Supreme Truth

As we see from the case of the Branch Davidians, extreme isolation from and often hostility toward the rest of society is a common hallmark of many predatory cults. As best we know from the case of the Branch Davidians, they appeared content to await the end of times. Arguably, given the implied threat in their collection of illegal firearms and explosives as well as the allegations of abuse of minors, the federal government had ample reason to intervene. However, there appears to be little evidence that the Branch Davidians constituted an immediate threat to those outside their compound at the time of the 1993 raid. Conflict was, in effect, initiated by the government, not the cult. Whether the government was right or wrong to do so remains a topic of very strong opinions.

Around the same time as the Branch Davidian compound was burning, a Japanese apocalyptic cult called Aum Shinrikyo was beginning to make waves across the Pacific. This cult formed in the 1980s, beginning as a kind of yoga studio but eventually developing into a death-oriented faith incorporating elements of Tibetan Buddhism, Hinduism, Christianity, and New Age ideas. The group was led by a con artist named Shoko

Asahara. Born partly blind, Asahara was raised in humble surroundings and had a childhood history of bullying others before turning to scams to get rich. As a youth he acquired the ability to control others, particularly those who were in pain and in need of connection. Unfortunately, he turned this ability toward his own twisted ends.[35] He ran his cult as predators do, isolating his members, taking from them their money and cutting their ties with family and friends, threatening them spiritually and even physically if they did not obey him.[36]

With the unquestioned obedience of his followers, Asahara focused increasingly on collecting wealth and power, as well as on doomsday visions including a fantasy about controlling a nuclear device.[37] Resentment over his blindness and for being sent to a school for the blind, which he may have interpreted as socially isolating, apparently fed into a deep hatred and resentment toward society. As a consequence, as Aum Shinrikyo grew to more than a thousand full-time members, much of its activities were directed toward acquiring means of destruction on a grand scale.

Here we can ask of Asahara the same question as David Koresh. Did Asahara truly believe the religious gibberish he sold to his idolizing members? With Koresh, his steadfastness to his visions even when he might have saved his own life by moderating them argues for delusional content. This does not mean Koresh wasn't a psychopath as well, but it does suggest some authenticity to his claims even if they hardly represented a coherent doctrine. With Asahara, the impetus appears to have been for gaining wealth and power and turning his influence toward damaging a society he hated. This argues that Asahara was more classically a psychopath who exploited religion toward his own personal ends.

Aum Shinrikyo pursued its interests in gaining a nuclear weapon for a time, seeking sources of uranium deposits and making contacts with disaffected Russian scientists.[38] Fortunately, this came to nothing, and the cult had to make do and consider biological or chemical weapon alternatives. During the late 1980s and early 1990s, the cult is known to have murdered at least one critic of the group and his family and considered assassinations of other critics.[39] By the early 1990s, it attempted to cultivate and disperse several biological weapons, including botulism, Ebola, and anthrax.[40] In each case, the attacks succeeded mainly in creating bad smells, failing to sicken anyone. It turns out that weaponizing biological agents is more difficult than imagined and Aum Shinrikyo lacked the technical prowess to pull off such an attack. As such, the group finally turned to chemical weapons.

Why was the group so intent on creating mass casualties? Most of the rank-and-file members likely had little idea what the leadership was doing. The direction appeared to come from Asahara himself who, as noted, harbored a seething resentment toward society. He infected his followers, many of them also alienated from society, with a vision of society as decadent and wicked. Violence was rationalized as bringing on the end times and salvaging humanity from wickedness. Former members of Aum Shinrikyo spoke of turning a blind eye to evidence of Asahara's duplicity and malevolence, so desperate were they for the transcendental spiritual experiences they craved and received as part of the group.[41]

Even among predatory cults, Aum Shinrikyo represents the most malignant combination of a charismatic but psychopathic leader combined with members so alienated from society that they are willing to commit murder to please their leader and secure access to the afterlife. Spirituality became twisted to settle personal vendettas and vulnerable people exploited to commit atrocities. Unfortunately, a small number of people become lost in modern societies, alienated and sometimes lacking the social skills to succeed. Such individuals often describe conversion to a cult as transformative, of having been "found" after being lost for so many years. The experience means sacrificing the previous identity and autonomy in favor of the loving, if demanding, new faith in the personage of the prophet.[42] Few resources exist to help them before they become involved with predatory groups. Most predatory cults mainly take advantage of their members, but a few such as Aum Shinrikyo lash out violently against society.

By 1994 the group had gotten reasonably proficient at developing the neurotoxin sarin. As with many nerve agents, death by sarin poisoning is brutal and painful. The highly toxic nerve agent interferes with communication between nerves and muscles. Death typically occurs by suffocation when the muscles that control breathing no longer function and is accompanied by painful contractions, searing pain, and loss of control of bodily functions. The group is believed to have murdered individual opponents during this time, potentially using sarin in some assassinations.

In June 1994, Aum Shinrikyo carried out its first mass attack using sarin, releasing a cloud of the gas from a refrigerated truck into the town of Matsumoto. In this case the motive appears to have been a legal dispute. Aum Shinrikyo was on the losing side of a real-estate quarrel and sought to eliminate the judges involved in the case before receiving a negative verdict. The gas cloud killed seven people in the town and sickened five hundred more.[43] Amazingly, the group managed to avoid the attention of authorities for this heinous crime.

In March 1995, Aum Shinrikyo carried out a more audacious attack on the public. Packages with sarin were left on five Tokyo underground trains. Cult members pierced the packages before escaping, allowing the contents to spill out and vaporize, spreading through the trains. Twelve people died, and at least a thousand others required hospitalization, some with long-lasting injuries.[44] This time, police were alerted to Aum Shinrikyo's involvement in the attack and quickly raided the group's compounds, placing dozens of members under arrest, Asahara among them. Several attacks by Aum Shinrikyo involving hydrogen cyanide weapons continued after Asahara's arrest, though they were not successful. Many cult members were found guilty of various levels of involvement in the sect's crimes, and thirteen including Asahara were sentenced to death by hanging for their involvement in the Toyko sarin attack or other murders perpetrated by the group. All were hanged in the summer of 2018.[45] Nonetheless, the renamed cult still survives and is designated a "dangerous religion" subject to surveillance in Japan and is considered a terrorist group in the United States.

Madness in a group such as Aum Shinrikyo functions on two levels. First, in the psychopathic leader such as Asahara, who cynically uses the vulnerabilities of others to amass power and exact retribution on those he feels have wronged him. And second, among the vulnerable members who subvert their own identity to the will of a charismatic leader, engaging in horrific crimes to please him and ensure their own path to the afterlife. Unfortunately, research on cult activity remains too sparse to fully understand how governments, therapists, and loved ones can best intercede to prevent tragedies like the 1995 Toyko sarin gas attack from occurring in the future.

A Bombing in Boston

The one thing we can say with some degree of definitiveness is that individuals who feel alienated, alone, and despondent are particularly vulnerable for recruitment by dangerous religious ideologies. Such individuals may find meaning and acceptance in a dangerous group, connections denied to them through more conventional social contacts. This motivates such individuals to engage in violence rather than return to their prior isolation.

No religion has a monopoly on violence, and even faiths with deep pacifist messages such as New Testament Christianity and Buddhism have been associated with politicized violence. Thus, I argue, religiosity is more window dressing than cause of human violence, and it's unlikely that the historical course of human atrocities would have been tallied much differently had humans evolved as atheists. Instead, religion can focus as a rallying point for those whose minds are filled with hateful madness a kind of moral virtue for acts they would have committed anyway.

Discerning the degree to which religiosity can predict violence has been controversial in modern history. For instance, in the United States, most terroristic violence has been domestic. That is to say, committed by mainly quasi-Christian[46] Americans against other Americans. According to a 2017 report by the U.S. federal government,[47] these were about equally distributed between violence perpetrated by far-right extremists (e.g., nationalists, racist hate groups, etc.) who accounted for 106 deaths and Islamist extremists who accounted for 119 deaths. It is worth noting that most of the Islamic extremists were themselves residents of the United States, not invaders from other countries. In past decades, far-left groups such as Weather Underground also engaged in terroristic violence in the United States, but that is far less common today. Further, to add to the confusion, it is worth noting that many of the incidents included as domestic terrorism also would be included in tallies of mass shootings. For example, the June 2016 mass shooting at Orlando's Pulse nightclub perpetrated by a Muslim American man. Do such incidents count as domestic terrorism or as mass shootings?

How a crime gets defined depends a lot on politics. If we're talking gun control, the Pulse shooting is considered a mass shooting. If we're worried about Islamic terrorism, then it's a terrorist attack. By contrast, the Columbine massacre, in which two teen boys killed twelve fellow students and a teacher at their high school in 1999, isn't remotely considered terrorism. Is Columbine different from Pulse because the Columbine killers were unaffiliated whites with no political cause and the Pulse shooter vaguely pledged allegiance to the radical Islamism group Islamic State of Iraq and the Levant (ISIL)?

Interestingly, recent research suggests that answer is no. Research has indicated that suicide terrorists such as the Pulse shooter or 9/11 bombers are psychologically similar to people who commit mass or school shootings such as the Columbine killers.[48] Specifically, they share the traits of extreme antisocial personalities, deep mental health issues including suicidal ideation, and a sense of grievance toward others. Suicide terrorists are willing to die, not just because of the promises of some heavenly reward, but because they already want to die. But, as with mass shooters, they blame others for their mental state and intend to punish those others with violence on the way out. In effect, the madness of the suicide terrorist and the mass homicide perpetrator is more similar than different.

This raises the tricky issue of ethnic profiling when it comes to terrorism. Terrorism is nothing new to history and has been used by multiple cultural and religious groups to intimidate other groups. It is used both by governments in power and various nongovernmental groups. Depending on politics, military strategies, economics, and other forces, terrorism can flare up in one region then die down only to flare up elsewhere. However, within the United States and Europe, considerable attention is focused on terroristic violence perpetrated by Islamist groups such as al-Qaeda and ISIL. Attacks such as 9/11, which killed roughly three thousand Americans, as well as bombings, shootings, vehicle ramming, and other attacks throughout Europe have associated terrorism with the Middle East and Islam in the minds of many. This occurs because the human mind tends to work in terms of broad strokes rather than details. We use heuristics to make snap judgments about a situation. To a large degree, these are necessary and adaptive, allowing us to quickly estimate risk. Although we might recognize that domestic terrorism in the United States is about equally split between far-right and Islamist terrorists, the 9/11 attacks remain vivid in the memories of many, as do more recent, albeit smaller, attacks throughout Europe. It can be difficult for people to remain nuanced in their perceptions under such conditions.

On one hand, it is clear that radical Islamist groups such as ISIL are promoting terrorism and that such groups provide a unique challenge at the time of this writing. The inability to acknowledge that particular regions or cultures are currently struggling with violence more than others only does disservice to our ability to focus resources and attention. At the same time, we must also recognize that the vast majority of people from the Middle East or the Muslim faith are not violent terrorists and are as repulsed by radical violence as much as anyone. Our brains have difficulty navigating such nuances, however, and it is easy for alertness to descend to Islamophobia and racism on one side and politically correct naivete on the other. Fostering discussions among stakeholders of all backgrounds about reducing terroristic violence is more fruitful than taking rigid ideological standpoints, but such also requires a degree of rationality on the part of humans that is often in short supply. To examine how religious extremism can spill over into terroristic violence, we'll consider the case of Tamerlan and Dzhokhar Tsarnaev, Chechen American brothers who, in 2013, killed four people in connection with bombings of the Boston Marathon.

Between 2002 and 2003, the two Tsarnaev brothers arrived in the United States with their family from Kyrgyzstan, a politically conflicted country near Russia. Their parents received asylum in the United States and the family settled in as many immigrant families do. Dzhokhar adjusted reasonably well at first, doing well in school, but his older brother Tamerlan struggled. He did poorly in school, associated with a fundamentalist Islamic mosque, and was arrested for assaulting a girlfriend. Increasingly, he showed interest in violent, jihadi internet sites. By 2011, the U.S. federal government received warning that Tamerlan was becoming radicalized and planning to travel to Russia to join anti-Russian insurgents in Chechnya. The investigation at this time, however, concluded without detaining him.[49] He was placed on a terrorist watch list but nonetheless allowed to travel to Russia in 2012.

At some point during this time, Tamerlan succeeded in radicalizing his younger brother Dzhokhar. Some speculate that the brothers, or at least Tamerlan, may have been involved in a 2011 triple murder. Three men, two of whom were Jewish, were viciously killed in Waltham, Massachusetts. The victims were nearly decapitated and marijuana and money were left behind at the scene, suggesting lack of a financial motive. Given affiliations between Tamerlan and one of the victims, suspicions later were raised that Tamerlan may have been involved. Another suspect was killed by police in 2013 shortly after allegedly confessing that he and Tamerlan had committed the killings. The suspect allegedly lunged at the interviewing officers after confessing. However, this triple murder officially remains unsolved.[50]

Boston Marathon bombing. *Photo:* Aaron Tang, Creative Commons License.

On April 15, 2013, Tamerlan and Dzhokhar detonated two improvised explosive devices placed in backpacks along the path of the Boston Marathon. Three people were killed and 264 wounded, including sixteen who experienced traumatic limb amputations from the blast. The two brothers fled the scene. However, they were identified both by witnesses and by security camera footage at the scene. Their photos were released to the public three days later.

That night, April 18, the brothers engaged in a shootout with a university police officer, killing him. They later carjacked an SUV, but the owner of the vehicle escaped and called the police. The owner told police that the suspects had been discussing the Boston Marathon bombing. Police quickly trapped the vehicle and another shootout began. The brothers fired on officers and threw homemade bombs. Multiple officers were wounded, some seriously. Tamerlan was first wounded by gunfire then, while wrestling with police, run over by his own brother as Dzhokhar fled the scene in the SUV. Tamerlan later died at a hospital.

Dzhokhar ditched the SUV soon after, provoking a house-to-house search of the nearby area. The next evening, a resident called police, stating that he believed someone was hiding under a tarp in a boat outside his house. Officers fired at the boat, which was determined to have a human occupant. Once firing stopped, negotiations led to Dzhokhar surrendering to authorities.[51] He was sentenced to death in 2015.[52]

During the sentencing, U.S. Attorney Carmen Ortiz said, "The bombings were not a religious crime . . . even though the bombers claimed to represent Islam. It was a political crime committed by a pair of adults who adopted an ideology of hate."[53] In this sense, antireligion crusaders have it wrong when they imply that religion is a cause of human violence. Religion can act as a rationale for violence, to be sure, but it's unlikely that the atheistic world would be any less brutal than the theistic one. The worst we might say for faith is that, despite many of the world's religious movements ostensibly emphasizing pacifism, they have been less than successful in stemming the tide of human aggression.

The case of the Tsarnaev brothers isn't the only one in the United States or Europe in recent years to carry with it an aura of Islamist-inspired violence. For instance, in 2015, married couple Rizwan Farook and Tashfeen Malik opened fire at an office party in San Bernadino, California, killing fourteen and injuring twenty-two.[54] Farook may have been motivated by arguments at his workplace, which was hosting the party. Yet the couple also proclaimed allegiance to groups such as ISIL and had been preparing for terroristic violence for months, stockpiling weapons and making explosives, some of which they hoped to deliver on radio-controlled toy cars. The couple left their six-month-old daughter with Farook's mother before carrying out the attack. The couple were later killed in a shootout with police. This case highlights the often muddled, intermingled motives of personal grievance and religious extremism. It also provides a rare example of a husband-and-wife team in mass homicide.

Undoubtedly humans will continue to violently clash over faith for the foreseeable future. But conflicts that are ostensibly faith based have declined in number in recent decades. Underlying many of these were struggles between cultures over land and resources. In answer to the question of whom among us are correct in their faith: whether Christian, Muslim, Hindu, Buddhist, or atheist, there is only one empirical way to test our hypotheses about god. It's an experiment we are each destined to undertake.

CHAPTER SIX
MADNESS ON THE COMMUNE

I n the mid-nineteenth century, German philosophers Karl Marx and Freidrich Engels developed a philosophy of social structures rooted in class struggle and utopian egalitarianism. Throughout most of history, governments of all sorts—whether democracies or despotic autocracies—tended to cater to social elites at the expense of the masses. This became increasingly true under modern capitalist states in which elites, or the bourgeoisie, controlled the levers of production to the detriment of the masses, the proletariat, the oppressed laborers. Marx and Engels laid out ideas by which capitalist societies could experience a revolution of the proletariat, with control of production passing to all members of society, or socialism. This would eventually lead to a classless utopian society of common ownership, or communism.[1] Instead, communism as it was practically applied throughout the world in the twentieth century, left a legacy of misery, death, and world conflict.

In fairness, the goals of communism as established by Marx and Engels include a fair number of items that we might consider reasonable today, such as progressive taxation, abolition of child labor, and free education for children. Other goals, including the abolition of land ownership, state centralization of credit banking and communication, and the redistribution of the population in order to eliminate urban/rural distinctions may come across as a bit authoritarian. In 1917, communism obtained its first large-scale opportunity to apply itself to state rule in the crumbling tsarist Russian state.

Tsarist Russia had been involved in World War I since 1914, and a combination of military defeats and long-term social and economic problems led to considerable discontent. This was exacerbated by the failure of Tsar Nicholas's wife Alexandra to provide coherent leadership of the government in St. Petersburg while he was away failing to provide coherent leadership for the armies fighting at the front.[2] Ultimately, this dissatisfaction with the monarchy led to the breakout of revolutionary movements throughout 1917. The tsar and his family were arrested and, in 1918, shot. Sadly for Disney princess fans everywhere (not to mention the tsar's family), the remains of all Tsar Nicholas's household, including the mythical daughter Anastasia, have been located.[3]

In swooped Vladimir Lenin who, living largely in exile at the time, nearly missed the revolution owing to bad transportation back into Russia.[4] Once back, Lenin united other Russian communist exiles with local malcontents such as Joseph Stalin and pushed for Bolshevik Communism as the organizational government of Russia. The October 2017 revolution brought bolshevism to the forefront of government, but it would be several more years of civil war with interventions by the governments of the United Kingdom, the United States, and others attempting to stop a communist takeover. But Lenin and his cronies proved victorious and communism was established firmly in Russia, or what would soon become the Soviet Union.

Lenin obviously was influenced by Marxism but also adapted it to his purposes. Putting it a bit bluntly, Lenin believed (perhaps not without reason) that the masses of ordinary people were too dumb to carry out the revolution faithfully on their own. They needed to be guided by the strong hand of an ideologically pure few in the Communist Party. Therefore, party membership and ideological adherence became cornerstones of Marxist-Leninism. Deviations from the party line were to be met harshly with condemnation, humiliation, expulsion from the party, and sometimes violence. If this is starting to sound less like rings-of-people-holding-hands-and-singing-together-in-egalitarian-bliss envisioned by some communist faithful, well, you're not wrong. Under Lenin, Russian communism developed into brutal, authoritarian one-party rule, providing an unfortunate model for communism everywhere.

Lenin enjoyed a mythical position in the Communist Party and, while he lived, a steadying if authoritarian force for the Russian state. Nobody would mistake Lenin for Santa, but he wasn't an advocate for the kind of meat grinder horror that was yet to come. But Lenin was also primarily a thinker and gradually delegated greater and greater amounts of practical authority to just one of his disciples: Joseph Stalin.

Comrade Stalin

Between 1922 and 1924, Lenin suffered a series of strokes, the last of which killed him. At some point during this time, he may have begun to realize he'd created a monster. In one of his final writings, he criticized Stalin and suggested removing him from his powerful post of party secretary general. Lenin was struck down by strokes before he could put these thoughts into action, but the existence of this letter became a controversial affair after Lenin died in 1924. Nonetheless, Lenin's last-minute objections were too late. The monster he'd helped create assumed power in Soviet Russia by creating a terror state on a scale seldom before seen.

Joseph Stalin, born Joseph Djugashvili,[5] was born in 1879[6] in a small town in the region of Georgia. No, not the state north of Florida. This Georgia was then a region of Russia with its own non-Russian ethnic group. Today Georgia exists as an independent nation just south of Russia in the same sense that a mouse lives an independent existence just south of a cat. Stalin's family was poor, and his father was a violent alcoholic who beat Stalin and his mother regularly. Some who knew him in those years suspected that these beatings helped turn him into the heartless and suspicious creature he was to become, both resentful toward others in authority and inured against the suffering of others.[7] Stalin's mother also beat him, though this seemed mixed with some genuine affection as well as ambitions that he might become a priest. Parenting practices at that time were generally harsh and it is thought that Stalin was likely exposed to continuous neglect and abuse by both parents, including painful and unhygienic infant swaddling, which often left infants in their own filth for hours then bathed in icy waters.[8] When he grew in authority in the Communist Party, Stalin saw that his mother was taken care of, though he rarely visited her and did not attend her funeral when she died in 1937.

Stalin contracted smallpox as a child, leaving him with facial scars. He also suffered a permanent injury to his arm in an accident. Sent to school, he excelled and showed himself to be a hard worker. His callousness also emerged with a demonstrable cruelty to animals. He established a fascination with power, particularly over his classmates. He began to refer to himself as "Koba" after a Georgian folk hero.

Stalin's relationship with his native Georgia would prove to be a difficult and complex one. Once he assumed power, Stalin emphasized the needs of the Soviet Union (or more directly, himself) rather than giving priority to his Georgian roots. This was most notable during Georgia's incorporation into the Soviet Union in the early 1920s, during which Stalin successfully quashed Georgian communists' appeal for semiautonomous status. On the other hand, others have seen Stalin's relationship with Russia as synonymous with that of his father. The argument is that Stalin assumed control of Russia as the father-like authority figure in order to punish it through a terror campaign.[9]

Stalin emerged into early adulthood as a troublemaker for tsarist Russia. Even before World War I, discontent in Russia was widespread and the Bolshevik Communists sought to take advantage of this. Stalin organized strikes and demonstrations among industrial workers, eventually organizing a gang of likeminded individuals, which resembled a mafia as much as a political party. Stalin was involved in bank robberies and other organized crime efforts to fund the communist cause. Stalin aligned himself with the Bolshevik Communists, instead of a rival group of communists, the Mensheviks, perhaps because the Bolsheviks tended to be more disruptive and welcoming of violence. Although he used aliases and moved about, Stalin was arrested several times, sometimes being sent to exile in Siberia.[10]

Nonetheless, between periodic exiles, Stalin remained active in the Bolshevik movement. He proved to be an excellent organizer, a skill that would come in handy once the communists assumed power. He was not the literary genius or deep thinker that Lenin proved to be, but neither was he the unthinking brute often portrayed when juxtaposed with Lenin. In particular, he proved to be a strategic mastermind in the theater of cutthroat politics. His writings did attract Lenin's attention, aiding Stalin's ascendancy among the Bolshevik Communists.

Tsarist Russia experienced significant reverberations in 1905 as strikes, protests, and military mutinies spread throughout the country. These were sparked by Russia's defeat against Japan in the Russo-Japanese War, as well as the flagrant abuses, corruption, and unfairness of the tsarist system of government. The tsar, Nicholas II, managed to retain power, but the conflicts of 1905 were a sign of the weakening monarchy in Russia. By the time of the revolutions of 1917, Stalin's star had risen considerably among the Bolsheviks who, being more militant than their rival Mensheviks, ultimately assumed power, transforming Russia into the Soviet Union.

The Death of Lenin

Lenin's death in 1924 raised the question of who would succeed him. Stalin was a contender, although there were others, most notably Leon Trotsky, who shared Lenin's capacity for deep theoretical thought and personal charisma. Trotsky held great influence among the Bolsheviks. Here, Stalin's incredible gifts for strategy and organization played well to his advantage.

Stalin had been fortunate in that Lenin's death had occurred before Lenin might have reduced Stalin's power. Stalin quietly had gotten the levers of the Communist Party and governmental bureaucracy under his control during the Lenin years. Many of the posts he had taken might have seemed less than exciting or flashy while Lenin was alive, but these gave Stalin an excellent power base once Lenin was dead.

After Lenin's death, Stalin did not assume complete authority immediately but had to contend not only with Trotsky but with many other leading Bolsheviks as well. Here Stalin displayed a masterful gift for cutthroat diplomacy that would have made Machiavelli proud. Nominally, much of the fighting revolved around which leaders were more faithful to the ideas and legacy of Lenin. This allowed Stalin to use charges of factionalism, or, in effect, heresy to reduce the influence of his opponents. He initially formed an alliance with two other Bolsheviks, Zinoviev and Kamenev, whom he used to publicly denounce Trotsky while Stalin himself remained in the background. Trotsky was humiliated and disempowered. By 1929, he had fled into exile. He would be assassinated in 1940 on Stalin's orders, killed with an ice axe.

Stalin immediately turned on his erstwhile allies Zinoviev and Kamenev. He had their supporters removed from positions of power, placing his own men in their stead. Zinoviev and Kamenev found themselves outmaneuvered by Stalin and his new allies. Once again, the charges focused on ideological purity, though mainly as an excuse for Stalin to shove

Joseph Stalin.

rivals out of positions of power. At first, he was content to humiliate and disempower his rivals. As his power and confidence grew, he had them tortured into giving public "confessions" of treachery and treason and then had them executed. At each turn, Stalin split his rivals, forming alliances with some, such as Zinoviev and Kamenev, only to turn on them later.[11] Their deaths were public spectacles, show trials of public confession and humiliation. Some victims were promised leniency in exchange for making confessions only to find themselves sentenced to death at the trials.

The Great Purge

By the early 1930s, Stalin emerged as the undisputed sole ruler of the Soviet Union. The Soviet Union was no longer an oligarchy ruled by a single-party system based on communism. Although lip service was still paid to the ideology of communism, in effect, the Soviet Union became a terror regime subject to the whims of a single man: Joseph Stalin.

If his political machinations during the 1920s demonstrate the brilliant Machiavellian aspects of Stalin's personality, the 1930s brought greater emphasis to two other aspects: lack of conscience or empathy for others and extreme paranoia. Coupled with the clear narcissism that drove his lust for power, this created a dangerous mixture. Stalin exhibited the dark triad of antisocial, narcissistic, and Machiavellian personality traits that were discussed earlier in the book with unquenchable paranoia. This made the 1930s one of the most brutal and controversial periods of Stalin's rule. It was marked by two issues. First, massive suffering and loss of life due to Stalin's policies, for which he showed little concern. And second, his astounding failure to turn his paranoia toward the developing threat of Nazi Germany, where it would have been well placed. Instead, Stalin focused his fury mainly on his own people.

One difficulty that became apparent was the issue of agricultural peasants.[12] Marx and Engels appear to differentiate between the proletariat, or wage-earning laborers, and peasants who worked land they owned. Marx and Engels considered peasants or serfs part of the "lower middle class" and appeared to argue that they at least had some ability to rise up into the bourgeoisie. Lenin and the Bolsheviks saw reason to find common cause with the peasantry in promoting the communist revolution, although, as a practical matter, communist fervor did not spread widely through more agrarian regions of Russia.

Stalin sought to incorporate the principles of communism, at least as he fancied them, into the agrarian sector. First this occurred by identifying land-owning farmers, or kulaks, with the bourgeoisie and purging them. This involved uprooting entire families from their homes and shipping them into exile in remote regions like Siberia without adequate food, water, or clothing to survive the arduous journey of sometimes thousands of miles. Many were simply shot. The ownership threshold for who was a kulak also was, to say the least, vague and shifting. Many poorer farmers who initially might have been delighted to see their richer neighbors hauled away eventually found themselves on the list of kulaks. Neighbors were encouraged to report each other to the government, stoking an atmosphere of terror among the agrarian classes.

Stalin then focused on the collectivization of agriculture. Agricultural production continued to fall during the purging of the kulaks, which was hardly surprising. Stalin blamed this on hoarding but also saw the issue of private ownership of farmland as problematic. The Soviet Union began a process of forcing peasants off their farmland and onto government-run collective farms. Naturally, this was not received well and resulted in both armed uprisings as well as decreased production. In some regions, most notably the Ukraine, massive famines resulted. Stalin also launched programs to eliminate the national identity of some regional populations, such as the mass execution of Ukrainian bards. Millions died, either by outright executions, the forced exile of the kulaks, or starvation during the famine. Estimates of the death toll ranges around eleven million.[13] The Ukraine, specifically, is estimated to have lost one-fifth its total population.[14] Stalin expressed not an ounce of concern for such unfathomable human suffering.

During the 1930s Stalin turned his reign of terror inward toward the mechanisms of power itself. This included the Communist Party, the army, academics, and even the secret police. Discredited individuals were arrested, tortured, forced to confess as well as to implicate others in "factionalism," "Trotskyism," and collaboration with external powers, whether capitalist countries or Nazi Germany. Many of those weeded out included foreigners, people who had joined the Communist Party for career advancement, national and local party leaders, and, of course, any remnants of the old communists who had criticized or challenged Stalin. People were forced to confess their crimes; many were executed and many more imprisoned or exiled to prison camps.

Most famously, Stalin turned much of his ire onto the military, wherein he decimated the officer corps. Numerous talented officers, both high and low in rank, were cast out of the armed forces, imprisoned, and executed. The high command was particularly hard hit. Although a fair number of the imprisoned officers were eventually allowed back into the military,[15] this purge certainly unsettled the officer corp. Stalin's motives for this purge aren't entirely clear, although his paranoia and desire to discombobulate a potential rival seat of power presumably played a role. More controversially, this purge of the officer corps led to widespread assumptions that the Soviet army was weakened, dangling low fruit in front of Hitler's face a few years later.

Even those who carried out the purges were not immune. The Soviet secret police, then called the NKVD,[16] were themselves subject to Stalin's purges. NKVD leaders Genrikh Yagoda and Nikolai Yezhov were each arrested and shot for anti-Soviet activities. Truly, no one was safe in Stalin's Russia.

Historians aren't sure how many died during the purges of the 1930s, although figures in the range of one million, give or take, are common.[17] These figures are mainly for the late 1930s and don't include deaths due to the famines or forced relocations of agricultural collectivization. What did Stalin hope to gain from such unfathomable horror?

Real paranoia was undoubtedly a factor. Stalin had made his bid for dictator of the Soviet Union by the early 1930s, but potential enemies remained everywhere. The Old Bolsheviks who rode in with Lenin during the 1917 revolution and sometimes challenged Stalin during the 1920s were an obvious source of worry and had to go. Military commanders controlled the army and might launch a coup against Stalin. They, too, had to go. The Soviet Union was surrounded by the hostile military powers of Germany and Japan, and it wasn't unreasonable to suspect both countries were developing networks of spies in the Soviet Union. But the terror regime of Stalin didn't merely round people up and shoot them. That might have provoked resistance. Under torture, it forced people to confess and, more importantly, name others who were coconspirators. Cruelly brilliant, this strategy shattered any trust people had in one another. Any errant comment whispered to a friend might result in the NKVD learning of it, resulting in arrest, torture, exile, or death. By setting people against one another, making them frightened to confide in one another, smashed any possible resistance to the Stalinist regime.

Stalin in World War II

The Soviet Union and Nazi Germany were classic enemies. Ideologically their political systems were opposed and, more importantly, Hitler had publicly advertised his intentions of turning the Ukraine and western Russia into a German slave empire. To the east, the Soviet Union sparred with the Japanese armies in Manchuria for control of parts of China and Mongolia. At this juncture, Stalin's famous paranoia deserted him, and he made one of the most remarkable deals in history.

The 1939 Molotov-Ribbentrop Pact, bringing a peaceful agreement between Nazi Germany and Soviet Russia, stunned the world. In this agreement, Germany and the Soviet Union promised to remain neutral to each other and secretly agreed to carve up Eastern Europe into separate spheres of influence. The Western powers of England and France were shocked by this development and even Germany's nascent ally Japan[18] felt betrayed by Germany, given that Japan was in sporadic conflict with the Soviet Union at the time.

The Molotov-Ribbentrop Pact brings up two interesting counter-factuals. First, Hitler tended to be secretive and did not inform his allies, particularly Japan, what he was doing. As a consequence, Japan ultimately signed its own nonaggression pact with the Soviet Union. This was amazing luck for Stalin; when war broke out between Germany and the Soviet Union in 1941, he didn't have to worry about being squeezed by Germany and Japan from both sides. The Axis powers were notoriously uncoordinated in their efforts and this worked to the advantage of the Allies. Had Germany worked harder to include Japan in its plans and mollify it regarding the Molotov-Ribbentrop Pact, a coordinated German-Japanese attack on Russia might have produced a different outcome than a German attack alone.

The second is the possibility that the Soviet Union actually might have joined the Tripartite Alliance of Germany, Italy, and Japan. There's some chance this might have happened had Hitler been willing to drop his fantasy about turning western Russia and Ukraine into a massive slave camp. But this he was not willing to do. Cooperation between the Soviet Union and the Axis powers might have turned the entire European-Asian landmass into a zone impenetrable to the British and American allies.

But, of course, neither of these things happened and the world is better for it. Stalin took advantage of the Molotov-Ribbentrop Pact to expand Soviet control of eastern Europe. After Germany invaded Poland in September 1939, Soviet forces invaded eastern Poland and occupied territory assigned to Russia in the pact. The Soviets were ruthless in their treatment of the Poles, as evidenced by the Katyn Massacre, during which fifteen thousand Polish army officers, prisoners of war, were summarily executed.[19] The Russians later expanded into the Baltic countries of Latvia, Estonia, and Lithuania, with similar repressions there. Most infamous was the Winter War of 1939 and 1940 against Finland. Although the Soviet

Union ultimately prevailed against the much smaller Finnish forces, the campaign was clumsy and Soviet losses against the Finns were high. This war reinforced the belief that Soviet armed forces were seriously diminished by the Great Purges of the 1930s.

In hindsight, it seems obvious that the Molotov-Ribbentrop Pact couldn't last. Nonetheless, in uncharacteristic naivete for such a paranoid man, Stalin was shocked by the 1941 German invasion of the Soviet Union. After all, Hitler had been advertising his intentions to expand Germany's living space into Russia and the Ukraine for years, buildup of German troops on Soviet borders wasn't a secret, and some of Stalin's spies had warned a German invasion was imminent. Stalin dismissed these signs and was taken completely by surprise by the German invasion. Early during the invasion, Stalin's initial reaction vacillated between disbelief, paralysis, and despondency, issuing unrealistic orders for suicidal counterattacks that resulted in significant Soviet losses. Soviet forces were savaged by the Germans until the Germans were stopped at a line running roughly between Leningrad (formerly St. Petersburg) to Moscow to Stalingrad. Stalin's leadership during this period was erratic and poor. Fear among Soviet commanders prevented them from challenging Stalin's unrealistic orders and failures by the Soviet military unsurprisingly resulted in scapegoating of Soviet officers.[20]

Stalin eventually got his head together and organized more competent defense of Russian soil, employing scorched-earth tactics, appointing better commanders to Soviet armies, and shifting industry east of the Ural Mountains and out of range of German bombers. He also was able to shift military units from eastern Russia to face the German armies to the west. Despite its massive losses during the initial German invasion, Russia could count on overwhelming manpower and natural resources. Stalin was further aided by the ideological racism and cruelty of the Nazis. Had the Nazis been evenhanded in their treatment of the Ukrainians and Baltic peoples, the German armies might have been treated as liberators. Instead, their vicious treatment of native populations only united resistance against them.

In this sense, Stalin got lucky as the Germans undid themselves. But did he really think he had made friends with Hitler? Did he believe that peace would last between the Soviet Union and Nazi Germany? This has been a point of contention among historians. Author Victor Suvorov, a former Soviet military intelligence officer, has written several books stating that Stalin had been planning to invade Germany in the early 1940s.[21] Other scholars, however, have been more doubtful of these claims.[22] Nonetheless, some evidence suggests that Soviet forces were massed on the border with German-controlled territory, suggesting an impending plan to attack Germany no later than the summer of 1942.[23]

The most likely scenario is that both Hitler and Stalin intended to attack each other. Neither was provoked by self-defense. Stalin's surprise came from being beaten to the punch, not out of any true belief in Hitler's honesty or intention to abide by the Molotov-Ribbentrop Pact. Hitler always intended to invade the Soviet Union to create a German-run slave state. Stalin always intended to invade Germany to continue Soviet expansion into Europe, though may have been held back waiting for what seemed an opportune time to take advantage of German weakness.[24] Both men were cynical and duplicitous and intended to stab the other in the back. Hitler merely struck first, enjoying initial success due to the poor state of the Soviet army at the time. To think that Stalin was credulous about Hitler's good intent or had any intention of abiding by a pact himself is failing to understand Stalin's basic nature, which was cruel, paranoid, and selfish.

If Stalin's handling of the war, particularly in the early years of the German assault, was erratic, his handling of his own allies was deft by comparison. During the war, Stalin met several times with his counterparts, Winston Churchill in the United Kingdom and Franklin Delano Roosevelt in the United States. Although unsuccessful in pushing them into opening a second European front in the war before 1944, he had greater success in navigating the Soviet Union into a dominant position during the postwar period. Churchill was suspicious of Stalin's motivations but also aware of the United Kingdom's declining power as a first-rate nation. Roosevelt was motivated to pacify Stalin, particularly as he wanted Soviet involvement in a final assault on Japan after Germany was defeated. Stalin played his hand well, obtaining a de facto Soviet sphere of influence over eastern Europe.[25]

Most egregious, considering that World War II started in Europe over the German invasion of Poland, was that the Soviet Union was allowed to keep the portions of Poland taken as part of the Molotov-Ribbentrop Pact. Poland and the Poles were simply, and quite literally, moved west at the expense of defeated Germany. Part of German East Prussia around the city of Konigsberg (now Kaliningrad) was annexed to Russia. This region remains an odd, isolated bit of Russia today, surrounded by Poland and the Baltic states, not physically attached to the rest of Russia. Some other areas of eastern Europe also were annexed to the Soviet Union, and the Soviet Union also established several client states from East Germany through Bulgaria. Granted, occupation of these territories by Soviet troops would have made dislodging Soviet interests practically impossible, but the western Allies largely acquiesced. Perhaps sadder was the Soviet demand to return Soviet prisoners of war, some of whom had switched sides to fight for the Germans in order to escape certain death in German POW camps. The allies sent these men back to the Soviets despite their pleas (correctly, as it would turn out) that they would receive a less-than-warm welcome home.

After the war Stalin focused on making the Soviet Union a powerhouse of heavy industry and keeping it on an equal strategic footing militarily with the West. This obviously involved acquiring nuclear weapons. Soviet-U.S. nuclear rivalry would go on to inspire decades of fear of impending world destruction and lots of great '80s music about the same.[26] Some poor sods in Russia might have figured that, having achieved victory in the Great Patriotic War and getting on in years, Stalin might now mellow out and rest on his laurels. In this they were sadly mistaken. Stalin returned to a regime ruled by terror and paranoia. The best that might be said about the post–World War II era was that things weren't as bad as the 1930s. Naturally, Stalin claimed considerable credit for the war's success for himself and ultimately sidelined some generals he thought were outshining him.

After the war, Stalin's paranoia increased to the point that some claimed he was quite literally afraid of his own shadow. Some have argued that this is likely due to the development of dementia, possibly brought on by small strokes during Stalin's last years.[27] By that time, he was reportedly eschewing medical advice and instead taking cures from a bodyguard trained in veterinary medicine. Stalin had never exactly been a health nut, given to excesses of food, alcohol, and smoking. Stalin died in March 1953 of a stroke, and autopsy evidence suggested he likely had a series of small strokes impacting his mental performance in his final years.[28] He was not, to say the least, missed. The Soviet Union returned to a single-party oligarchy and, under Stalin's successor Khrushchev, repudiated his legacy. The Soviet Union didn't exactly become a pussycat among countries, but the mass slaughter died down to a manageable fear-inducing stream.

In understanding Stalin's psychology, diagnosis is straightforward. The likely diagnosis of paranoid personality disorder has been made for decades.[29] Combined with his shrewd political skill and callousness, his personality fits well with modern science's theory on the dark triad of narcissism, antisocial, and Machiavellian traits. He was the epitome of a totalitarian autocrat. If the final numbers of the deaths he caused are in dispute, what is not is that he was directly responsible for the deaths of millions. He ruled his country through sheer terror. Like Hitler, he saw himself as fulfilling a unique role in human history.

Stalin's relationships with his family were mercurial and complex. He appears to have loved his first wife, who died of typhus, but quarreled with his second wife, who ultimately committed suicide. Stalin appeared to take his second wife's suicide personally, as if she had been motivated to wound him. Stalin abandoned his oldest son Yakov when he was captured by the Germans during the early stages of the war, refusing a German offer to exchange him. His younger son died of alcoholism. Only with his daughter Svetlana did Stalin attempt to maintain cordial relations, although he could be controlling and difficult even with her. He may have been surrounded by people and could be convivial when he wished, but Stalin's personality isolated him in a sea of terrorized followers.

Chairman Mao

In the great contest for most despicable madman in history, Mao Zedong ranks up there with Hitler and Stalin and, in terms of sheer body count, may win the title. Mao seized the reigns of Chinese Communism in the 1930s and went on to lead Communist China until his death in 1976. During that time, he massively expanded China's influence and role in the international scene. His policies also resulted in the deaths of tens of millions of people, mostly Chinese citizens.

The legacy of Mao is more complex than that of Hitler and Stalin. Several factors play into this. First, the modern People's Republic of China is a direct successor to the reign of Mao. Thus, there is no clear break with Mao's past in China as occurred with Germany post-Hitler or even Russia's de-Stalinization. This muddies an objective read of Mao's past. Second, Mao himself arguably created a number of myths about his history as part of his cult of personality in China. Sifting through what actually happened versus what Mao wanted people to think happened can be difficult. Third, although few people are inclined to give Mao a halo, there is some disagreement about the degree to which the deaths that occurred during Mao's reign can be attributed to either purposeful or callous indifference as opposed to simply ill-thought policies. "Whoops, I accidently starved to death tens of millions of people" perhaps is a valid defense to some. As a result, there is some disagreement as to the degree that the positive outcomes of Mao's regime balance the unquestionably high death toll.[30]

As an example of this, consider the controversy that erupted over one popular biography of Mao. The account by Jung Chang[31] and Jon Halliday,[32] often relying on interviews with people involved, paints a harrowing picture of Mao as a conniving, lying, self-absorbed psychopath entirely unconcerned with the welfare and suffering of others. They accuse him of direct involvement in torture and terror schemes as well as considerable backstabbing of his fellow Communists. Their vision of Mao portrays a man obsessed with historical mythmaking to make himself look like a hero in ways undeserved. In the fashion of academics who like to squabble about who's smartest, Chang and Halliday's biography of Mao provoked a *whole other book* simply to criticize Chang and Halliday's tome.[33] Although a few of the essays were supportive, most condemned Chang and Halliday for exaggerating Mao's negatives and relying too much on interviews. Many essays complain Chang and Halliday are not "fair" to Mao or, as one contributor put it "Chang and Halliday eschew any attempt to balance the good and bad in his legacy."[34] This argument left me unsatisfied. Would we be demanding "fair" biographies of Hitler had Germany won World War II and survived into a modern Nazi state? Stalin created a powerful superpower out of the Soviet Union yet is not given a free pass to "balance" his legacy against the millions of deaths he caused. Other critiques—mainly that Mao's assent to power must be understood in the context of the cultural and political forces at play in China at the time—are fair but this argument does not discount the powerful role that a unique personality such as Mao's played in China's history. Let's take a look at Mao's history and personality as best we can to clarify this muddied picture of conflicting accounts.

Like many of the madmen[35] in this book, Mao was raised in a difficult home environment. He was beaten viciously by his father, likely an early introduction to the role of violence and callousness in shaping behavior.[36] Very likely, genes that shape antisocial personality traits were passed down from father to son, which combined with the harsh upbringing to shape a cold and uncaring personality. In his teen and early adult years, Mao wandered a bit, looking for a life course. He found a love for learning and books but did not like the Confucian classics, and his lack of stick-to-itiveness infuriated his father. At about this time China went through a revolution, ejecting the old Manchu Qing dynasty[37] in favor of a republican government. During this period, Mao also married his first wife, an unhappy arranged marriage. He quickly abandoned her, and she died just a few years later.[38]

The Communist revolution in Russia began to spill over into China, and Mao joined the Communist Party. During the 1920s, Mao began his ascent, often at the expense of fellow Communists. Some accounts note a genuine concern in Mao for the well-being of the peasants and lower classes, but he also developed a skill for cutthroat politics. True to form with Soviet Communism, Chinese Communism developed a knack for brutal infighting. In their scathing biography, Chang and Halliday claim Mao developed a taste for brutal violence during a tour of the Hunan countryside between 1926 and 1927. Much of the violence was revolutionary in nature by peasants against landlords, involving sadistic torture and humiliation of the victims. Like Stalin in the Soviet Union about the same time, Mao appears to have understood how violence and terror can suppress masses of people who might otherwise rise.

At about this time, the Chinese republic also began to split politically. The Communists became increasingly separated from the majority rule of the Nationalists, by now led by Chiang Kai-Shek. Beyond these two factions, multiple independent warlords controlled vast areas of territory. China was on the verge of becoming a failed state. China was also under pressure from Japan, increasingly an aggressive militarized country with designs on China's natural resources. By the late 1920s, China was in civil war, complicated further by Japanese invasion and occupation of Manchuria in 1931. Mao had married a second time, but once again largely abandoned his wife and their children. His second wife would be executed by Nationalist forces in 1930.

The losers in this scenario were the Chinese people. Stuck between three bad choices—the bloodthirsty Communists, the corrupt Nationalists and the invading Japanese—many Chinese bravely resisted and died, standing up for their republic. Lost in the muddy struggles between Mao, Chiang, and the Japanese are literally millions of stories of good, courageous people who fought and died for something better. Unfortunately, most of their stories will never be told.

China's civil conflicts lasted, on and off, for twenty years and eventually were absorbed into World War II. Here, Mao's mythmaking went into overdrive, creating stories of remarkable success, courage, and military genius, particularly during the famed Long March of 1934 to 1935, when Mao led Communist forces out of a potential encirclement by Nationalist forces. In fact, Mao tended to take credit for others' successes and pass blame to others for his failures. It's possible that, far from a desperate flight, Chiang might have let the Communists escape, using their movements to invade and assume control of territories ruled by other warlords.[39] If so, this was a colossal mistake on Chiang's part.

Mao had married a third time as well. This marriage turned out no less tragic for the lucky lady than the previous two. Although He Zizhen, his wife, had revolutionary zeal, she had to abandon several children she gave birth to at different points of the Communist army's travels, including on the Long March. Like his previous two wives, she was discarded by Mao, and reputedly went mad.

Mao was well supported by the Soviet Union, which generally stuck by him even as other Communist leaders complained about him. Using violence, spies, blackmail, and subterfuge, Mao managed to outmaneuver his rivals, becoming head of the Chinese Communist Party. The Communist Party employed brutal indoctrination techniques and bloody purges to maintain a terror-based loyalty in regions under its control.

The Soviets pressured the Communists and Nationalists to ostensibly work together to fight the Japanese during World War II. At one point, Chiang Kai-Shek was arrested by a local warlord, who forced him to work together with Mao as a condition of his release. Nonetheless, cooperation between the Communists and Nationalists remained minimal and clashes continued. Both sides remained as concerned about jockeying for power as they were fighting the Japanese. And arguably, neither side was particularly effective in fighting Japanese armies. Although Japan found itself in a quagmire in China, the Communists largely avoided pitched battles, whereas Chiang Kai-Shek retreated to China's interior, where Allied commanders found him slovenly, corrupt, and always asking for resources without taking decisive action.[40] Japan was ejected from China only after Russian armies invaded in August 1945.

The defeat of Japan brought the Chinese civil war back to the forefront. Initially the Communists did poorly, but Mao maintained brutal control over his forces and the lands under Communist control using ruthless repression to maintain absolute obedience. Chiang was gradually undercut by the reluctance of the Americans initially to support him and then by the incompetence or possible subterfuge of his own generals. Mao's tactics were vicious, including the 1948 siege of the city of Changchun, which led to the purposeful deaths of perhaps 160,000 civilians. Communist soldiers reportedly shot any civilian trying to leave the city. Residents resorted to eating tree bark, leather belts, and possibly even their dead.[41] By 1949, Chiang and his remaining supporters retreated to the island of Formosa, turning it into what Pink Floyd musician Roger Waters once called "a shoe factory called Taiwan."

Mao initiated a unified (aside from Taiwan) People's Republic of China in 1949. For some reason Communists and other autocrats have great affinity for including words like "democratic" and "republic" in the names of their countries, confusing schoolchildren everywhere. Presumably still smarting over Chiang's escape to Taiwan (the political separation of mainland China and Taiwan remains a thorny issue to the present day), Mao set about purging everyone in China who had anything to do with the Nationalists. Included in this bloody purge also were many landowning peasants. Public executions became common, Mao presumably wondering why these had gone out of fashion after the Middle Ages.

Detailing a litany of Mao's many abuses against his own citizens would (and has) take volumes. Two events naturally stand out, namely the Great Leap Forward (which left countless millions in the ground, not leaping) and the Cultural Revolution. Both are controversial, as some scholars point to these events as playing a role in modernizing China. But they also resulted in the deaths of millions.

The first, the Great Leap Forward, was a plan to create massive collectivization of agriculture from 1958 to 1962. If this sounds vaguely like Stalin's disastrous effort to collectivize agriculture in the Soviet Union during the 1930s—well, there certainly were similarities. The effort was also wrapped into deliberate purges and persecution of undesirable people. Once farms were collectivized, as in the Soviet Union, grain production fell, leading to mass starvation. Amazingly, during this time, China *exported* significant amounts of food to other countries rather than feeding its own citizens. Afraid of being purged, many officials exaggerated the amount of grain being produced on farms in regions under their control rather than report the failures to those higher up. Nonetheless, significant evidence suggests that Mao was aware of the massive scale of deaths and exhibited little concern for the suffering of his own people. It has been estimated that between forty-five and fifty-two million Chinese died, perhaps 5.5 percent of the population of China at the time.[42]

Repression of the population likewise continued, which included torture and executions. Local party cadres used their control of the limited food supply to starve those whom they didn't like or who were expendable, such as the elderly or those too ill to work. Terror continued to be the norm for most Chinese.[43]

Mao Zedong, early 1960s.

The Cultural Revolution came later, roughly from 1966 until Mao's death in 1976. Mao unleashed this revolutionary force against party and cultural elites, resentful that his status had been reduced after the failures of the Great Famine. Mao focused on his cult of personality, collecting his sayings in his *Little Red Book*, and released indoctrinated youth Red Guards onto the populace. These youth unleashed mayhem and chaos onto China, attacking older adults, forcing them into confessions, torturing, and murdering them. Party elites and educated professionals were particularly targeted. At least four hundred thousand people died,[44] though others put the total in the millions.[45] Many, shamed and physically tortured, committed suicide and Mao expressed little concern for these people.

By 1969, Mao shifted focus and now ordered the People's Liberation Army (PLA) to reassert control. They did so with enthusiasm, arresting many and sending them to reeducation camps. However, the army leader Lin Biao turned on Mao, planning a coup. Lin fled the country, believing his plot detected, and died in a plane crash. At least, that's the official story, although much of this affair remains mysterious.[46] Mao now purged the PLA of presumed rivals and supporters of Lin Biao.

Rather amazingly, some scholars still argue that these atrocities must be balanced against China's growth during this period. True, Mao did see China into a period when it was freed of imperial colonies and increased industrial production. So sorry about the tens of millions of dead, but at least we've got these cheap Chinese toys.

All good things must come to an end and in 1976 Mao died, setting off a power struggle among potential successors (including his final wife who was disgraced, arrested, and ultimately committed suicide in 1991, thus completing the Mao Marriage Curse).[47] Attempting to cover everything that happened in modern China since Mao would be yet another book, but suffice to say, if you ignore human rights and focus only on economic and geopolitical power, China is indeed a remarkable island of success in the dismal sea of failure that is otherwise communism. And, hey, who needs human rights when you can build your own islands from nothing in the South China Sea, right?[48] Unlike with Stalin or Hitler, there hasn't been a clear break between Mao and modern China. Likely this is why we see such continued hagiography of Mao, including among some non-Chinese scholars, and attempts to find his "good side." Maybe Mao was a feminist? Probably not.[49] To be fair, if we blame Mao for the atrocities that swept across China in the mid-twentieth century, we must begrudgingly credit him for creating the scaffolding for China's undeniable rise. Post–World War II, China was largely freed of imperialist clutches (among which we might include the Soviet Union) and began to develop as a military and economic power to be reckoned with. But, as the saying goes, even Mussolini made the trains run on time.

Like Stalin, Mao appears to have had dark triad traits of narcissism, antisocial personality, and Machiavellianism. Paranoia is perhaps less a dominant trait (relatively speaking, that is) compared to narcissism and callousness. Naturally, his rise must be understood in the historical context of twentieth-century China. China emerged in the twentieth century as a massive but chaotic nation beset by hungry imperial powers, including Japan. Leadership, political and military, was weak despite China's vast resources. Some have suggested Mao used Chinese culture to present himself as something close to a deity.[50] More than most madmen and -women, Mao remains a considerable lightning rod, both beloved and hated by many.

Why Communism? (Or, What Was the Proletariat Thinking?)

The basic psychological profiles of Stalin and Mao are, in many respects, fairly similar. Both were, in essence, narcissistic psychopaths who turned their massive countries into personal fiefdoms, selfishly unleashing terror when they felt they might be losing those fiefdoms. We might look through communism's long list of dictators from Cuba's Fidel Castro to Cambodia's Pol Pot[51] and find a general theme of megalomaniacal jerks who turned their nations into hell on Earth. All systems of government produce nightmare regimes from time to time, but the track record of communism is outright astonishing. Only a handful of communist countries remain, some of which, like China and Vietnam, have embraced the global market and some capitalist ideas, though none are places I'd personally care to pack my bags to move to permanently.[52]

It's not like *nobody* knew of the disasters befalling the Soviet Union by the 1930s. Why did so much of the world seem eager to give communism the good ole college try in the latter twentieth century?

Part of it is that Marx and Engels were on to something in *The Communist Manifesto*. Not the solution—no, no—communism sucks, let's just put that out there. But they recognized the problem. During the nineteenth century, industrialized capitalism could be brutal and protections for workers were few. Other than a lot of cool Dickens novels (and a few lemons, admit it), the benefits of capitalism for the low-skill, low-wage worker were nearly nonexistent. Desperate people do desperate things. Potentially burning everything down can seem better than the status quo.

Of course, not everyone—even among the lower classes—is attracted to communism, and communist parties typically have had to use brute force to control large populations. So who is attracted to communism and why? One early paper from the mid-twentieth century found evidence that, in the United States at least, adoption of communist sympathies was a way to express hostility without feeling guilt.[53] Some have suggested that, beginning with *The Communist Manifesto*, paranoid ideology has been a unifying force for communists and those drawn to that movement.[54]

Research by the eminent psychologist Hans Eysenck discovered that, despite their hostile ideological differences, the personalities of self-avowed fascists and communists tend to be similar.[55] Both groups tend to be authoritarian, emphatic in their beliefs, intolerant of ambiguity, and generally "tough minded," aggressive, rigid, and dominant. These similarities between the two groups may not be surprising since—whatever their differences—both theories of government tend to produce authoritarian police states abusive toward their own citizens.

Not to put too fine a point on it, but communism tends to attract individuals who are ideologically rigid bullies. Sure, there are undoubtedly some very nice communists in the world, but the ideology itself tends to draw in troubled souls. Thus it is perhaps no surprise that handing these individuals power almost always results in disaster. Granted, many individuals undoubtedly join a dominant party for personal gain rather than ideological purity. As generations change and these individuals rise through the ranks, their more moderate beliefs may soften communism a bit. Hence, the bloody massacres of the twentieth century are largely a thing of the past, replaced by a more mundane grinding repression and control. Progress, I guess? Both Stalin and Mao appeared to have been alert to these tendencies, leading to purges of their own communist parties.

In general, though, it is time to put the communist experiment to rest. Nice try, Marx and Engels, maybe a little less dictatorship, paranoia, and bloody revolution next time.

CHAPTER SEVEN
MADNESS AMONG THE 1 PERCENT

B y this point it is abundantly clear that despotic systems of government—whether monarchies, fascist dictatorships, or communism—inherently invite madmen and -women into positions of power. Sure, there are examples of enlightened tyrants or benign monarchs, but absolute power seems to attract those with a kind of narcissistic madness and places few restrictions by which to restrain it. On a broader level, few governance structures are truly equal and even more representative forms of government can see the emergence of a ruling elite. Whether aristocratic families, politicalized dynasties such as the modern American Kennedys, Bushes, and Clintons, or the uneven enfranchisement such as seen in ancient Athenian democracy (which we visit in chapter 10), governance can often take the form of power struggles between the haves and have-nots.

As we saw in chapter 6, fixing inequality was the appeal of communism, the notion that the have-nots would spark a revolution to overthrow their betters and rule as a mass of coequals. Rather soon, communist leaders realized that too many people among the masses were doofuses, and some kind of ruling class in the form of the Communist Party was needed after all. But one of the lessons of communism is that there is inherent strain between the elite and the masses, and when the elite lose sight of this, chaos can reign.

For stable government, it's in the interest of the elite—even if only in their own cynical self-interest—to show compassion toward the masses and to give the masses respect, reasonable resources, and some agency in their own welfare. Nonetheless history is resplendent with examples of elite arrogance, callousness, and short-sightedness. Often, this madness of the 1 percent has led to considerable disaster for the countries they ruled.

The Fall of the Roman Republic

Earlier in this book we considered several Roman emperors, particularly Caligula and Elagabalus, who exemplified the risks that come with dynastic autocracies. Indeed, it seems we tend to give much more attention to the middle third of Rome's history.[1] Other than a few great stories like Spartacus or Hannibal,[2] we mainly hear about the Roman *Empire* and often forget Rome was a *republic* for centuries before that republic sacrificed its constitutional protections and slid into autocracy. In that sense, the Roman Republic is a case example for our own modern republics and how encroaching madness can cause us to throw away everything.

The terms *democracy* and *republic* tend to be used interchangeably. However, there are some notable distinctions between the systems, and, in fairness, in some cases (such as in many modern governments including the United States), elements of the two can be blended together. A true democracy involves rule by the majority decision of enfranchised individuals (which may include all citizens or just a subset of them, typically wealthier males). In essence, whatever the majority wants is what happens. Ancient Athens and many other Greek city-states (though certainly not all) represent the closest examples of true democracies.

By contrast, a republic typically differs in two important ways. First, the enfranchised masses typically elect a much smaller group of representatives, usually skilled politicians, to make decisions on their behalf. And second, republics are often limited by charters or constitutions, restricting the types of decisions the representative government can make. By restraining decision-making power, charters and constitutions typically bestow certain rights upon their citizens that cannot be removed by a majority vote. So, for instance, let's say Ted is a jerk. In ancient Athens, the enfranchised majority could decide that Ted is such a jerk that he represents a threat to the moral well-being of youth[3] and vote to have him executed,[4] perhaps on some trumped-up charge. By contrast, in today's modern republics this would not be allowed because although we might all agree that Ted is a jerk among jerks, he has certain unalienable rights to life and freedom that we can't just vote away. Hell, we might even make him president one day.

Exactly where the city of Rome came from is a bit of a mystery. The Romans themselves thought they were descended from refugees fleeing the sacked city of Troy.[5] They appear to have emerged as an independent entity surrounded by tribes of Latins, Etruscans, and others, so perhaps they weren't wrong. In their early history, they threw off monarchical rule by the dreaded Tarquins and established a republic that combined elements of oligarchy and democracy.[6]

The early history of the new republic presents a remarkable lesson in class struggle and compromise. Governance of the republic was complex, with power distributed among the Senate, elected magistrates such as consuls and later tribunes, and various peoples' assemblies. During times of crisis, a dictator could be appointed for a limited time, typically six months. In general, the republic disdained long-term magistrates, and even the consuls were elected two at a time for one-year terms in office.

At the outset, the aristocratic class, or patricians, controlled most of the levers of power and, human nature being what it is, demonstrated little regard for the general masses of people, the *plebs* (which refers to them as a class), or plebeians. The plebeians eventually became frustrated under both unrelenting debt and lack of power and became understandably upset about the state of things. Rather than revolt or assassinate leading Roman patricians, the plebeians came up with a novel solution: they effectively went on strike. En masse, they seceded from Rome and moved to a nearby hill where they basically hung out and waited.

Deprived of anyone to stir their lemonade or massage their feet, the Roman patricians panicked. They agreed to reforms that would guarantee some protections and power for the plebs. This didn't all happen in one sitting, but over multiple generations of strife and compromise, the Romans managed to keep their class struggles from blowing up into open civil war. The plebs ended up with their own peoples' assemblies as well as tribunes, elected plebeian officials who could veto laws that plebs didn't care for.

Rome also was clever insofar as it extended citizenship (albeit of a lesser status) to defeated neighbors and rivals, thereby reducing their resentment. This worked particularly well for their Latin neighbors, who, after initial warring, came to see the benefits of remaining allied to Rome even during darker times.

Rome ended up almost accidentally expanding across the Mediterranean. Rome liked to think it always had a just cause for going to war, although its rationale for this could be a bit loose. During significant periods, the republic was almost continuously at war with its Italian neighbors, Greek city-states in southern Italy or Sicily, or foreign powers. Perhaps the most famous wars were those against the Greek general Pyrrhus, who sought unsuccessfully to protect the Greek city-states in southern Italy from Roman domination, as well as the multiple wars with the Phoenician city-state of Carthage. During the second war with Carthage (or Punic War), the celebrated general Hannibal invaded Italy, demolishing one Roman legion after another. Here, though, the Romans' political acumen paid off. To Hannibal's surprise, the Latins remained loyal to Rome and continued supplying troops for new legions even as Hannibal cut them down. By contrast, Hannibal had poor access to reinforcements. Eventually, Rome attacked Carthage directly, and Hannibal was defeated by Scipio Africanus at the Battle of Zama. The effect of this was to expand Rome's reach to Sicily, North Africa, and Spain. Rome was on the rise.[7]

Given that we've covered two later mad emperors, we already know the Romans managed to mess up their republic and end up with a famous autocratic empire. By what madness did this happen? The republic was far from perfect, but it was firm in its opposition to autocracy. So how did the republic cast away such core values? How this happened is an object lesson for today's politics.

The expansion of the republic's territory was a considerable boon, naturally. However, it brought with it several unexpected challenges. One was the sudden increase in slaves in Rome. It turns out that slaves are cheaper for given jobs than are free citizens who irritatingly expect to be paid. The increase in slavery put a fair number of lower wage Romans out of work, which they didn't like, though one presumes the slaves weren't too happy about this, either. This creates a vague echo of modern immigration/jobs debates and the perception of the lower classes being left behind by cheap labor benefiting the wealthy. Nobody suggested the building of walls and such, of course, but the fact remained that poorer Romans got left out of the economic boon times and became resentful.

The second concern was the expansion of the army during the Second Punic War. Under the talented but flamboyant general, Scipio Africanus, it became clear that the army potentially could be a political force all its own, particularly if the army remained loyal to Scipio rather than Rome. Fortunately for Rome at this moment, Scipio had little interest in politics or world domination. Indeed, though Scipio had his faults, he is a clear antithesis of a madman, having resisted the obvious allure of a grab for power. The moment for a military takeover passed, for now at least, but raised the potential of the army as a threat to the constitutional republic.

Rome's newfound riches also led to increased corruption. This was revealed in the case of the Gracchus brothers, Tiberius and Gaius, each of whom in turn became reforming tribunes of the people and in turn were assassinated. Tiberius initially sought land reform, transferring tracts of land from wealthier Romans to poorer.[8] This, naturally, was quite popular with the poorer plebs and less popular with the wealthy patricians. Tiberius pushed the limits of the powers of the tribune more than most tribunes and in doing so provoked the Senate. Naturally, both sides interpreted the actions of the others in the worst possible light.[9] This eventually resulted in a violent mob clash provoked by the Senate that resulted in the death of Tiberius and many of his followers.

Some years later, Tiberius's brother Gaius became tribune and tried to push Tiberius's reforms further. In addition to solidifying land reform, Gaius sought to root out corruption (which was becoming rampant) and bring about judicial reform. Gaius also sought to extend greater citizen rights to non-Roman peoples throughout Italy, which went over about as well as minority-rights efforts tend to do at pretty much any point in history. Violence once again naturally ensued, with Gaius meeting the same tragic end as his brother. The historian Plutarch suggests that one senator offered to pay the weight of Gaius's head in gold to whomever killed him and, signifying the times, the killer in question filled the skull cavity with melted lead to make it heavier.[10]

The Gracchus brothers pushed the limits of tribunal power. But they also clarified the class struggle of the plebs for a new generation. More than in the past, the result was class violence in which the patricians asserted their control over the levers of power.

Naturally, things deteriorated from there. The next phase of conflict was epitomized by two talented generals: Marius, who represented the

The Death of Gaius Gracchus by Francois Topino-Lebrun.

populist plebs, and Sulla, who represented the Senate. Both were excellent commanders. Being older, Marius's star shone first, and he instituted important reform to the Roman army, making it increasingly professionalized and, as such, more loyal to its commanders than to Rome itself. He was, in effect, a populist, representing the interests of the people against the greedy and corrupt patricians. Eventually he was opposed by his protégé Sulla, who made the unprecedent step of marching an army on Rome itself, assuming dictatorial powers. Both cases—the popularists under Marius and the patricians under Sulla—shattered constitutional norms. Roman armies waged war against each other and Sulla, upon assuming dictatorial power, initiated a bloody purge of political rivals. Surprisingly, he retired willingly from office, dying of natural causes.[11] One has the sense he was not greatly missed.

By now, the protections of the Roman constitution were in tatters. In short order, control of Rome fell to the triumvirate of Pompey, Crassus, and Julius Caesar. Pompey and Caesar were both excellent generals. Crassus, not so much, but he was rich. In fairness, he had defeated the gladiators' uprising led by Spartacus, but he died campaigning against the Parthians in the East. Unfortunately, Crassus was the glue that kept the triumvirate together, and Pompey and Caesar soon ended up at war with one another.[12]

The rest is literally the stuff of Shakespearian plays. Caesar defeated Pompey, who fled to Egypt seeking refuge with the Egyptian pharaoh Ptolemy XIII. Ptolemy, thinking it would get him in good with Caesar, had Pompey killed. Naturally, this was a spectacular misread of the situation, for despite their civil war, Caesar still had affection for his rival Pompey. Caesar then threw his support behind Ptolemy's rival, wife, and sister (yes, all three), Cleopatra VII (yes, *that* Cleopatra). With Cleopatra, Caesar returned to Rome, had himself declared dictator for life, and was promptly assassinated. Pro-republican forces briefly had the upper hand but were soon defeated by Caesar's protégés Marc-Anthony and Octavian, his grandnephew. Fresh off victory, Marc-Anthony and Octavian had a falling out and Octavian defeated Marc-Anthony and his lover Cleopatra (yes, still *that* Cleopatra). Basically, everybody died except for Octavian, who renamed himself Augustus and became the first emperor of Rome.[13] And that, of course, is the end of the republic.

So what happened? In this case, although certain specific individuals ranging from the Gracchus brothers to Octavian/Augustus played important individual roles as leading figures, none, save perhaps Sulla, qualify as madmen the way we've defined it in the book here. Some of these individuals, such as Julius Caesar, were narcissists and not beyond brutality when it suited them. But they don't quite rise to the level of a Hitler, Mao, or even Alexander the Great. In this case, the death of the republic can't be blamed on the crucial actions of a single individual.

Instead, it was the republic itself that went mad, gradually and in a series of steps that may not have been seen as consequential at the time. A lot of this developed through anger, as the respective classes of plebs and patricians increasingly became resentful toward each other. Each grasped for power and overreached, provoking greater fury in the other. Undoubtedly each side constructed narratives for why they were morally right and the other side scoundrels. Increased corruption decreased faith in public institutions and leaders.[14] Gradually, constitutional norms were broken, and the structure of social fabric built on compromise unraveled. Each side became focused on "winning" without considering the long game of what their efforts might do to the republic. The corruption of the republic didn't happen overnight but accumulated through a series of emotional, selfish, and rigid decisions and a decrease in the culture of public service and compromise. Coupled with the rise of a powerful permanent army, the situation became ripe for the eventual loss of protected freedoms, however imperfect they may have been under the republic. People began to look for strongmen to protect their interests. Be careful what one wishes for!

The fall of the Roman Republic thus presents a test case for how increased emotionality, sense of personal grievance, rampant corruption and greed, centralization of power among a few individuals, and unwillingness to find common cause can undo a constitutional society. Its story is a warning for us all in the modern age.

Having depressed the reader with this morality tale of republican corruption in an oligarchical system, we turn to the Renaissance. Here we look at how madness among the ruling class led to the brutal downfall of one of the world's greatest monarchies.

Let Them Eat Cake

Marie Antoinette probably never uttered the infamous words, "Let them eat cake!" often credited to her in response to the starvation of peasant mobs in eighteenth-century France. But the fact that so many were willing to believe she had tells us much about her place in the French Revolution of 1789, as well as of the French aristocracy more broadly. Unlike the contemporary American Revolution, which sought the overthrow of a remote regime, the French Revolution was a homegrown affair born of desperate class conflict. Predictably, it turned personal and cruel and, whatever its leaders' initial intent, did not lead to anything resembling democracy.

Developing a full picture of Marie Antoinette is difficult given the juxtaposition between the degree to which she was vilified at the time of the French Revolution and some attempts to entirely rehabilitate her in modern scholarship. She was an archduchess of Austria and daughter to the famed Austrian empress Maria Theresa. She arrived in France in 1770, betrothed to the awkward heir to the French throne, Louis XVI.[15] Quickly, she was shunted largely from view in the isolation of the royal palace at Versailles, subject of considerable gossip. The king, Louis XVI, was shy around women, particularly his wife, and their marriage was not consummated for years. This fact did significant harm to both their reputations.[16] Only the kindly advice from Marie Antoinette's brother, the Austrian emperor, Joseph, to Louis seems to have given Louis the courage to consummate the marriage, and the couple had their first child in 1778.

The finances of France already were strained due to decades of war and mismanagement. Yet Marie Antoinette's behavior contributed to the view that she was, at very least, indifferent to the financial suffering of the average person. Even her defenders acknowledge that Marie Antoinette was a frivolous spender who seemed aloof from concerns about her behavior. Perhaps worse at the time, she was often seen going out on the town without her meek husband, giving the perception that she was unfaithful. Some evidence suggests the perception is accurate and that two of her children may have been fathered by one of her lovers instead of Louis, although these claims aren't without controversy.[17]

If Marie Antoinette's behavior contributed to some of the negative impression about her, she was also the victim of a most unfortunate ruse. The "affair of the diamond necklace" involved the theft of an amazingly expensive necklace by several con artists. Forged correspondence convinced the jewelers that they were selling the necklace to Marie Antoinette, to be paid in installments. In fact, Marie Antoinette had no knowledge of this arrangement at all. The necklace was stolen and never seen intact again. The main con artist, Jeanne de la Motte, was arrested and convicted, but negative press nonetheless cast Marie Antoinette as a villain in the affair. It was said, falsely, that she had been willing to further bankrupt France for a frivolous necklace. Whatever else we might say about her, the damage done to her reputation by this situation was unfair.[18] Nonetheless, the story stuck due to her own unrestrained spending, which was true enough.

Despite the considerable attention paid to her, including excellent biographies, getting a full picture of Marie Antoinette's psychology can be a bit frustrating. She took an interest in the Austrian hypnotist Franz Anton Mesmer,[19] who foolishly rebuffed her offer to support his work.[20] It is less clear to what extent her own anxieties may have led her to be interested in his work.

It can help, perhaps a little, to imagine what historical figures might have seemed like had they been taken out of their own historical context and put instead into an entirely mundane existence in the current era. Stalin the greengrocer almost certainly would have remained a difficult man even if deprived the levers of power to do harm to anything beyond cabbages and perhaps his own family. Marie Antoinette largely comes across as a somewhat naïve teenage girl, and later woman, well out of her league in facing historical events. Her and her husband's early lack of knowledge about sex caused her brother to refer to them as "two complete blunderers."[21] Her main limitations include her spendthrift nature, her disconnect from the popular people, her inability to figure out how to combat the negative gossip about her, and an unfortunate conservatism in politics. She had been poorly educated as a girl, leaving her unprepared for leadership. Her tendency to favor her home country, Austria, made it easy to paint her as a traitor to France. She may have been unfaithful to her husband, though that evidence is not without controversy. She may have had some rather understandable neuroses that led her to an interest in mesmerism.

Plunked down in modern society, Marie Antoinette probably would fit in with any modern university sorority. She was not evil, even if she could be vain and short-sighted. She was not mad in the same sense that Hitler or Stalin was; her madness was one shared by much of contemporary high society. Those in power had placed the burdens and pains of maintaining society on those least able to bear them, and, despite warning signs, remained stubbornly on this path. Those errors in thinking stretch back to France's multiple wars across the sixteenth through eighteenth centuries and its regressive taxation system, and Marie Antoinette can't be blamed for bringing these into being. Yet, like her contemporaries, neither could she see a way past them. Her madness, as it were, was one of short-sightedness, an inability to fully appreciate the suffering of others nor to see how her own behavior contributed to the downfall of her country. In this she had many colleagues among the French aristocracy. She deserves neither full blame nor complete exoneration.

The rest, of course, is well-known history. Anger in France exploded with the storming of the Bastille on July 14, 1789. The royal family was placed under a kind of house arrest while France developed an ostensible constitutional monarchy. In 1791 the royal family attempted to escape Paris and join royalist supporters. They were captured and returned to Paris amid accusations of treason. With war against Austria breaking out soon after, Marie Antoinette was increasingly viewed as a foreign collaborator. Her husband, Louis XVI, was executed by guillotine in early 1793.[22] The writing, for Marie Antoinette, was on the wall.

By October 1793 she herself was tried for treason, found guilty, and beheaded by guillotine. Her role in provoking the revolution remains controversial to this day. Yet at the very least she is symbolic of the selfish madness that can overtake those in power when a rigid grasp on both

The Execution of Marie Antoinette.

power and financial resources cause the frustration of the masses to over-flow into violence and chaos. In this case, the madness was not so much her own, but one that had overtaken all those in power in French society.

iMadness

As I've noted a few times in this book, not all cases of madness result in calamity. As with Alexander the Great, they end with a truly inspired moment in history on occasion. Now we turn to one of those and the case of a man whose vision for personal computing played a major role in the evolution in how we engage with computing, communication, music, and movies.

Indeed, it's hard to have a discussion of Steve Jobs without hearing or using the word "vision" or "visionary."[23] Jobs, the legendary cofounder of Apple, is one of the heroes of the millennial surge in personal technology use. But he was also known as a difficult, callous, and eccentric personality. During his life he both built and burned a fair number of bridges. In this sense he appears to exemplify a particular personality style that hasn't gotten a lot of coverage in the psychological literature but that seems to exemplify a "roll big" approach to innovation and business. Let's have a look.

Jobs was an adopted child raised in a loving and supportive home. Unlike many of the other folks in this book, there's little reason to believe that Jobs's harder edges were shaped—even partially—by untoward harshness in the home. Nonetheless, Jobs had a reputation for misbehavior and resistance to authority, perhaps some early signs of his prickly adult personality shining through. In general, we likely overestimate the impact of environment on personality development, and Jobs may be a good example that genes tend to trump environment where this is concerned.

By high school he'd begun to show an interest in electronics and made a fateful friendship. This was Steve Wozniak, the tech wunderkind who formed the design side of the Apple cofounding team. Jobs performed the role of visionary, pushing the products to ever-reaching heights. The Apple Computer Company was formed in 1976 (famously in the garage of Jobs's family) and had its first real hit with the Apple II computer beginning in 1977.

It's probably hard to overestimate the impact of the Apple II on home computing. I remember it well from my own youth, both playing video games and learning how to code in BASIC, making my own programs. It was an iconic machine that revolutionized how we incorporate technology into our lives.

By this time, the full range of Jobs's personality characteristics had become apparent. First, he tended toward eccentricities and even what psychologists sometimes call "magical thinking" (belief in phenomena that are not scientifically supported). He was a strict vegetarian who believed that this obviated a need for bathing. He had strong opinions and could be brutally critical of others, sometimes publicly humiliating them. Some reports suggest Jobs bilked his partner Steve Wozniak out of an early bonus for their work, though Jobs denied this. When he didn't get his way, he threw tantrums. Jobs was an amazing visionary and also a perfectionist, but some of his visions resulted in odd designs for his products that didn't work out so well. For instance, at Jobs's insistence, the early Macintosh lacked cursor control keys or an internal hard drive, greatly limiting its memory. Some accused him of taking credit for others' ideas. He was known for creating a "reality distortion field" in which he could convince

Apple II computer, Computer History Museum.

others of wild ideas and make them sound reasonable, only for people to come to their senses once he had left.

Jobs could be erratic in his personal life as well. Perhaps the most famous example surrounds his first daughter, Lisa, whom he initially disavowed despite a DNA test proving his paternity with 94.4 percent certainty. When she was in elementary school Jobs acknowledged her, but the quality of his parenting remains an issue of some contention. Accounts by Lisa sometimes portray him as callous, erratic, even inappropriate at times, though other family members contest these accounts.[24]

This personality style combining great vision and passion with harsh, erratic leadership and eccentric beliefs is one that isn't well described in the psychological literature. It evokes elements of several personality disorders such as narcissistic, schizotypical (those who tend to endorse bizarre beliefs and have awkward social skills), and obsessive-compulsive, without fitting comfortably into any of them. Although direct comparisons are fraught, echoes of Jobs's management style can sometimes be found in descriptions of other visionary leaders such as Amazon's Jeff Bezos[25] or Elizabeth Holmes, an innovator who promised her company Theranos would revolutionize blood tests but ended up indicted for fraud.[26] When successful, these inherently iconoclastic personalities can revolutionize whole industries, becoming heroes. But the likelihood is that we mostly hear only the successful cases, and visionary leadership likely crashes and burns (albeit not so dramatically as with Holmes) in most cases. This leadership style is something of a Hail Mary pass for novelty. When it works, it's amazing. But more often, it does not work.

By 1985, struggling with other executives at Apple, Jobs was forced out of the company he helped create. This was a devastating personal blow for Jobs, but it also drove him to reinvent himself. He founded NeXT computers, but its expensive products, though pioneering, failed to find a customer base. Jobs had far more success with Pixar, particularly when that company started making charming animated films like *Toy Story*.

During the years without him, Apple began to struggle. By 1997, its fortunes plummeting, Apple bought NeXT, bringing Jobs back to the company he helped found then was ousted from. This second coming touched off one of the most brilliant phases of his life and Apple's development. Although there were some missteps, Jobs righted Macintosh's convoluted line, bringing in the iMac. Over the next decade and a half,

Apple introduced the iPod music device, iTunes, which changed the music delivery system from albums to individual songs, the ubiquitous iPhone, and the iPad. Ultimately, Jobs played a major role in revolutionizing how we compute, watch movies, listen to music, and communicate. Perhaps he was mad in his way and certainly his relations with others were often strained, but no one can say that's a bad track record for invention.

Jobs married Laurene Powell in 1991 and the couple had several children. Between his successes with the rebirth of Apple and his developing family life, Jobs seemed to have it all. However, in 2003 he was diagnosed with pancreatic cancer. He initially resisted treatment and didn't disclose his illness publicly, both choices that attracted controversy. When first diagnosed, Jobs rejected surgery in favor of alternative treatments, diet, and acupuncture. Although fear of surgery is obviously natural, Jobs had a rare slow-growing cancer and surgery, if done early, might have saved him. Naturally, we can never know for sure. Jobs eventually did seek conventional medical treatments, but the cancer progressed. In October 2011 he died leaving a legacy of both amazing revolutions and mercurial personal and professional relationships.

Elite Men and Their Contempt for Women's Rights

In October 2017 dramatic allegations came to light accusing famed Hollywood producer Harvey Weinstein of multiple sexual assaults and rapes of aspiring actresses stretching back decades. In many cases, others around Weinstein were accused of being complicit or at least having knowledge of the assaults and not speaking up.[27] Producer of many famous films such as *Pulp Fiction* and *Shakespeare in Love*, Weinstein would be accused by dozens of women and charged with sexual assault and rape (as of this writing). Victims told spine-chilling stories of being lured to private meetings with Weinstein to discuss film matters only to be groped or forced into sexual activity. Many feared their careers would be ruined if they rejected Weinstein's sexual advances.[28]

The accusations against Weinstein were hardly the first to strike the entertainment industry. Within recent months and years, other famous men in the entertainment industry such as Bill O'Reilly and Bill Cosby had also been accused of sexual harassment or, in the case of Cosby, a long stretch of bizarre rapes. Cosby, the beloved father figure on *The Cosby Show*, had been accused of and eventually convicted in 2018 of drugging then raping unconscious women, with allegations stretching back to the 1960s.[29] This particular MO led to speculation that Cosby might have had somnophilia, or "Sleeping Beauty syndrome," a preference for sex with unconscious partners.[30]

Yet the Weinstein case touched off a larger series of allegations against dozens, perhaps hundreds, of high-profile men in the entertainment industry, news media, politics, and business. Launching what has been called the #MeToo movement, accusations of sexual assault against multiple high-profile men created awareness of the continued presence of sexual threat in the lives of women.

Understanding this phenomenon is difficult. How common is sexual assault (a broad category of behaviors that range from unwanted sexual touching through rape) in elite environments, and what does this say about gender relations more broadly? Some observers suggested, rightly, that sexual assault and harassment may be, if anything, more commonly experienced by women in service industries, such as among bar or restaurant staff. I am optimistic enough to believe most men are appalled by the revelations of widespread sexual assault and harassment still experienced by women. Although some women do commit sexual assaults, men vastly outnumber women as sexual assault perpetrators.[31] This suggests there is something gender-specific about sexual assault.

Many contemporary discussions focus on social causes of sexual assault, patriarchy, and "rape culture." Yet, popular as they are, they are difficult to substantiate. Rape is not culture specific, nor even specific to humans; rape (or analogous behaviors) are seen in many other animal species ranging from insects to mammals.[32] Ducks, for instance, are notorious rapists, so don't feel guilty the next time you have an opportunity for l'orange.[33] Although sexual assault is more common among males than females, most males do not engage in sexual assault nor approve of other males who do (even if they often remain ignorant of the scope of women's experiences).

Biological explanations for rape behavior, thus, appear to be more salient. Such arguments are complex of course but basically boil down to what can be called the "dads and cads" argument.[34] This theoretical approach suggests that the best chances for male reproductive success comes from securing consenting romantic partners and contributing to the welfare of the resultant offspring. These are the "dads." But a small number of males (the "cads") are either socially or temperamentally unable to succeed at such an approach. Such males may lack the social graces to court women consensually or simply may be antisocial. Although for males, sex through consent is most efficient at reproducing one's genes, women certainly can become pregnant through rape, and thus a motivation to rape can be passed down through generations among a small number of males. Most people don't like thinking of either sex or rape in such reductionist biological terms, but my feeling is that this is the direction in which the best evidence points. Again, to be clear, this is merely a biological explanation for why rape occurs based on available data. In no way does this mean rape is acceptable, desirable, or not deserving of punishment when it occurs.

As for why there seems to be more clustering of sexual assault among elite men, it bears repeating that, even among elites, most men are not assaultive. However, as we've already seen in this book, power tends to attract certain personality types related to narcissism and antisocial traits. So the coupling of invulnerability that comes with elite status along with such status tending to attract more inherently callous men could be expected to make sexual assaults more pronounced among some elite-status men.

To summarize to this point: rape and sexual assault probably have many biological and personality determinants but can also thrive in social environments in which reporting of rape (and thus deterrence) is discouraged or punished. Most men do not commit sexual assaults nor approve of them but, living different social and emotional experiences, may nonetheless be oblivious to the degree to which women experience sexual threats in their day-to-day experiences. Sexual harassment and assault clearly occur at rates far higher than most of us men could have imagined and men of good faith need to band together with our women friends, family members, business partners, and spouses to make sure a clear climate of deterrence exists regarding inappropriate sexual behavior. I remain optimistic this is inherently doable and most people, male or female, want this.

Now things take a twist. I sometimes say that all movements end up being defined by their loudest and least rational elements. This has been an issue that has plagued feminism for decades (and to be clear I identify myself as feminist). The practical goals of feminism—from equal pay, to freedom from violence, to expanded roles for women in business, entertainment, and politics—are all worthy and likely enjoy popular support. But the academic side of feminism sometimes allows itself to get bogged down by rigid ideological systems that, with some justification, make it easy to portray the entire movement as "male bashing." Again, I am *not* saying that feminism is about male bashing, but rather that the ill-considered public statements and treatises of some perpetuate that image.[35] Therefore, many people engage in the cliché, "I'm not a feminist but . . ." wherein they obviously support the practical goals of feminism but reject the label.

Likewise, the #MeToo movement saw controversy when some individuals made statements appearing to show disinterest in due process for those accused of sexual misconduct. One of the most infamous quotes was by *Teen Vogue* writer Emily Linden who tweeted, "Sorry. If some innocent men's reputations have to take a hit in the process of undoing the patriarchy, that is a price I am absolutely willing to pay." Though by no means representative of the larger #MeToo movement, these comments got considerable attention. They are undoubtedly an angry reaction to the absence of due process that female victims of male sexual aggression have experienced since the dawn of time, but they nonetheless harmed the #MeToo movement by portraying it as more interested in mob rule than justice.

Accusations of sexual assault against several powerful women also complicated the story (though it should be noted that they are as entitled to due process as are accused males). In an ironic turn, these included Asia Argento, one of the actresses who had originally accused Weinstein of rape.[36] Even if these allegations against women are true, a few women engaging in sexual assault does not mitigate the behavior of many men doing the same. But it does highlight a tendency for social movements, particularly those fueled by emotion, to construct simplistic narratives and often to stumble when those narratives become more complex.

The 2018 confirmation hearings for Supreme Court justice Brett Kavanaugh further divided opinions. Kavanaugh was known to be a conservative judge, and his nomination predictably split opinions among conservatives and liberals in the United States. Just as he was about to be confirmed, he was accused by several women, most notably Dr. Kristine Blasey Ford, of sexual assaults when he was a college student (1982 in the case of Dr. Ford). Once again, the nation became divided over the issue of whether sexual assault allegations were inherently true or whether the

Harvey Weinstein and Asia Argento. Argento was one of many women to accuse Weinstein of sexual assault, only to be accused of assault herself against a male minor. *Photos:* Georges Biard.

accused deserved some degree of benefit of the doubt until due process could examine the claims.

Arguably both congressional Democrats and Republicans played the issue for their own political advantages. Some accused Senate Democrats, particularly Dianne Feinstein, of sitting on a letter from Dr. Ford accusing Kavanaugh of assault for weeks and not referring it to the FBI and instead "weaponizing" it to use against Kavanaugh at a critical moment during his confirmation hearings.[37] Dr. Ford gave moving and credible testimony before a Senate hearing. Later, Kavanaugh defended himself in testimony some felt came across as too angry. A subsequent, albeit brief, FBI investigation was unable to verify Dr. Ford's claims and Kavanaugh was confirmed. Nonetheless, the FBI investigation was so quick and limited that it did little to allay the concerns of Kavanaugh's critics. In a blow to the perception that assault claims are almost always good faith, several other claims (involving both male and female claimants) against Kavanaugh were found less credible and were themselves referred for criminal investigation for filing false claims.[38]

So did Kavanaugh assault Dr. Ford when they were young? We might say that only the two of them know for sure, but even that may be mistaken. Much of the debate on sexual assault allegations focused on low percentages of malicious false reports. Indeed, malicious false reports are rare, although contrary to some claims, there are no credible figures on their exact prevalence.[39] However, the issue of sexual assault claims isn't merely one of one party lying, but also one of memory. We know that many good-faith accusations are faulty due to the low reliability of human memory. DNA evidence has exonerated many men falsely convicted of rape based on eyewitness testimony.[40] But many of these cases are stranger rapes. Can this happen between individuals who are at least acquaintances as well? The issue of a false identification was raised by some Kavanaugh supporters and dismissed by his critics.[41] The truth is we don't have a lot of clear evidence about the reliability of memories of rape among acquaintances, particularly when so many years had passed (Ford accused Kavanaugh of attempting to rape her in 1982 and the allegation was made public in 2018). In fairness, this observation also applies to Kavanaugh. Particularly if he was intoxicated at the time, he may have no memories of actually perpetrating an assault. But memories, even those for traumatic events, are well known to be malleable over time.[42] That Dr. Ford didn't name Kavanaugh as her attacker until 2012 during therapy does raise the possibility that the identity of the attacker could have been mangled over thirty years. I have little doubt that Dr. Ford experienced a real sexual assault in 1982, but whether Kavanaugh is lying, whether Kavanaugh lost the memory of assaulting Dr. Ford, or whether Dr. Ford's own memory was malleable, we may never know.

Due process is necessary for both parties in such a case. Accusers deserve due process to have their cases heard and investigated in an efficient and dispassionate manner. Too often, victims of sexual trauma have been denied due process by having their claims dismissed out of hand, their credibility tarnished, and their concerns swept under the rug. But being heard and being uncritically believed are two different things. An accused individual also deserves due process and the right to answer charges made, to expect an impartial investigation, and, if the facts warrant, to go to trial.

As with free speech, due process is not only a legal concept but a moral and ethical one, and jettisoning it in either direction outside of legal proceedings still carries social risk.

We cannot definitely say what happened between Ford and Kavanaugh but perceptions about this issue tend to become filtered through our own tribal lenses. Neither conservatives nor liberals were immune to interpreting a singular event through their own sociopolitical worldview and emotional reaction rather than a dispassionate assessment of the facts, however limited, of the case. In this sense, the moment was fully democratic and demonstrated how democracies can descend into social madness, indulging in rage, fury, and mob rule, suspending the rule of law, and polarizing a community so that it turns on its own as enemies. But we return to this issue in chapter 10, when we consider the madness of the masses.

CHAPTER EIGHT
WHEN THE MIND GOES: DEMENTIA AMONG THE RULING CLASS

On August 23, 1899, an article headline in the *New York Times* blared, "Emperor of China Insane." Unfortunately, the ensuing article isn't much longer than the headline; aside from a claim that the emperor had developed symptoms of dementia, the reader is given little further information. Presumably, the emperor in question was the Guangxu Emperor, only twenty-four at the time, rather young for dementia. China in the late nineteenth century appeared to be in perpetual decline, largely at the mercy of the imperial European powers as well as Japan, and rife with corruption and a chaotic government. At the moment of the *Times* headline, the Guangxu emperor effectively was being placed under house arrest by his powerful aunt, the Dowager Empress Cixi, who was opposed to his reform efforts. Nine years later, he was murdered by arsenic poisoning, probably also by his aunt.[1] So we might take the convenient claim of his unusually early dotage with a grain of salt. But what exactly is dementia, how does it differ from other forms of madness, and how has it influenced the behavior of the powerful?

Throughout most of the book this far, we've looked at madness wrought in most cases by disorders of the personality as well as a few unfortunates stuck in positions of authority or influence despite the presence of debilitating mental illness. By contrast, dementia refers to organic brain disease that is typically gradual, in most cases irreversible, and increasingly impairing. Most cases of dementia, such as those brought on by Alzheimer's disease, occur with advanced age, but some

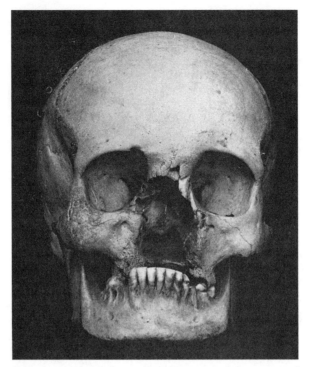

Skull demonstrating bone destruction caused by untreated syphilis. *Photo:* Joseph Bryant and Albert Buck.

specific diseases, such as Huntington's disease or even untreated syphilis,[2] can bring on dementia earlier.

Like it or not, advanced age inevitably brings on some level of cognitive decline. That's why, when we see a centenarian, we tend to remark how "sharp" or "alert" they are so long as they can put on their own pants or stir their own coffee. I'm not trying to be ageist (I'm getting there, too!), simply noting that we all have an awareness that some decline in some cognitive skills is a natural part of aging. Normal cognitive decline is predicted by some factors including genetics, smoking, lack of exercise, and lower B-12 vitamins. However, the effects of these predictors are generally quite small, so I'm not sure I'd pound the B-12s just yet.[3] As we age we tend to lose little bits of reaction time, new memory formation, processing speed, and novel learning, but, hey, we get wisdom in return. Given that this makes us more alert to what we're losing in all the other realms, this hardly seems like a fair trade but whatever. One centenarian, upon being asked the benefits of advanced age replied, "much less peer pressure," which is not only wise but perhaps one of the funniest observations of all time.[4]

Dementia refers to cognitive declines that are atypical for the person's age. These can result from neurodegenerative illnesses such as Alzheimer's disease or Parkinson's disease or more acute damage such as from strokes. Some infections can cause dementia. Untreated syphilis can bring on dementia, as can HIV. Prions, little errant proteins that make copies of themselves while destroying brain tissue in the process, are responsible for dementia due to Creutzfeldt-Jakob disease. In most cases, this is genetically inherited but can be transmitted by contact with brain or spinal tissue (including from other animals such as with mad cow disease or "zombie deer" chronic wasting disease). A particularly vicious variant, fatal familial insomnia, mainly attacks the thalamus region of the brain, which is responsible for sleeping. As the name suggests, these poor souls lose the ability to sleep—even sedatives don't help—and they effectively die from exhaustion within months or a few years at the outside. Fortunately, this is rare, appearing more common in Italian families (good news if you're not Italian, not-so-good news if you are).

Dementia can also be inflicted through repeated injuries to the brain. Famously, chronic traumatic encephalopathy (a fancy way of saying getting hit on the head a lot) has been found to be common in high-impact sports such as boxing and football.[5] Certainly, chronic substance use, such as drinking alcohol, can bring on variants of dementia such as Wernicke-Korsakoff syndrome.

Dementias, particularly those due to neurodegenerative diseases or stroke, are more common during the elderly years. However, rarer forms of dementia can strike at any age, including childhood. Leukodystrophy, which damages the myelin coating around the axons of neurons, can appear in childhood.

In many cases, dementia can develop slowly, becoming obvious only after symptoms reach a state of advancement. This means that, when occurring in a world leader, dementia could begin to set in, potentially influencing policy decisions, before the diagnosis is clear. The possibility that dementia has influenced the course of history has been raised a few times. But first, let's examine whether a case of neurological decline might have influenced art.

CHAPTER EIGHT

We're All Ears

Okay, yeah, we're about to discuss Vincent van Gogh. Van Gogh is famous for two things. First, being one of the most talented painters of the late nineteenth century. And second, for cutting off part of his ear and giving it to a prostitute he fancied. It's hard to say for which of these he is more eminent.

Van Gogh's short life (he died at about age thirty-seven) was marked by extraordinary pain and chaos. He began life as an unruly child and things largely got worse from there. Never very successful with women (it turns out girls don't like ears as presents), he was often alone, isolated, and despondent. He mainly survived on the goodwill of his brother Theo, who always believed in Vincent's amazing talents even if Vincent was difficult to deal with at times.

Van Gogh's issues weren't, strictly speaking, a dementia in the purest sense (we get to a few examples of that later in the chapter). But his problems related to a broad overlap between traditional mental illness and neurological disorder exacerbated by misuse of the powerful but popular alcohol drink absinthe. As such, his neurological and psychiatric decline are worth considering here.

First, it's important to note that van Gogh had many positive qualities as an individual. Obviously, he was an exceptionally skilled artist. He maintained an emotional closeness with his brother despite sometimes turbulent relations. And he sustained a deep emotional and spiritual longing and awareness throughout his life. Inevitably, as we delve into van Gogh's darker side, it's important to remember that van Gogh was a complex and multifaceted individual.[6]

That said, van Gogh's life was one shrouded in considerable darkness. Several times he became infatuated with women who had little interest in him, and their rejection sent him into cataclysmic spirals. He had understandably better luck with prostitutes, though this created scandal for his family. He commonly neglected his hygiene, threw tantrums of anger, sunk into deep depressions, and experienced delusions of paranoia and terrifying hallucinations.

He also experienced seizures, particularly what are called complex partial seizures. Such seizures tend to result from localized lesions in the brain. They generally don't cause full loss of consciousness and violent muscle spasms that are witnessed in the more dramatic grand mal seizures. Rather, individuals with complex partial seizures may seem disoriented or unaware of their environment, engage in odd or purposeless behaviors, experience psychotic symptoms, and have no awareness or memory of actions that occur during the seizure.

In van Gogh's case, the symptoms of epilepsy were worsened by his regular consumption of absinthe, a popular European alcoholic drink long thought to cause convulsions. More recently, these beliefs have been challenged in scientific studies.[7] Nonetheless, the uniqueness of absinthe aside, the sheer volumes of alcohol consumed by van Gogh almost certainly contributed to his neurological decline. Evidence from his letters suggests his experiences with seizures and mood disorders were associated with periods of higher absinthe consumption. Or put another way, heavy alcohol consumption undoubtedly made a touchy neurological situation worse.

Despite his talent, van Gogh was not a success during his lifetime. Setting the stage for tragic artists ever since, his art only became famous after his death.[8] The most famous incident of van Gogh's life occurred during a moment of significant delirium. Van Gogh had been living with the artist Gauguin and predictably had a violent falling out. As Gauguin left their shared living space one evening, van Gogh followed him threateningly with an open razor. Upon being rebuffed, van Gogh went home, cutting off part of his left earlobe, which he then presented to his favorite prostitute, a presumably startled woman named Rachel. The next morning, he was taken to the hospital, where he claimed to have no memory of the incident.

Van Gogh was, by this point, on his final downward spiral. He spent time in an asylum, which doesn't seem to have helped him much. In July 1890, van Gogh shot himself in the chest and died two days later. His supportive brother died six months later of natural causes, and it was his brother's widow who preserved most of van Gogh's paintings.

How might van Gogh have progressed had doctors managed to save him from his suicide attempt? Naturally, we can only speculate, but educated guesses are fairly straightforward. First, we must be clear that van Gogh wasn't necessarily doomed. Were he able to cut back significantly on his alcohol consumption, it's entirely possible he might have slowed or even arrested his neurological and psychiatric decline. Absinthe consumption appears to have worsened both his seizures and psychosis.

Vincent van Gogh, self-portrait with bandaged ear.

Unfortunately, recidivism among those with alcohol issues is quite high. Particularly given the acute nature of van Gogh's problems and the lack of empirically supported treatments available for them at the time, I fear that the prognosis for van Gogh would never have been good. By the time of his death, it's likely van Gogh's brain had already experienced significant damage. Even if he avoided suicide, continued heavy drinking would have damaged his brain leading to worsening symptoms of dementia, a condition called Wernicke-Korsakoff syndrome,[9] or "wet brain." Typical symptoms include memory loss, difficulty forming new memories (anterograde amnesia), and a clumsy, staggering gait. Such a condition would not have helped his preexisting psychiatric problems nor his seizure disorder. Put simply, unless van Gogh changed his lifestyle considerably, he was already a man on the road to alcohol-induced dementia by the time of his suicide.

How World War I Was Lost

Dementia doesn't always come on slowly and predictably, as is the course of chronic alcoholism. Sometimes dementia can drop like an anvil. This can occur to a wide variety of sudden insults to the brain, although the one most people live in fear of is a cerebral vascular accident (CVA), or stroke. Strokes can happen at any age. One of the more famous and inspirational stories is that of Sarah Scott, an eighteen-year-old woman who had a stroke while reading aloud in an English class. She suddenly lost the ability to speak or move the right side of her body. Fortunately, she was rushed to the hospital and her life was saved. Nonetheless the stroke left her with aphasia, a condition that makes it difficult to speak, read, write, do math, handle money, and so forth. Scott has since released a series of YouTube videos documenting her recovery and brought considerable awareness to stroke prevention.

Nonetheless, strokes become far more common among older adults. Risk factors include high blood pressure, smoking (which is a risk factor for pretty much everything), high cholesterol, obesity, and diabetes. One of history's most famous strokes occurred in 1919, when one largely destroyed Woodrow Wilson's ability to function as president of the United States.

Most representative republics see the need for some kind of executive head of state and typically elect them to specific terms in office. The Roman Republic elected consuls for one-year terms, but most republics use longer terms of, say, four or six years. This turnover period allows enfranchised citizens to reconsider how their executive is doing and elect a new one if they are unsatisfied with the job performance. The trick is, if executives are elected to fixed terms, what do we do when the executive implodes halfway through a term? Oddly enough, not all republics seem to have foreseen this possibility and include a mechanism for easy replacement of an impaired but not dead executive.

Woodrow Wilson is generally regarded as a competent U.S. president, though how favored he is by history tends to wax and wane a bit. Accolades come mainly for effectively managing the U.S. economy during his term, keeping the United States out of World War I until absolutely necessary,[10] and for a sensible vision for peace after the war that, predictably, nobody listened to. By contrast, he failed to get the United States to ratify the League of Nations, despite the concept being largely his idea, and he is also criticized as a proponent of racial segregation.[11] He is also widely remembered for his misfortune of having a stroke during his final years in office, remaining president while his wife secretly made many of the decisions of running the country for him.

Compared to some of the colorful characters in this book, Wilson's background is a rather unremarkable one. He was no madman, to be sure. Well, unless you consider academics to be inherently mad, and then perhaps you're not too far from the truth. Wilson was descended from Scotch Irish parents, his father a Presbyterian minister and theologian. Wilson was born in the South, but his family didn't have particularly strong roots there, so Wilson was able to traverse some of the ongoing north/south regional divides. Wilson gave law school a shot, didn't much care for it, then got a PhD in political science and spent most of his life in academia, arguing over a few pennies' worth of departmental budgets and obscure points of abstract political science. In this role, he was extremely successful and became a rising professorial star. In 1902 Princeton made him its president. Back in those days, people actually listened to Ivy League college presidents, so this raised Wilson's stature significantly.[12]

Eight years later, as a steppingstone to the presidency, Wilson was elected governor of New Jersey. Not inclined to settle for *that*, Wilson ran for the presidency of the United States just two years later in 1912. He had staked out a reputation as an anticorruption, antitrust, social justice (which mainly meant he championed poorer or middle-class whites in those days) progressive. Wilson benefited from a split, four-way election. Republicans were split between the official nominee and incumbent president William Howard Taft[13] and former president Teddy Roosevelt, who figured he'd give the presidency another shot. Thinking Taft was a bit of a wet noodle, Roosevelt figured only he could save the Republican Party from itself and, miffed at being rebuffed for the nomination, ran anyway under the Bull Moose Party. Looking back, I can't believe more people didn't vote for him just because of the party name. Wilson also faced an outside challenger in socialist (yes, they had them back then too) Eugene Debs[14] but Debs didn't do Wilson as much damage as Roosevelt did to Taft. Roosevelt actually outpolled Taft, returning one of the most impressive outcomes for a third-party candidate in U.S. history. But it wasn't enough to beat Wilson, who became president in 1913.

First, let's acknowledge that Wilson deserves eternal damnation for reviving the State of the Union speech, preempting far more worthy network television shows for decades.[15] Technically not required in the Constitution, which only mandates the president file an occasional report with Congress, the State of the Union has devolved into a weird demagoguery grudge match between the president and his or her[16] congressional opponents. Aside from this travesty, Wilson got his presidency off to a good start, challenging business trusts, lowering tariffs, and creating the federal income tax (okay, maybe that's not so popular), the Federal Trade Commission, and the Federal Reserve. All this economic stuff is a bit boring, I admit, but in short, he made the U.S. economy run better at the time.[17]

Blah, blah, economics, blah, blah . . . what really loomed large during Wilson's presidency was World War I. Entire libraries' worth of books have been devoted to what caused World War I, who's to blame, and whether it inevitably led to World War II. Summarizing it in a few lines, Europe's great powers were locked in paranoid power struggles and had developed two unwieldy alliance structures to try to maintain peace. People probably weren't stumping for war, but all it took was one lit match, a bunch of misunderstandings, and dumb decisions to start it. The 1914 assassination of Austrian Archduke Franz Ferdinand by Serbian terrorists likely aided by elements of the Serbian government provided the match. Even after the assassination, nobody thought it would *really* lead to a global war until Austria's demands for recompense proved unreasonable and nobody could back down from confrontation. Germany egged on its ally, Austria, although Germany itself wasn't entirely set on war, but the alliance systems all kicked in and soon enough most of Europe, Ottoman Turkey, and colonial possessions were in all-out war. This may seem like a big no-fault situation—and, granted, World War I doesn't have an obvious bad guy like Hitler—but Germany usually gets more blame for deciding to brutally invade neutral Belgium on its way to France.[18]

The United States didn't have a dog in this fight, so Wilson sought to keep the country out of it. Considering the meat grinder it turned into, with eight and a half million soldiers killed over four years,[19] it's hard to argue with this decision. Both sides made it difficult for Wilson. The British blockaded Germany and stopped ships and confiscated property heading into Germany. Granted, they were generally rather prim and proper about it, even paying for the stuff they confiscated. By contrast, the Germans torpedoed ships and inevitably sent some Americans to the bottom. In fairness, the Germans had few options. Though they had sought to develop a surface fleet on par with the British,[20] they hadn't managed it by the breakout of war in 1914 and had to rely on U-boats to blockade the British. Submarines of the day were rather slow and frail, so if they had gentlemanly surfaced to warn ships they were about to be torpedoed, their targets could have sailed away or blasted them to smithereens with deck cannons. Nonetheless, the finer points of the limitations of U-boats were lost on American civilians as they sunk to the bottom of the sea.

The United States also had divided national loyalties. Social and political ties to the United Kingdom were significant, and the United Kingdom and France were the two governments closest to the American republic in form. Most Americans weren't overly excited to protect any of the monarchies of the Central Powers (Germany, Austria, and Turkey, primarily), nor the Russian allies of the British and French, for that matter. But the United States did have a significant German immigrant population, as well as a fair number of Irish who weren't too keen on the United Kingdom.[21]

Germany ultimately made it difficult for the United States to stay out. Unrestricted submarine warfare sinking ships with Americans on them was one part of it. The other was the Zimmerman Telegram, a clumsy effort to get Mexico to join the war on the Central Powers side. Mexico had enough internal chaos of its own at the time to avoid taking on the big country to the north, but Germany hoped Mexico might be tempted by getting back parts of the southern states lost to the United States in the Mexican-American War.[22] If Mexico had been dumb enough to let itself get trounced in a North American war, that would tie up the U.S. Army for the foreseeable future. Mexico, it turned out, was not that dumb, but when the letter got in the hands of the U.S. government, it was too much for even Wilson to bear. In April 1917, Wilson asked Congress to declare war on Germany, although American forces wouldn't arrive on the continent in large numbers until 1918.

The thing about World War I is that Germany *still* nearly won it; 1917 was a good year for Germany. By then it had knocked three allied powers—Russia, Romania, and Serbia—out of the war. Its Austrian allies and the Italians[23] were beating each other into a stalemate. That left Germany to take on France and the United Kingdom, but France was already reeling, its armies having mutinied once in 1916. A German offensive in spring 1918 sought to smash the allied lines before American troops could arrive in great numbers and very nearly did so. Nonetheless, American troops turned the tide in Europe, something we brag about every chance we get (doing it again in 1941 didn't help matters). By then, the other Central Powers were exhausted and capitulated one by one. The German Army was never solidly defeated in the field, but its populace was starving under the British blockade and it had no real hope of fighting off a fresh American army. So an armistice was declared beginning November 11, 1918.

During the war, one unsavory element deserves attention. Congress, with Wilson's support, passed the Sedition Act and the Espionage Act of 1918, which severely curtailed free speech and political expression during the war. None other than Wilson's one-time presidential rival Eugene Debs was arrested and jailed under these laws for opposing conscription for the war. To be sure, this wasn't the first time a president played a role in suspending constitutional protections during a time of conflict—both Adams and Lincoln did as well. But, along with his segregationist policies, this assault on free speech and debate is one of the darker elements of Wilson's presidency.

Wilson had a vision for a postwar reconciliation and reconstruction that pretty much nobody agreed with, it turns out. Nonetheless, his instincts are credited with having been quite good, particularly with the wisdom of looking back. Wilson really wanted the creation of a League of Nations to prevent future similar outbreaks of war. He also took a line that was more generous to the Central Powers than was the perspective of the main Allied nations. Ultimately, neither line of thinking worked out. The Allied Powers, Britain and France particularly, wanted reparations from Germany and wanted to carve up the colonial territories of the former

Central Powers for themselves. Japan grabbed bits of Pacific Islands owned by Germany as well as former German interests in China. Italy had eyes on bits of the former Austro-Hungarian Empire but was frustrated by the other great powers in these ambitions despite earlier promises.

Wilson proved grudgingly willing to compromise on some of these territorial acquisitions with an eye on his League of Nations. But here he was thwarted on the home front. Isolationist feeling as well as partisan politics ultimately doomed the League of Nations in the United States. Despite it being an American idea, the United States never joined the League of Nations.

I said earlier that Wilson was a rather ordinary fellow in many respects. But his presidency was certainly anything but ordinary. And now began one of its most remarkable chapters. Wilson had experienced some health issues for years, even before assuming the presidency. High blood pressure had been a long-standing problem for him, and he may have had some small strokes dating back to 1896. In April 1919, while still at the Paris Peace Conference, he had another stroke, which set him to spending inordinate time in a confused state arranging and rearranging the furniture in his apartment. But he quickly recovered and continued with the conference. Upon his return to the United States, he faced a difficult battle getting the League of Nations ratified in Congress. Here he stumbled, becoming stubborn by refusing to negotiate with Republicans in the Senate to get their support. Instead, to pressure them by galvanizing public backing, he undertook a grueling public tour of the western United States to make his case directly to voters.

During this tour in late September or early October 1919, he suffered a massive stroke. He experienced paralysis and reduced speech and cognition. Fascinatingly, a small cabal around the president, including his wife Edith, private secretary, and physician, hid the details of Wilson's incapacity for about seventeen months, until near the end of his presidency. His wife Edith acted as an intermediary between the president and the outside world. Although she declaimed having done so, it is widely assumed she made substantive policy decisions on his behalf during this time.[24] Stripped of its main advocate, the League of Nations died in the U.S. Senate. Without it, the United States pulled back from moral leadership in the postwar world and would remain isolationist until World War II. Wilson did survive a few years after leaving the presidency in 1921,

Woodrow and Edith Wilson, who may have effectively served as an uncredited U.S. president for a time.

turning it over to Warren Harding, beginning twelve years of largely rubbish Republican rule in the White House. Wilson died in 1924.

The tantalizing question is: what might the world have looked like had Wilson not had his stroke in 1919? The failure of the United States to take part in the League of Nations largely doomed that enterprise to

163

irrelevance, particularly as it had been an American idea in the first place. A more mentally vigorous Wilson might have either compromised with his Republican opponents or galvanized public support to see the Senate ratify the League. It's not inconceivable that a healthy Wilson might have run for a third term,[25] bringing his leadership to the postwar world. Could Wilson have guided the world toward a more prosperous and generous twentieth century that would never have seen World War II? Without his declining neurological health, he might even have kept the Allies in line during the Paris Peace Conference, limiting their harsh treatment of Germany. Or perhaps that's too much to ask of him, even on a good day. What we can be sure of is that his stroke eliminated him as a force to be reckoned with at just the moment the League of Nations most needed him. Without him, it was doomed to failure.

America Will Never Make Concessions to Terrorists—Except Maybe Sometimes

I grew up, entering my preteen and teen years, in the 1980s, which means I still have a fondness for Duran Duran, the Atari 2600, and *Raiders of the Lost Ark*. It also means I became politically aware during the presidency of Ronald Reagan with its clear dividing line of good and evil (the Russians were evil, sorry guys) and seemingly impending nuclear holocaust. It's fun to look back on those days, when parents smoking pot in their bedroom in *Poltergeist* was good PG-movie entertainment and playing war games on a dial-up modem with a national security supercomputer seemed the height of technology (movie reference, if you didn't get it). But Reagan loomed large during those years, and I still remember his genius as a politician, both affable and strong. He is one of those examples wherein history needs not a madman but a determined, confident leader, and that's exactly what the United States got in Reagan. Mostly.

Reagan was born and raised in Illinois to Jack and Nelle Reagan. His mother, Nelle, was a stable and positive influence in his family. Highly religious, she put on morality plays in which she cast young Ronald, possibly giving him an initial taste for acting. By contrast, his relationship with his father was more difficult. Jack Reagan had difficulties with alcohol. At one time, Ronald came home to find him passed out on the front porch, another time Jack stumbled into the house leaving the family car running in the street with the door open.[26] Some researchers have suggested that growing up with an alcoholic father explains some of Reagan's weaknesses as president, particularly his aloof, disengaged style and stubborn loyalty to subordinates even when they failed him.[27]

Reagan's life is undoubtedly a fascinating one. First radio actor, then movie star, then governor of California, and finally president of the United States. Not too shabby, one must admit. He married twice and had five children, one whom died in infancy. I'll spare delving into the Reagan family's home life much, save to say at least one daughter seems not to have been overly content with it.[28]

Most people agree that the Reagan presidency was one of the most influential of the twentieth century. To give credit where it is due, Reagan restored America's confidence and worldwide reputation. Most notably, he is credited with playing a significant role in ending the Cold War with the Soviet Union by escalating the arms race to a point at which the Soviet Union collapsed economically. By contrast, others criticize his economic policies and related disengagement from social welfare issues. Reagan survived an assassination attempt in 1981 by John Hinkley Jr., an actual madman in this story. Hinkley apparently believed that shooting Reagan would impress the actress Jodie Foster enough to kindle a romantic relationship.[29] Reagan survived his injuries, although his press secretary James Brady was critically wounded and would die of his injuries thirty-three years later.

However, the episode we are most concerned with is the Iran-Contra Affair. Without getting too involved, let's try to hash out the major players in this muddled mess. Iran, by the 1980s, had developed into a fanatical Islamic regime hostile to the United States. Iran also had significant influence with some of the terrorist groups in the Middle East, some of which had kidnapped American citizens. Reagan received considerable credit for the release of American hostages held by Iran once he was inaugurated, although it seems more likely that the Iranians timed it to spite outgoing president Jimmy Carter rather than out of any particular fear of Reagan. Okay, so Iran, bad. We've got that down.

The Contras are a bit murkier. During the Cold War, both the United States and the Soviet Union funded nasty little proxy wars, sometimes using rebel groups to overthrow regimes friendly to the other side. One of these was Nicaragua, where a communist regime friendly to the Soviet

Union was being confronted with Contra rebels financially supported by the United States, particularly through the Central Intelligence Agency. This all seemed reasonable until it dawned on Congress that the Contras were mainly a bunch of brutal but ineffective thugs and decided to cut off funding in 1985.

Okay, back to Iran: bunch of crazy jerks, right? But in fairness, the United States had spent years propping up a pro-U.S. monarchy, the shah, which was bumbling and corrupt. When the shah was overthrown by the Islamic Republic in 1979, Iran inherited many American-made weapon systems, particularly planes, that had been sold to Iran by the United States under the shah. Iran soon ended up in a big war with its neighbor Iraq and needed spare parts. So despite all the "death to America" stuff, there was a market for U.S. goods there. The United States pressured other governments not to sell spare parts to the Iranians—after which they promptly started doing exactly that themselves. They also sold Iran missiles and other equipment. Funds from these sales were then funneled secretly to the Contras, to whom, we will remember, Congress had just cut funding. Later, officials would try to explain this all as an effort to help free American kidnapping victims in the Middle East, but this explanation generally didn't wash with congressional investigators.[30] It didn't help that Reagan had made previous bold pronouncements declaring that there would be no deals negotiating with terrorists. In the subsequent investigations, he appeared to have a poor grasp of at least some of the details of the Iran-Contra Affair, fueling speculation that early symptoms of dementia played a role in his loss of control of his own administration.

So, basically, the United States tossed away much of its credibility for a lousy deal. The shenanigans didn't really help the American hostage situation in the Middle East. As for the Contras, they plodded along, and Nicaragua eventually began holding free elections so that's a win, in fairness. Iran came out of the deal with supplies for its military. And the United States mainly ended up holding the bag. We can debate whether the blow to U.S. prestige was worth free elections in Nicaragua, if we even assume that the Iran-Contra funding was central to this. The more interesting question is how much control Reagan had over this whole fiasco.

One of the more controversial views to come out of Iran-Contra is not that Ronald Reagan directed an illegal scheme to fund the Contras by selling arms to Iran, but rather that by that point in his presidency, he

no longer had the mental faculties to fully understand what his administration was doing.[31] This involves speculation that Reagan was already
experiencing the earliest stages of dementia and ultimately lost control
of his administration.

In 1994, six years after leaving the White House, it was announced
that Reagan had been diagnosed with Alzheimer's disease, a progressive
neurodegenerative disease that begins with memory loss and leads to a
complete loss of mental faculties and death. Alzheimer's is inherited in
most cases. Its exact cause is somewhat speculative, typically involving
the accumulation of proteins in the brain that result in neuron death. The
brains of people with Alzheimer's disease noticeably shrink as the cells
die. Usually death results within about a decade of diagnosis (Reagan died
in 2004). However, the date of diagnosis typically does not indicate the
actual start of the disease. Typically, Alzheimer's may have been slowly
developing for years prior to the symptoms becoming acute enough to
be diagnosed.[32] So it's entirely possible that Reagan was experiencing
preclinical symptoms of Alzheimer's even a decade prior to his diagnosis.

This, not surprisingly, has been a matter of considerable controversy
and speculation. Many, and not unreasonably, find the question of Reagan's mental health during his presidency to be unfair.[33] And doctors who
knew him during his presidency declare not having seen clear signs of Alzheimer's disease at that time.[34] Then again, without a magic Alzheimer's
detecto-wand, it's entirely possible they missed it. There's no blood test or
other test for Alzheimer's and early symptoms easily can be disregarded
or dismissed as normal aging or forgetfulness. Even later Alzheimer's is
diagnosed largely as a process of elimination; only examination of brain
samples at autopsy can render a definitive diagnosis.

The question of Reagan's possible early symptoms while in office
has even split his family, with one son claiming to have seen signs of dementia during Reagan's second term, although other children disagree.[35]
Reagan was known to have shown at least occasional signs of confusion
or memory loss during his second term, most notably during the 1984
presidential debates against Walter Mondale. More recently, an analysis
of Reagan's speech while he was in office provides some evidence for
early markers of Alzheimer's disease.[36] This isn't definitive evidence but
adds weight to the argument for its presence. We may never definitively
know for sure but if you were to pin me down to an educated opinion, I

Ronald Reagan. *Source:* National Archives and Records Administration.

suspect that, yes, Reagan likely was experiencing some early preclinical Alzheimer's symptoms while in office.

I suspect much of the controversy arises from the false impression that dementia is a binary condition. In other words, people may feel that even an early hint of Alzheimer's disease makes someone a kind of "unperson" incapable of any rational thought. The end stages of Alzheimer's are indeed tragic, but patients with the disease can live full and productive lives for years after diagnosis, not to mention during the pre-diagnosis period. It's not beyond thinking that, particularly in one of the highest stress jobs imaginable, early Alzheimer's symptoms may have increased Reagan's likelihood of making a few mistakes. But that needn't tarnish his legacy as president. Many presidents have labored under medical and neurological conditions as bad or worse than early Alzheimer's. And, Iran-Contra aside, Reagan's presidency remains one of the most consequential of the twentieth century, probably *the* most consequential of the latter twentieth century. If we can remove the stigma of dementia from the legacy of the Reagan presidency, it may make it easier for us to evaluate the potential presence of early symptoms of Alzheimer's in Reagan during the late 1980s and, by doing so, more fully to understand early markers for Alzheimer's disease that may otherwise go unnoticed.

Some Concluding Thoughts

Parsing the role of dementia in history is made difficult given that a scientific understanding of dementia only really emerged in the twentieth century and that dementia clusters together a number of phenomena with varying symptoms and causes.[37] To be fair, scholars throughout history recognized that dementia was a thing but were often at a loss to explain it.[38] Unfortunately, it still carries considerable stigma and potential for ageism, which makes analysis of its role in history even more fraught.

Because people's conceptualization of dementia in the past was often vague and sometimes muddled with normal aging, we don't have as clear a record of dementia as we do the sorts of personality disorders and acute mental illnesses that created cruel or bizarre behavior earlier in life. Some individuals such as George III (whom we visited in chapter 4), had early diseases that degenerated into dementia. Others such as Henry the

VIII (the English king with six wives, most of whom didn't emerge from matrimony with him for the better), experienced behavioral changes that are sometimes posited as dementia. In Henry's case, everything from untreated syphilis to McLeod syndrome are suggested as causes.[39] Of course, most people throughout history simply didn't live long enough for dementia to become a factor.

In the tally of horrors madness has unleashed on humanity, dementia probably plays a lesser role than personality disorders. There are descriptions of emperors and kings who appear scattered or disengaged in their latter years, and, at times, others took advantage of this. But there's little evidence that dementia unleashed horrors on the scale that distorted personalities have, such as with Hitler, Mao, Stalin, or even Alexander the Great. As may have happened with Iran-Contra and more clearly happened with the League of Nations, dementia may precipitate a loss of central control and the onset of entropy. Perhaps dementia causes fear mainly due to its relative commonness and the sense it looms over us all. That is its greatest horror.[40]

MADNESS AS A POLITICAL FOOTBALL

In the antebellum southern United States in the 1850s, physicians were confronted with a peculiar mental illness previously undescribed in the medical lexicons. Specifically, against all logic and reason and to the befuddlement of southern doctors, some black slaves were tossing their tools and running away from service in hopes of reaching the non-slave-owning north. Given that—as the thinking went at the time—black slaves were clearly both in their rightful place and benefiting from the security and guidance of their white masters, this irrational motivation to flee could only be explained through mental illness. Dutifully, a southern physician, Samuel Cartwright, published details about the condition he called "drapetomania," or, essentially, an irrational desire among slaves to run away.[1]

Technically, the disorder at the time did indeed meet the ostensible criteria that we use to judge when a behavior is a mental illness. It was deviant, meaning that it violated the predominant (white) social conventions of "normal" behavior. The behavior involved an obvious sign of distress. And it was maladaptive, given the significant risks black slaves took in engaging in the behavior. Cartwright believed that white slaveowners who were either too lenient or too cruel likely would see an increased incidence of the behavior among their slaves and recommended the lash treatment.[2] Northern medical professionals largely mocked Cartwright's absurd diagnosis, with one sarcastically suggesting it might also be applied to schoolboys who ran away from headmaster whippings found some purchase among southerners at the time for whom it fit with a convenient social narrative.

Looking back, we can laugh or cringe at drapetomania as an obviously ridiculous and racist pseudoscience notion. But it also serves as a warning: what we consider to be madness is often shaped by politics, history, and social narratives. Madness itself is a political and politicized issue. What role does the government have in treating or housing those who are mentally ill, and how does it balance due process with the ostensible requirement to protect society from the unsafe mad? How do we define and classify mental illnesses, and is our system for doing so (whether the American Psychiatric Association's *DSM* or the World Health Organization's *ICD*) based on sound science or more akin to social narratives and just-so stories? Does the invocation of madness distract society from practical debates such as gun control in the United States or, for that matter, simply absolve horrible people of their personal responsibility?

Back in chapter 2, we considered how madness was treated through history (most often badly) to the controversies surrounding modern reliance on pharmaceutical interventions. In this chapter, we consider the politics of madness itself. We examine different governmental approaches to madness from the use of asylums to the deinstitutionalization movement of the 1960s and its ramifications. We look at the intersection between madness and violent crime and how prisons and jails came to be primary delivery systems for mental health services. We look at the role of madness in mass shootings and terrorism, events that strike fear not just in the United States (though we have our abundance of the former, in particular), but throughout the world. We look at modern classification systems like the *DSM* and *ICD* and see to what degree they reflect the reality of mental illness. And we consider some options for how we might do better.

What to Do about Madness?

In the twenty-first century we typically have a perception that governments and societies have a responsibility to help their most vulnerable members even if we're not that good at it in practice. But even that philosophy hasn't always been a given throughout history. We don't know a lot about what prehistorical societies did with their mentally ill (aside from drilling holes in their skulls), but for premodern societies, the answer seems to be: not much at all. For the most part, madness was seen as spiritual, religious, or curse related by most early societies and there was little perception that governments ought to do something to take care of the mentally ill. Most governments were too busy invading their neighbors or squeezing taxes out of their subjects, particularly the poor. Even when a society such as the ancient Greeks conceptualized mental illness as a disease, this didn't really result in a plethora of government-sponsored treatment options.

It wasn't really until the Renaissance that politics entered the realm of mental health,[4] and people began to think that governments ought to *do something* in order to—well—*do something* about the mentally ill roaming the streets or interrupting a relative's salon time with their raving delusions. I keep saying *do something* because nobody actually *knew* what to do. Thus, we enter the age of confinement, when the obvious thing to do with a population of odd folks that leave the everyday taxpayer a bit flummoxed is to stow them away in some kind of prison, out of sight and mind. Hence, we enter the period of flourishing government asylums.

One of the most famous of these is Bedlam, or Bethlem Royal Hospital, a place developed for "lunatics and idiots"[5] (hey, maybe it's for politicians after all!). Bedlam began in the thirteenth century as a priory in London but by the fourteenth century had begun to settle into its role as a hospital for the mad, making it one of the first asylums in history. Nobody's exactly sure what they did with inmates way back then, but Bedlam would eventually lend its name to a term for chaos and confusion. Granted, much of this comes from Bedlam's latter periods.

In fairness, *you* try designing a hospital for individuals with psychosis in the fourteenth century and see if *you* can do any better. Bedlam suffered from some of the straightforward issues of any early asylum: lack of funding,[6] poorly trained and paid staff, and, frankly, no freaking clue what it was doing. None of the techniques of modern psychology or psychiatry[7] were available to them. Hospitals like Bedlam were confronted with conundrums of what to do with psychotic patients who could be aggressive, act out sexually (or just, you know, want to have sex every now and again like any adult), engage in suicide attempts, and such. Lacking any real options, the asylums experimented with the kinds of brutal treatments we discussed in chapter 2 and used mechanical restraints and straightjackets on the unruliest.[8]

What comes across as well is that the staff was often not much better—at least as a source of stability—than the patients. Violence and fear were instrumental in securing the good behavior of inmates and the mentally ill were treated as if they were animals. There was also a distinct moral harshness to places like Bedlam. Indeed, some court evidence suggests that low-class women who were perceived as loose in sexual morals could find themselves adjudicated to such places.[9] Let's stick a pin in that point for a bit: that some of the inmates may not have been mentally ill at all by modern standards but likely were simply low-functioning and sexually licentious during Tudor-era England.[10]

Controversial as it may be to say, the internment of the critically mentally ill isn't necessarily an inherently terrible idea on the surface. A humane, dignified regimen of care geared toward curative goals or comfortable care with maximal agency if that is not possible shouldn't be dismissed out of hand if the alternative is mainly homelessness. But asylums generally ran afoul of two ongoing issues in mental health care. First, where a clear cure may not always be possible, frustration may set in for both patient and treatment staff, and this can lead to abuse and aggression in both directions (although treatment staff ultimately wield outsized power). And second, although the public are often very earnest in believing that policy makers must *do something* about mental health, the public is often less enthusiastic about paying for this something in the form of taxes.

This combination of poor funding and frustration coupled with clueless management created the difficult situations for which Bedlam became infamous. The popularization of the word "bedlam" to mean chaos or madness came in the form of contemporary plays, including references in Shakespeare,[11] but also from occasional publicized audits of the hospital. A 1598 inspection found the place to be quite literally falling apart with holes in the roof and not enough eating utensils. By the early 1600s, one "keeper" (i.e., the dude in charge) of the hospital was sacked for siphoning funds away from the hospital and largely leaving the inmates to starve.[12]

Hygiene was also a problem for the hospital, which had inadequate water supplies and bathroom facilities, such as they were. Bathing was likely rare, and most inmates had access only to a chamber pot, though this did provide ammunition when one wished to catapult his or her displeasure toward the staff or visitors. In fairness, routine bathing was uncommon among even the general public during these earlier centuries. Given

Bedlam at its "improved" location in the seventeenth century. Engraving by Robert Hooke. *Source:* Wellcome Library.

how sensitive we are to body odor today, it's a wonder any socialization at all got done during the Tudor and Stuart England years.

It would be nice to say things got better over time, but that didn't really happen until at least the nineteenth century. Granted, some keepers might be humanely inclined, but treatment remained brutal, involving procedures like bloodlettings and blistering. Health care and food resources remained low, and Bedlam was often financially thin. There are reports Bedlam opened its doors and charged admission to the public to increase income. The actual location moved a few times, though this didn't bring with it much by way of improvements for the inmates.

Things briefly improved during the early nineteenth century before a return to more brutal treatments and restraints in the late nineteenth century. In the early nineteenth century, a reform effort by the Quaker Edward Wakefield exposed the appalling conditions of the inmates, many of whom were chained up for years. Things got better but ultimately Wakefield went to his heavenly reward and people forgot about Bedlam and the chains returned. Being nice to the mentally ill didn't necessarily make them less mentally ill, so some genius probably figured *why be nice?* Spare the rod and all of that.

By the twentieth century Bedlam joined the ranks of other modern asylums, being no better or worse. Whether this is a good thing, I suppose, depends on what you think of modern asylums. Not that there's many left, but we come to that in a moment.

In fairness to Bedlam, the hospital was probably not exceptional for its day in its maltreatment of the mentally ill. From the story of Bedlam, we can see a few truisms that may help us to understand current politics. First, people aren't that excited about paying for mental health services, at least not for someone else. Second, mental health issues are ripe for due process problems. Rosenhan's spectacular field report from 1973 in which he and his students posed as patients with schizophrenia was itself a response to a problem already speculated about. As you may recall from chapter 2, hospitals were reluctant to let Rosenhan's researchers leave, even when they stopped displaying their fake symptoms. Asylums are already scary places but add to that the potential for being unfairly locked up in one with no recourse, and they become terrifying indeed.[13] Arguably, mental health staff have obvious incentives for *never* releasing anyone from involuntary commitment. Should they do so, and that person immediately killed themselves or someone else, society certainly would ask why no one waved the magic psychiatry wand and predicted it in advance. Third, mental illness is frustrating for all involved. Certainly, for the person suffering, but also for their families and for mental health staff. Frustration breeds aggression and aggression breeds both real risks as well as the potential for abuses.

So despite periodic efforts to reform them, asylums remained difficult and unpleasant places until the mid-twentieth century. About that time two things happened. First, states decided they *really, really* didn't want to keep paying for these expensive buildings that always ended up as the settings for bad horror movies. And antipsychotic medications like Thorazine became widely available, holding forth the promise of controlling serious mental illness in community settings. Coupled with this, kind-hearted advocates saw an opportunity to return the mentally ill to the community where hopefully they would be productive citizens. I sometimes imagine well-intentioned animal rights activists breaking into SeaWorld aquarium and releasing the penguins from their temperature-controlled pens into the 95-degree Orlando heat crying, "Be free, be well!" the whole time. The deinstitutionalization movement that shut down most of the asylums was a bit like that, but let's take a close look at it.

Out'cha Go!

Alright, so let's acknowledge that, aside from a few brief moments of reform, the age of confinement was all too often a horror show. Certainly any change would be welcome, and the government couldn't possibly screw things up worse, could it? Never challenge the government on that score!

Deinstitutionalization began in the 1950s and followed through the 1960s in various legal and professional lurches. This happened through both the federal and state governments, which became concerned about tossing good money after bad at the asylums. At the same time, the legal system increasingly became concerned about due process issues for the mentally ill. Deinstitutionalization was supposed to have two parts. First, move people out of the asylums. Second, move them into a community mental health system that would take over for the asylums. Oh, don't forget to fund part two with tax money; let's not forget that very important second part.

The whole idea was part of something called the Community Mental Health Act.[14] There were two arguably unforeseen obstacles (well, three if you include the tax issue) for transferring the mentally ill to community centers. First, nobody wanted them. This is a phenomenon sometimes called NIMN (not in my neighborhood) or NIMBY (not in my backyard). Community mental health centers were envisioned as smaller, more open facilities that would function amid the general public, unlike the large, prison-like, isolated asylums. Community mental health centers could include everything from halfway houses to residential school-like facilities. Communities, particularly more affluent communities, blocked the building of these community mental health centers. If we're being honest, can we entirely blame them? Even if we assume they wouldn't increase local crime (we get to that in a bit), they still would likely reduce home values. So, although people might support mental health centers in the abstract, they get edgy when their home values are on the line. I get it; I've got a mortgage, too.[15]

But the other issue is that the new system created a messy bureaucratic web. Asylums had one benefit, sorta, in that whatever services were being provided were all under one roof and the mentally ill were never expected to play a role in coordinating them. But now a person might have a social worker and a psychiatrist, live in some community facility, have to go to court for monitoring, and maybe need to work with insurance or social security. And of course, each of these entities might do a lousy job communicating with one another (think about the last time you had a medical procedure that required a hospital visit and all the organization that required). This would probably be frustrating for any of us to try to imagine; now try to imagine doing it with schizophrenia.

The result was what most folks agree was a spectacular failure to transition people from the asylums to any kind of functioning community mental health system. Instead many previously committed mentally ill individuals became homeless, incarcerated, or, in some cases, ended up dead due to neglect.[16] I'm not saying no one made out okay or even for the better, and a lucky few may have been taken back in by family. But overall the result was pretty bad.

How many were affected? Good estimates are hard to come by. In 1987 one scholar guessed that perhaps one and a half million chronically mentally ill people effectively got dumped in the transition between asylums and the largely missing community mental health centers during a twenty-year period.[17] Another figure puts the population of asylums in the United States in any given year at their peak at about half a million.[18] On any given night there are roughly 550,000 homeless individuals in the United States, which is lower than in past decades, so that's good news.[19] However, perhaps one third of those individuals are chronically mentally ill.[20] So that's the population of interest now: folks who likely would benefit from some kind of structured, dignified, humane state living facility but got bupkus instead.

Aside from homelessness, deinstitutionalization is sometimes referred to as *transinstitutionalization* insofar as that many of the chronically mentally ill simply moved from state hospitals to prisons and jails. Indeed, correctional facilities today are often the largest providers of mental health care in the counties in which they operate.[21]

The development of new drugs for the treatment of psychosis and other mental health conditions arguably played one role in the deinstitutionalization movement. These drugs held the (probably oversold) promise that individuals could return to "real life" so long as they stayed on their medication. This outlook neglected two facts: first, that the drugs mainly treated some symptoms but not others, and second, that they often had severe side effects that discouraged persistence in taking them. The degree to which pharmaceutical agents propelled deinstitutionalization is controversial, and movements toward deinstitutionalization had begun prior to the advent of such drugs.[22] Post–World War II, many states experimented with the idea of community-based clinics to supplement hospital stays. However, many patients were readmitted, suggesting that the transition to community care often did not work out very well. Nonetheless, these problems continued past 1954, when antipsychotic medications became widely available.[23] It was only in the 1960s that asylum populations began to decrease in the United States.

Much of the impetus appears to have been political. A 1961 government report, the *Joint Commission on Mental Illness and Health*, argued against building any further large state hospitals. A push was made for greater federal investment in a community mental health system. President Kennedy got in on the act with a speech in 1963. By 1980, the population of state asylums had declined from roughly 550,000 to about 140,000.[24] One detail: the federal initiatives forgot to include any mechanism for directly transferring care from state hospitals to a community mental health system. So too often, folks were released from state hospitals into the waiting arms of, well, nothing.

People talk a lot about the importance of reforming the mental health care system. And there have been some improvements, such as considering mental health syndromes as being on par with physical health conditions for insurance reimbursement. But often the talk is just talk. Reform would involve tax money, functioning bureaucracy, and good science to determine what works and what doesn't. It would also require a careful balancing of due process with the need for confinement. Is return to an asylum system necessary? Honestly, probably so, but not a return to the brutal asylums of the past. Any confinement system should work on the principle of least restrictive environment— that people should be confined only to the degree minimally necessary for their well-being and care—in humane conditions with well-trained and compensated staff and with clear due process and judicial oversight. This, of course, would take money, and folks in the United States are excited neither by taxes nor bureaucracy. So we'll see.

Interestingly, the discussion about reforming mental health often comes up after tragic violent events, particularly mass homicides. This is another kind of weird football people play with mental illness. To what degree is mental illness associated with violence in society? And to what degree do people bring it up (along with nonsense stuff like video games) in order to distract the populace from other issues such as gun control?

Madness Unleashed on the Masses

In December 2012, the lead-up to the Christmas holidays was tragically disrupted for many families in Newtown, Connecticut. On December 14, a troubled twenty-year-old young man walked into Sandy Hook Elementary with a Bushmaster AR-15 style sporting rifle.[25] He had already murdered his mother in their home. Now he engaged on a rampage, killing twenty young children and six school staff before committing suicide. The Sandy Hook shooting became one of the deadliest mass homicides in U.S. history (though not the record) and set off a nearly year-long debate about gun control, mental illness, and (more foolishly) action video games before sputtering out without accomplishing anything.

The Sandy Hook shooter[26] had a long history of mental health problems, depression, social isolation, and autism spectrum symptoms. In fact, the presence of mental health issues, often undiagnosed or poorly treated, is nearly universal among mass homicide perpetrators.[27] This precipitated a long discussion that we should *do something* about the nation's mental health system. But what? And was mental illness the best lens through which to view the mass shooting problem? Or merely a distraction from the gun control debate?

First, though, let's dispense with the third excuse people came up with for the Sandy Hook shooting. It took eleven months for the official investigation report to release an official report on the shooter.[28] During that time, it was reasonable to conclude that the shooter must have played some action-oriented[29] video games. Indeed, many news headlines proclaimed anonymous sources close to the investigation found that the Sandy Hook shooter had played thousands of hours of games like *Call of Duty* and was obsessed with such action-oriented games. Ultimately, it turned out he mainly played *Dance, Dance Revolution*. In fact, the belief that action-oriented games (or television or movies) are linked to violent crimes is pretty much a scientifically dead issue, promoted irrationally—as all moral panics are—largely by cranky old people. Time to move on.[30]

So back to mental illness: can mental illness be linked to crime? Well, that rather depends on what you mean by both mental illness and crime. In this sense, both the folks who want to pin all violence on mental health issues and the folks who portray the mentally ill as innocent lambs both have it wrong. The issue is a bit more nuanced than most people seem to want to believe.

Let's look at the common claim that only a small percentage of violent crimes are committed by the mentally ill. Typically, the suggestion is that only a small proportion of violent crimes, say around 5 percent, are committed by the mentally ill. For instance, a commonly cited 2006 study from Sweden came to this conclusion.[31] However, the trick is that this study limits mental illness to *severe* chronic mental illnesses, such as schizophrenia and other psychosis. Such disorders are exceedingly rare, typically occurring in less than 1 percent of the population. So if 1 percent of the population does indeed commit 5 percent of violent crimes, that sure does indicate an increased risk for violent crime among the mentally ill. People who raise this argument answer the question regarding links between mental illness and crime by considering *only one particular form* of mental illness. That's a bit deceptive, I feel.

It's deception with good intent, no doubt. To be sure, the vast majority of mentally ill individuals do not commit violent crimes. However, the implication that there's no elevated risk at all for violence among the mentally ill is not data based. Nor does it fit well with the experience of many clinicians, myself included, who experienced relatively frequent aggression in psychiatric settings. It's valuable to reduce stigmatization of the mentally ill but not with nonsensical claims.

By and large, the mentally ill are just trying to get by in life like everyone else but with some obvious extra challenges. The vast majority are not dangerous. At our university, Stetson University, someone with schizophrenia occasionally wanders onto campus from some nearby indigent or low-income communities. For some reason, other staff on campus usually direct these folks to the psychology department (note to academics everywhere: the psychology department does not have a magic wand to wave on mentally ill folks from the community). I've talked to a few and I let them know I've got about twenty minutes to spare (some folks with schizophrenia can talk for a long time). Mainly they want someone to talk to regarding their revelations on the Bible or whatnot. They're harmless even if, of course, ill.

But working in psychiatric settings, you also understand that suggesting there's *no link whatsoever* between mental illness and violence is also wrong. Assaults do happen in psychiatric settings (and among psychiatric populations outside of care) with greater frequency than in the general public. Research does find that, for instance, psychosis is a risk factor for violence, although this doesn't mean that everyone or even most with psychotic illnesses are violent.[32] Psychosis appears to elevate violence risk about three to five times that of the general population. In some of my own work, I find that a combination of depression with antisocial personality features is one of the stronger risk factors for youth violence.[33] Claims that there is no link at all often rely on shifting definitions of mental illness. For instance, if we limit mental illness to psychosis only, as that 5 percent statistic does, then the Sandy Hook shooter, a young man who was clearly disturbed, including autism and depression and antisocial features, would not qualify.

On the other hand, I have little doubt that the issue of mental illness can also serve as a distraction from other issues for some politicians, particularly gun control in the United States. This is not to say that the mental health system in the United States doesn't need reform; it almost certainly does. The Sandy Hook shooter's mental health issues had been known for some time, and his mother had struggled for years, obviously unsuccessfully, to address them. Should this shooter have been placed in a humane, caring asylum given his acute mental health issues? Possibly so, but again, the United States doesn't have anything like this kind of system in place.

Using mental health as a distraction from other issues is also a cynical ploy. We can have a conversation about mental health reform while also discussing sensible gun control issues. Unfortunately, both the left and the right tend to spend too much time seeking moral high ground to make this possible. Conversely, this makes both sides suspicious of the other. Probably most of us would agree that we don't want folks like the acutely ill Sandy Hook shooter having access to otherwise legal firearms. Perhaps there are reasonable ways to ensure this becomes less likely without unreasonably burdening responsible firearm owners. I don't claim to have the immediate solution, but it's certainly a conversation worth having. Of course, that would require the masses to calm down, stop trying to "win," and behave like rational human beings. As we see in the next chapter, that's not always an easy thing for people to do.

Defining Illness

As we saw at the beginning of the chapter, defining mental illness is itself a political/social process. Psychiatry has always struggled with categorizing mental illness. That's not to say mental illness doesn't exist as a real thing, but that its boundaries tend to be grayer and more fluid than for many medical illnesses. For instance, a disease like the flu or cancer can be ascribed directly to certain biomarkers or biological agents like a virus or damaged cells. Most psychiatric illnesses having nothing equivalent. There's no blood test for depression or an X-ray that can tell you whether your thoughts are normal or deviant. And that tends to make psychiatry messier. At the extreme, psychiatry has been accused of pathologizing many normal feelings and behaviors and profiting off the same. Let's have a look at this issue.

Psychiatry (as well as psychology) only emerged as a profession in the late nineteenth century, in large part from the physicians who helped run asylums. During this early phase, psychiatry was heavily influenced by Freudian thinking, with penis envy, Oedipus complexes, and all manner of similar nonsense. In fairness, Freudian theory has some interesting observations about human nature, such as the defense mechanisms like denial and rationalization. Yet diagnosing people based on this approach tended to be chaotic at best and put psychiatry in an awkward position in terms of public credibility. Any two psychiatrists might use widely varying terms and diagnoses to discuss the same patient. Naturally, this didn't appear scientific at all.[34]

Psychiatry needed a common nomenclature and in 1952, the American Psychiatric Association (APA) created it with the *Diagnostic and Statistical Manual (DSM)*. The *DSM* would become both an important cash cow for the APA as well as a source of ongoing controversy. The *DSM* still tended to feel a bit heavy on Freudian influences and was revised in 1968. Still it continued to have reliability problems, with clinicians disagreeing over the diagnosis of mentally ill individuals.[35] The psychiatrist Thomas Szasz opened a broadside against the concept of mental illness itself, suggesting that the medicalization of deviance and distress was a false path and mental health should not be confused with medical health.[36] Szasz's point was important but ultimately one largely rejected by psychiatry, as it sought greater credence for its profession in parity with medical doctors.

The trick about psychiatry is that, with a few exceptions, most mental illnesses don't resemble medical illnesses, either in terms of clear delineations or in identifiable biological markers. By the time of the *DSM-II* in 1968, psychiatry increasingly coalesced around the model of mental illness as synonymous with medical illnesses and all the talk of neurotransmitters and chemical imbalances with which we've become familiar. But this model has also been criticized as having sketchy data to support it as well as having done little to improve mental health outcomes.[37] It's hard to argue that the brain plays no role in mental health, of course, but some folks question whether mental illnesses are synonymous with medical illnesses. However, this model definitely opened up a lucrative path for pharmaceutical industries, and concerns about too-cozy relationships between Big Pharma and psychiatry and the APA specifically have persisted ever since.[38]

In 1980, the APA published the *DSM-III*, an attempt to make the diagnostic categories more rigorous, reliable, and based on data. Many categories were changed, added, or deleted, but overall the number of potential mental health conditions expanded, a trend that would continue in subsequent versions of the *DSM*. In 1987 the *DSM-III-R* presented a kind of midcourse correction. These new versions of the *DSM* provided evidence that, at the very least, carefully trained clinicians could achieve a reasonable degree of reliability in diagnosis, albeit by no means perfect.[39] However, they left unsettled the question of whether such diagnoses are *real*. In other words, did the diagnostic categories reflect real, distinct categories of disorders with identifiable conditions? Or were they simply voted on by committee, sometimes reflecting the special interests, worldviews, and prejudices of the psychiatrists at the APA? We don't need a committee to tell us that the flu is different from anthrax, because the different critters involved are identifiable under microscopes. But, for instance, depression and anxiety tend to both co-occur and look different in different people. Are depression and anxiety different disorders, aspects of the same disorder, split into dozens of individual little disorders, or something else?

Of course, homosexuality is the obvious model for this confusion. Originally included in the *DSM*, homosexuality (like drapetomania) had all the markers of a mental illness. The behavior was considered deviant by society at the time. It could cause distress in individuals who were told it was morally wrong. And the behaviors persisted despite obvious negative consequences ranging from social ostracism to jail or, in some parts of the world, execution. But here we can see Szasz's point: homosexuality wasn't a disease like colon cancer is a disease. It reflected a moral conflict between a conservative society and individuals who strayed from the moral values of that conservative society. Homosexuality was a disease because society wanted it to be a disease.

This is not to say that all mental conditions are like homosexuality in this sense, which finally disappeared altogether from the *DSM* in 1987. But we can see the problems with the boundaries of mental illness. Not only do mental conditions bleed over, one into another, but their boundaries with normality are likewise unclear. If I develop a depression because a beloved relative has died, is this a disease or a normal reaction to a tragic life event? If my personality is odd and eccentric (and I'm sure some people would say that it is), does this warrant a *DSM* diagnosis if I am otherwise functional? Why do we decide that overuse of video games is maybe a mental illness, but overuse of almost anything else, whether work, exercise, dancing, shopping, or cats (try an internet search for cat hoarder if you think I'm joking) isn't worthy of an official diagnosis?[40]

A central quandary for psychiatry is that most diagnoses remain constructs voted on by committees and diagnosed based on arbitrary observations rather than sensitive and specific medical tests. This is why mental health conditions sometimes seem to miraculously appear then disappear from different versions of the *DSM*. Asperger's syndrome, for instance, vanished from the *DSM* in its fifth edition, to much controversy. Mostly, new ones appear, as the number of diagnoses increased in the *DSM-IV* (released 1994) and *DSM-5* (released 2013—and yes, they switched to Arabic numerals).[41] The criteria for specific disorders such as ADHD and depression generally have become looser over time, once again raising the issue of financial conflicts of interest regarding potential overprescribing of pharmaceutical agents in treatment. By the fifth edition, individuals conceivably could be diagnosed with depression even if experiencing significant life trauma such as bereavement of a loved one. This raised concerns that the APA was continually medicalizing any normal life behavior at which a pill might be tossed.

By the time of the *DSM-5*, even psychiatrists involved in developing prior versions of the *DSM* had become concerned about the overreach of the APA as well as about the lack of scientific rigor.[42] Other professional bodies such as the British Psychological Society wrote open papers criticizing the *DSM-5*.[43] Obviously, individual opinions vary, but my sense is that, at least among my psychologist colleagues, the *DSM* categories aren't exactly "real." Certainly, mental illness exists but *DSM* categories are, at best, rough approximations of them and often are straight-out problematic with a tendency to overpathologize normal behaviors. So if it's so bad, why do we keep using it?

The answer is simple: insurance reimbursement. For psychologists, psychiatrists, and other therapists who seek reimbursement for treatment, a *DSM* code for diagnosis is necessary to receive compensation. This puts the APA in the unusual position of having a kind of de facto monopoly over the middle ground between therapists and insurance companies. *Therapists have to buy the* DSM *if they want to get reimbursed for therapy.* Among researchers, the *DSM* categories also provide a kind of handy language around which to organize research constructs. Researching "borderline personality disorder" sounds a lot better than researching "high-strung people who get moody and overreact a lot." The *DSM* creates a kind of illusion of definable categories of mental illness, which is more palatable than the shifting and confusing boundaries among mental illnesses as well as between pathology and normality that probably is reality.

So there you have it. A mental illness is quite literally decided by committee. This means that mental illnesses tend to occupy a muddy ground between real conditions of the brain, behavior, and personality and social constructions of what is desirable and what is not. Hence, we get rubbish conditions ranging from homosexuality to game addiction but also confusion about whether, say, the odd and socially isolated kid has a treatable condition or is just a bit strange. What gets to be a diagnosis remains very political, influenced by social and political pressure (remember the World Health Organization specifically noting political pressure as one impetus for its gaming disorder category), potential financial conflicts of interest, and groupthink and lack of skepticism among members of the APA.

Unfortunately, there's no easy road out of this. The WHO has the *International Classification of Diseases* (*ICD*), which is used more outside the United States. I'm skeptical that its approach to mental illness is much of an improvement on the *DSM*, particularly as the two tend to be linked to a great degree. The National Institutes of Mental Health (NIMH, just like in the movie *Secret of NIMH)* is developing a biologically based *Research Domain Criteria* (*RDC*) at least implicitly out of frustration with the *DSM*. The *RDC* appears to seek to make psychiatry both more rooted in biology and in science (those two may not exactly be the same), but it's hard to evaluate its worth until it is released. As clinicians we can dislike the *DSM* all we want, but abandoning it isn't financially viable for those who seek reimbursement from insurance companies.

Our understanding of mental illness has always been corrupted by politics and social conventions. The development of the *DSM*, though worthy in principle, has not done much to change this state of affairs. Likely, we'll continue arguing about the meaning of mental illness into the foreseeable future.

MADNESS OF THE MASSES

I n the late eighteenth century, two nations each took their first lumbering steps toward democracy. One succeeded, the other failed. In the United States, the colonists, reacting primarily to economic disputes and the heavy-handed response to them by the British Parliament, rebelled against their overlords in the United Kingdom. Fifteen years later, in France, the citizens likewise tossed out their aristocratic masters with an eye on equality and freedom. The United States' experiment resulted in a long-lasting democracy that persists, certainly with some warts, to the present day. The French experiment ended in terror, the guillotine, chaos, war, and, eventually, Napoleon, whose megalomaniacal rule was almost a relief by that time. What happened to make the outcome so different in these two new democracies?

To say that likening eighteenth-century America to France is an apples-to-oranges comparison doesn't even begin to scratch the surface. Nonetheless, there are some similarities. Both early movements saw a rise to prominence of firebrands and bloody infighting among former neighbors and friends. Indeed, during the U.S. revolution, some of the most vicious violence occurred not between British and American troops but between colonists who supported the rebellion and those (Tories) who supported the king.[1] Ascribing the U.S. success to any one thing is disingenuous but it appears that in the United States, level heads (Washington, Jefferson, Franklin, Madison, etc.) prevailed and, without a better way of putting it, were able to herd the passions of the masses into a productive direction. In France, arguably this didn't happen, and the chaos of mob rule invited the tyranny of the Reign of Terror and the corruption and autocracy that followed in its wake.

I sometimes joke that if we make policy decisions with the assumption that people are basically dumb, we'll seldom be disappointed. I don't mean individually dumb, of course, but rather that once we are reduced to an emotional, uninformed mass, bad decisions regularly follow. I happily include myself in that emotive, uninformed mass on most issues. People, even intelligent people, tend to make decisions emotionally rather than rationally, and when clustered together in groups, that bad instinctual decision making can become amplified. What else could explain the rush to war in Iraq in 2003 or adoption of the belief that kale actually is edible food?

As the old saying goes, democracy is the worst form of government, except for all the other forms that have been tried.[2] Democracy is a great idea—don't get me wrong—I fully support it! But it also does bring with it certain challenges such as just how much power to give to the citizenry, or demos, to make decisions, given that, as I mention above, they tend to be idiots and make bad decisions. Further, there are risks that pure democracies can degenerate into emotionalized, angry mob rule and effectively self-immolate. As I write this, the westernized democracies/republics seem to be almost universally struggling with nationalism, authoritarian leaders, immigration crises, and national identity and demagoguery. We'll have to see how this all turns out.

It may be instructive to look toward the roots of democracy in ancient Greece to see how things panned out for them. In particular, it can be instrumental to examine how the decision making of democracy can sometimes lead to its own ruin. Its tale can be a warning for us all today.

Did Athens *Really* Have an Empire?

Back in the 400s BCE the ancient Greeks emerged as a potential dominating force in the Mediterranean, not just culturally, but politically and militarily as well. They had just beaten back an invasion by the great superpower of the day, the Persians, and had developed an almost unbeatable system of heavy infantry fighting based on hoplite phalanxes. Had they been able to unite in common cause, they might have remained a power to be reckoned with, perhaps even swatting off those pesky Macedonians and Romans who would eventually eye their lands. The problem was that these Greeks, for all we tend to describe them as a unified group, were deeply divided and these divisions were part of their downfall.

The Greeks weren't all of the same ethnicity, for one thing, but incorporated varying waves of migrants and invaders. The two most influential were the Ionians, personified by Athens, who tended to occupy territories to the east, and the Dorians, personified by Sparta, who had invaded during a later period of the Greek Dark Ages. The Greeks were also divided by government type, with some city-states such as Athens moving toward democratic forms of government, whereas most others such as Sparta favored oligarchy, wherein power was held mainly by a few powerful or privileged individuals. To add to these divisions, the ancient Greeks never formed a nation-state in the modern way of thinking, but their loyalties remained with their city of birth, each of which was an independent political entity. Hence the term city-state.

Athens tends to capture the imagination of modern societies, primarily because it was a leader in the democratization movement in ancient Greece. Of course, ancient Athens wasn't Whoville. Enfranchisement was limited to native male citizens only, probably technically a minority of the people living in Athens. Thucydides, one of the greatest historians of this period, seems to have ascribed to the view that the common public are idiots. He complained democracies were prone to making grave mistakes. Given that he was, at one point, exiled from Athens, perhaps he may have had a bit of an axe to grind, in fairness.[3] Athens had a tendency to make a series of horrible democratic decisions, perhaps the most notable being the execution of Socrates for, in essence, being the "violent video games" of his day.[4]

Persia, then the regional superpower, invaded Greece twice in the fifth century BCE. Both times the motive was to punish the Athens, which had an annoying habit of stirring up rebellion among Ionian Greek city-states within Persian territory. Under their king Darius the Great, the Persians invaded Greece and did a considerable amount of damage, being opposed largely by only Athens, Sparta, and poor Eritrea, a little city-state that got razed to the ground for its troubles. The Spartans proved to be riven by internal chaos and too superstitious and delayed helping the Athenians. So it was up to the Athenians alone to defeat a Persian invasion at the

Battle of Marathon in 490 BCE.[5] The Athenians felt pretty good about this, while the Persians were left stewing in frustration.

The Persians invaded again in 480 BCE, this time under the king Xerxes. This is the war that was the setting for the famous film *300*, which is often rubbish historically but still lots of fun to watch. Here the Spartans were quite a bit more useful than the first time around. Their King Leonidas led about seven thousand Greeks in the famous Battle of Thermopylae, wherein part of the Greek force, including the famous three hundred Spartans, sacrificed themselves to cover the retreat of the rest of the army. The Persians pushed on and this time sacked Athens, although the Athenians themselves got out in time, evacuating to the island of Salamis. At Salamis, a Greek fleet commanded by Spartans and Athenians defeated the Persian navy, effectively leaving the Persian army helpless. The Greeks, led by the Spartans, then defeated the Persian army at Platea.

That was a very quick overview of the Persian wars but puts us in a good place to consider how the Greeks found themselves in an excellent position and managed to fumble it entirely. Part of the issue came from whether it was possible for the Greeks to develop a kind of cooperative confederacy after the Persian wars to see to their mutual defense, probably with Spartan leadership. But the Spartans weren't really a naval power and weren't too interested in continuing the war to kick the Persians entirely out of the Mediterranean. They abrogated leadership of this task to the Athenians and, in the process, accidently set up a dual state rivalry.[6]

Sparta and Athens facing off against each other for dominance of the Greek world got a lot of attention in the late twentieth century for the fairly obvious reason that it seemed to parallel the Cold War between the United States and the Soviet Union. Scholars examined the issue to try to figure out if superpowers in the position of Sparta and Athens were doomed to end up at war. Using the ancient Greek model, the chances didn't look so hot.

In fairness, Sparta wasn't exactly the Soviet Union (we'll presume Athens is the United States in this scenario). Although an oligarchy, it had numerous balances on power. Sparta had two hereditary kings, a council of officials called ephors, various other assemblies, and a small group of citizens who could also vote on policies. So Sparta wasn't exactly an autocracy, though control was left in the hands of the elites. Noncitizens tended to outnumber citizens. Because Sparta expected its male citizenry to be involved mostly in its professional standing army, basic sustenance work was left in the hands of helots, whose status was somewhere around serf or slave. The Spartan standing army spent more time making sure the helots didn't revolt than much of anything else. By contrast, Spartan women enjoyed unparalleled freedom and power, in contrast to their largely powerless sisters in Athens. Again, let's not glamorize Sparta too much; they basically ran a kind of big slave camp and certainly treated their children with great callousness, but they weren't all bad, either.

Neither Athens nor Sparta was really in the mood for war with the other. They did fight a fairly inconclusive war in the years after the Persian wars,[7] then settled down to a restless peace. Both had assumed control of respective alliances. The Spartans headed a league of allies mainly in the Greek Peloponnese. The Athenians held sway over the Delian League. This league was initially developed to fight the Persians, but the Athenians eventually came to dominate it, often bullying or outright invading wayward city-states who'd lost interest in donating. This, along with Athens' efforts to dominate areas in central and northern Greece, leads to talk of the Athenian Empire. In fairness, they were running something closer to a schoolyard bully's lunch money racket than a true empire, I'd say.

This story is really about how the democracy of Athens managed to goof things up, but in fairness, the early part of the Peloponnesian War as it develops isn't to be blamed on Athens. In fact, the whole Peloponnesian War begins with a series of misjudgments and errors exacerbated by Athens and Sparta's wariness of the other. But it could have been avoided. Really, it's mainly the fault of another city-state, Corinth, but let me explain. It all begins with a little place called Epidamnus.

What, you've never heard of Epidamnus? Well there's no good reason you should have, honestly. It was a little town toward the northwest outskirts of the Greek world, though placed along some important trade routes. Epidamnus fell into civil war, as Greek city-states tended to do. Those inside Epidamnus itself appealed for help to their mother city, Corcyra, of which it was a colony. Corcyra took no interest in getting involved and shooed the emissaries away. Now it happened that Corcyra itself was a colony of the bigger Greek city Corinth.[8] Somewhere since the founding of Corcyra, however, Corcyra and Corinth had a significant parting of ways and now hated one another. The emissaries from Epidamnus, being rebuffed by Corcyra, figured they'd give Corinth a try, because, well, why not? What's the worst that could happen?

Now Corinth really had no interest in Epidamnus. Quite literally, a volcano might have opened up and pulled Epidamnus into the sea and it wouldn't have influenced Corinth much at all. So it could have easily stayed out of Epidamnus's civil war as Corcyra had done. But here it saw an opportunity to stick it to Corcyra for no better reason than that it hated Corcyra. So the Peloponnesian War gets started with a big political middle finger. This was a dumb calculation on the part of Corinth and caused the Greek world no end of trouble, but people are kind of like this sometimes.

Consider the last time you had the opportunity to make a decision when you were feeling angry. Choice A was clearly the better practical choice for all involved including yourself but also required you to swallow your anger and be the better person. Choice B was an obvious disaster but gave you a chance to show everybody how pissed you were. Which did you pick? Generally, people make lousy decisions when they're feeling deep emotions. It's a kind of common madness that can influence us all, unfortunately. When it afflicts those in power, bad things can happen. And this is what happened to Corinth.

Corcyra could hardly stand aside while its hated rival and mother city[9] intervened and naturally picked the other side in Epidamnus's civil war. Things came to a head in Epidamnus when Corcyra, surprising pretty much everybody including itself, defeated a combined Corinthian and Epidamnian force. To say this outcome hardly settled emotions in Corinth would be putting it rather mildly. Corinth appealed to many of its allies in the Peloponnesian League (though not yet Sparta) and assembled a big force to teach Corcyra a lesson.

I kind of feel bad for Corcyra, since it hadn't wanted this and, really, this is all Corinth's stubbornness. Corinth had picked a dumb fight and lost and now started drawing in other powers into a bigger dumb fight that wouldn't profit anybody. Corcyra panicked and tried to smooth things over, but Corinth was having none of it. So Corcyra appealed for help from Athens (now you see where this is going). The typical Athenian probably couldn't have found Epidamnus on a map. However, Corcyra held a powerful navy, the second-best navy other than Athens itself. Athens couldn't let Corcyra's navy fall into the hands of a Spartan ally like

Corinth, so Athens joined in alliance with Corcyra, and together they kicked Corinth's ass a second time.

Seeing absolute crimson by this point, Corinth kept pressing the war. In a world where people aren't doofuses, someone might have pointed out that this was already a costly war over a remote town nobody really cared about. One of the antagonists, Corcyra, was still content to seek an arbitrated solution. But Corinth wanted revenge and whispered poison into the ear of its ally Sparta. How long would it be before Athens' obvious rise outshone Sparta? Wouldn't it be better to strike now, before Athens became too powerful?

For decades, Athens had been managed by an elected official named Pericles. Pericles was probably one of the better statesmen of the ancient world, being able to guide the chaotic democracy of Athens. Pericles worried that war with Sparta was inevitable but wasn't overly enthused about it. But as things escalated, he made a mistake by having Athens display power, bullying a few other local city-states. This, unfortunately, fueled the poisoned narrative Corinth was feeding Sparta. So Sparta declared war on Athens, beginning a twenty-seven-year mess that greatly weakened pretty much all the city-states in Greece, Sparta included.

If you thought the lead-up to the Peloponnesian War was a confused mess of idiotic decisions, it doesn't get better from there. With so many names and locations involved, it's clearly beyond what the current humble story hopes to achieve. I'll focus on the bits involving the foibles of Athenian democracy, since they're the most interesting at the moment.

The war itself was divided across three rough stages. The first stage, sometimes called the Archidamian War (because we need more Greek names to remember), got off to a bad start for Athens. In reality, neither Athens nor Sparta had any sensible theory of war regarding how to defeat the other. Sparta hoped to waltz into the region around Athens, pound the Athenian hoplites into jam, and be done with it. But safe behind their long walls, the Athenians prudently refused to fight the Spartans in open battle. Because the long walls extended to Athens' port, Athens could survive a land siege indefinitely. The Spartans could only burn the fields around Athens and shake their fists at the walls. As a naval power, Athens hoped to blockade Sparta and raid the coasts of Sparta's Peloponnesian allies. Sparta was pretty self-reliant and, though painful, the blockades weren't enough to crush Spartan resources for the war.

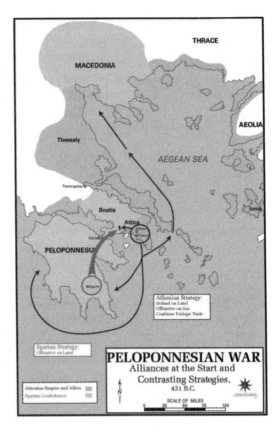

Map of the Peloponnesian War.

Athens initially got the worst of it. After shepherding all their peasants behind the crowded long walls, a plague promptly ravaged the city. The disease killed a substantial portion of residents, which was horrible luck for Athens. Throughout the rest of the war, the loss in manpower caused by this plague created a constant disadvantage in both hoplites and naval personnel. Worse, the plague killed Pericles, perhaps the only person capable of keeping the Athenian democracy halfway sensible. Even the Spartans packed up and went home for the year, fearful of catching the plague from the Athenians.

Things turned in favor of the Athenians after that. They managed to capture about three hundred elite Spartan and allied hoplites in battle, a rarity that gave them a significant bargaining chip. The Spartans managed to take some Athenian silver mines in Thrace. Of all people, the same Thucydides whose history of the Peloponnesian War is a major influence on our understanding of it led a force to take the mines back from the

Spartans, failed, and found himself exiled for his troubles. During his exile, he had a chance to speak with Spartans and other officials on all sides of the war, forming the experiences that led to his histories.

By this point, after about ten years of fighting, both sides were tired and broke, so a truce was signed that was supposed to last fifty years (spoiler: it didn't last nearly so long). Again, level heads might have observed that many lives and much treasure had been lost pretty much for nothing. Hell, most folks probably had forgotten all about Epidamnus by this point. But nope, this was just a lull in the fighting.

The war between the Greeks had brought them nothing but misery, death, and economic decline. Now begins one of the weirdest episodes in the war and an illustration of Athens' own contribution to this folly.

The Greeks had, for centuries, sent forth colonies throughout the Mediterranean including on the island of Sicily. Syracuse, a Corinthian colony and thus allied with Sparta's Peloponnesian League, dominated the island. In 415 BCE several smaller Sicilian city-states got into conflict and those opposed to Syracuse naturally called on the Athenians for help.

In fairness to Athens, the idea of dominating Sicily wasn't without some benefits, particularly as related to access to grain and other natural resources. But it would involve sending a large expedition quite a distance for the time, at great risk, including stirring up the whole Peloponnesian War again. Naturally the Athenian Assembly thought it a marvelous scheme.

One fellow, old and sickly Nicias, argued against the expedition, noting how much expenditures and resources it would suck dry. This only encouraged the masses to pour more investments into the project and to name Nicias one of the expedition's leaders, given how prudent he obviously was. To balance Nicias out, they also named as commander the younger, flamboyant Alcibiades, whom Nicias loathed with the flaming passions of hell. If this wasn't enough of a confused command structure, they also added a *third* commander, Lamachus, who mostly liked to break things. So the Athenian democracy[10] not only set out on a dubious expedition but managed to create one of history's worst command structures. As one scholar put it, "If their aim had been to sabotage the expedition deliberately, the Assembly could hardly have chosen better."[11]

But this particular folly isn't over yet. As the expedition was being prepared, someone vandalized a number of statues throughout the city dedicated to the god Hermes. This looked like a bad omen and got everybody whipped up. Eventually, it degenerated into an all-out witch hunt, with a wide range of people being accused, some imprisoned and possibly tortured, others fleeing Athens altogether. One false witness was eventually executed for the trouble he caused, but the vandal was never found.

Somewhere in the middle of this, one of the expedition commanders Alcibiades was accused by a rival of engaging in disrespectful blasphemies against Athens' religious sensibilities. Alcibiades demanded to be put on trial immediately to clear his name. Incredibly, his rivals were successful in arguing the trial should be delayed and that Alcibiades continue as one of the commanders of the expedition. Their aim was to secure false evidence against him while he was away, thus discrediting him fully without being able to defend himself. This was exactly what they did, and they sent a ship to collect him from Sicily once the expedition was under way. Alcibiades, sensing the fix he was in, jumped ship in Italy and fled. In sabotaging Alcibiades, the Assembly managed to remove an able commander from the Sicilian expedition and put it mainly into the hands of the sickly and unenthused Nicias.

Alcibiades went on to have a colorful career. Naturally, he defected first to Sparta, then, after having made enemies there, to Persia. In both cases he helped his overlords accumulate victories against his native city, Athens. Alcibiades was indeed a skilled military strategist. He tended to annoy people, however. Athens eventually recalled Alcibiades late in the Peloponnesian War, wherein he briefly helped revive Athens' fortunes until they remembered what a jerk he was and exiled him a second time.

Athens was generally a nuthouse during this time. One man castrated himself in public at the Alter of the Twelve Gods.[12] People were paranoid and saw plots everywhere. This was a bad environment in which to strategize a major military undertaking.

Athens' plight highlights some of the risks of pure democracies. Athens was under the strain of years of war and people were frightened and angry. As I noted, people generally don't make good decisions when emotional, and rash, emotional beliefs and schemes can wash through a democracy like a plague. In this sense, an entire citizenry can go mad. Groupthink, a process in which divergent views are discouraged or even punished, can exacerbate this situation. The populace often isn't very informed and can be swayed by demagogues. Thus, they can be persuaded to make uninformed, emotional decisions against their best interests and actively condemn anyone who tries to talk sense.

Perhaps the parallel in recent U.S. history is the 2003 invasion of Iraq. The United States had just experienced the trauma of the September 11, 2001, terror attacks, which killed thousands of citizens. The majority of citizens rallied behind President George W. Bush. The average person, being rather uninformed about Middle East affairs, had difficulty distinguishing between the radicalized Islamic terrorists of al-Qaeda and the secular strongman regime of Iraq, two unlikely bedfellows. Already frightened of terrorism, most people didn't question the Bush administration's dubious rationale for a war with Iraq, involving hinted ties to al-Qaeda and weapons of mass destruction. The resultant war was poorly planned, and despite an initial victory, the occupation devolved into an embarrassing fiasco. It's too much hyperbole to compare it to Vietnam, but the Iraq War is certainly an illustration of the limits of democratic decision making, even in a representative republic.

Without Alcibiades, the Sicilian expedition went badly. Unfortunately, strategy was left in the hands of the sickly and dispirited Nicias, who never wanted the expedition in the first place. Lamachus, the other remaining commander who advocated an aggressive strategy, was typically overruled. So the Athenians dawdled in Sicily, giving the Spartans time to reinforce Syracuse. The result was a complete disaster for Athens, with their navy destroyed and the army trapped on land, where it was eventually surrounded and destroyed. Both Lamachus and Nicias died or were executed.

The Sicilian expedition was a calamity for multiple reasons. First, it damaged Athens' navy, giving Sparta and her allies a chance to contest Athenian control of the seas, which was potentially fatal for Athenian strategy in avoiding Spartan blockades of resources. Second, the defeat damaged Athenian credibility and many city-states switched sides to Sparta. Persia also actively supported Sparta by this point. Third, it handed a valuable insider and commander to the Spartans in the form of Alcibiades.

Athens struggled on for nine more years but had mainly lost the initiative. It had a resurgence for several years, particularly under the restored Alcibiades, but, politically, Athens never again emerged from chaos. A coup in 411 BCE led to a short-lived oligarchy, but democracy was eventually restored. In 406 BCE the Athenians won a naval battle against the

Spartans but a storm prevented their triremes from rescuing sailors from their own damaged and sinking ships. As a consequence, many Athenian sailors drowned. On learning of this, the Athenian assembly became worked up into a fury by several agitators and had most of the victorious naval commanders executed. The idiocy of executing able leaders for events beyond their control does not need explaining. Coming to their senses too late, the Assembly eventually realized exactly this, then turned on the instigators, who mostly fled Athens before being tried.[13]

By this juncture, the Athenian democracy had, to put it in technical terms, completely lost its shit. This last act of blind emotional decision making marked the end of Athens' real ability to fight Sparta. In 405 BCE the Athenian fleet was destroyed by a Spartan fleet and, now unable to get grain from sea trade, Athens surrendered.

To their credit, the Spartans were fairly generous in victory, in the sense that they allowed Athens to continue to exist. The Corinthians, ever irascible, and the Thebans, allies of Sparta, wanted to see Athens destroyed. But the Spartans only demanded that the Athenians tear down their walls, abandon their navy, and turn over their overseas possessions to Sparta. Thereafter Athens was included in Sparta's larger confederation. According to one ancient historian, flute girls played music for the Peloponnesian workers as they tore down the walls, thinking this signaled an everlasting peace for Greece under Spartan hegemony.[14]

Not so fast, flute girls! It didn't take long for the Spartans to remind everybody that they were kind of asshats. The Spartans kept most of the spoils from the Peloponnesian War for themselves, not sharing much with their allies, and set out aggressively bullying pretty much everybody from their former allies in Corinth and Thebes to the Persians. By the early fourth century BCE, an alliance of Athens, Thebes, Argos, and Corinth, with Persia supporting them, checked Sparta's hegemony and ruined Sparta's efforts to become a naval power.

By 371 BCE, barely thirty-five years since the Spartans had achieved supremacy in Greece, this supremacy was shattered forever. The Thebans managed to figure out how to smash the Spartan phalanx. At the Battle of Leuctra, the Thebans massed their army on one side of their line. The weight of this massed force smashed through a thinner line of elite Spartan hoplites and crushed the Spartan army. Defeated decisively on land, the aura of Spartan invincibility was destroyed and now Thebes rose to prominence. This lasted until about 346 BCE, when, as we saw way back in chapter 1, the Macedonians rose to power under Philip and his son Alexander, ending the independence of the Greek peninsula pretty much for good until the nineteenth century ACE.[15]

Arguably all wars are dumb. Even if we say, for instance, World War II was a good war for the United States, the United Kingdom, and their allies, the decision by Germany, Japan, Italy, and their allies to start it in the first place was still dumb. But the Peloponnesian War was dumb all around and severely damaged all the Greek city-states and ruined their chances of avoiding Macedonian and, later, Roman control. The foolishness was spread quite thick, as none of the major powers went in wanting the war. Remember poor Epidamnus? Neither did most of the Greeks once things got going during the war.[16] Corinth deserves much blame early on for picking a fight for spite, which nobody, Corinth included, really needed.

But the affair of the Athenians, particularly once they lost their strategic leader Pericles, is instrumental in recognizing how democracies can come undone and contribute to their own downfall. Bereft of intelligent leadership, the Athenian democracy lurched from scheme to witch hunt to paranoia to scapegoating. Emotion ruled the day and the city's considerable financial and military resources were frittered away. In this sense, arguably, the affair of the Peloponnesian War is not very instructive regarding politics between rival states, but it does offer a warning about how internal politics can tear a democracy apart. This may be the real warning for the present day.

Are We Witnessing the Collapse of Democracy in the West?

I am going to do exactly the wrong thing for an author and answer my clickbait heading right away: no. But sometimes it can seem that way. As I write this, our society—whether the United States or many other industrialized nations—seems riven by an unprecedented level of partisan strife. The left hates the right, everybody is castigating everybody else based on race, religion, or gender. People are making up rubbish terms like "lamestream media" or "toxic masculinity" to smear people on the "other side." People are either "snowflakes" or "white supremacists" (even if not necessarily white). Conservatives on talk radio or television complain about the indoctrinating elements of universities, where university professors with little hint of irony talk about the indoctrinating elements of traditional society. It can seem like the social fabric is tearing and we are all looking for opportunities to be angry with each other while seizing a kind of irrational, paranoid, moral high ground for ourselves.

In fairness, the loudest voices tend to get the most attention, and this can create a distorting effect, insofar as that we may assume that the vocal hysterics of a few tend to represent the many.[17] This can have a pernicious effect on politics in some cases, such as when politicians feel pressured to cater to these loudest voices with more extreme policy recommendations. Take, for instance, the U.S. primary voting system.

Historically, the United States is one of few countries to use primaries to select political candidates for a general election, and voter turnout for primaries tends to be low.[18] Given this low turnout and the fact most of us have jobs and families that may make it difficult for us to go to vote in primaries, this has led to the perception that crazy, extreme voters are overrepresented in primaries and that most politicians have to cater to these extreme beliefs. Thus, in recent years both political parties have arguably shifted to their extremes. But is it true? Are the loudest, maddest people more likely to vote in primaries, giving them outsized control over our political process?

Unfortunately, the answer isn't clear because there just isn't a lot of data on primary voters. Part of the difficulty lies in differences in turnout between states, many of which have different rules about who can participate in primaries. Florida, for instance, allows only people who are registered with a party to vote in that party's primaries, thus cutting out moderate or independent voters. As to whether primary voters are more politically extreme, the evidence is mixed. One study using data from U.S. elections between 2008 and 2014 suggested that primary voters were not particularly extreme relative to others in their party.[19] However, that is in comparison with other voters in the candidate's party, not with the general mass of voters, many of whom identify as independents. So perhaps people who identify with one party or another have simply become more extreme. By contrast, an earlier paper suggested that primary voters are, in fact, more extreme than general election voters.[20] So it's probably wrong to think that primary voters are more extreme than the rest of their parties; perhaps people who identify with either of the major parties in the United States are more extreme than the rest of the electorate.

Either way, this runs a significant risk of creating a preference in primaries for candidates who are more ideologically extreme, then foisting two bad candidates onto a grumbling general electorate, which doesn't really like either one. This isn't really a recipe for great political outcomes.

Voters of all stripes also tend to make irrational, emotional choices rather than pragmatic ones. For instance, support for the avowed segregationist presidential candidate George Wallace in 1964 particularly centered among Caucasian Americans who lived in neighborhoods with heightened racial tension.[21] Angry and scared of change, some voters gravitated toward an obviously horrible candidate to preserve the status quo. Other analyses have suggested that catering to extreme voters is more pronounced in primary elections in which there is no incumbent candidate. It appears that parties feel the need to lock in a core group of die-hard (and potentially nuts) supporters before worrying about the broader masses.[22] Political parties may worry about "sour grapes" defecting—primary voters who refused to vote for the eventual nominee if that person is not the primary candidate they endorsed.[23] The irrational and emotional nature of such decision making comes in failing to realize that, even if one's primary candidate isn't the nominee, the actual nominee is still more likely to share values with the voter than the candidate for the opposing party.

So do primaries empower madness? Probably. This may be both because the party membership of both major parties has simply become more extreme and also because of the perception of candidates that they need to promise big (and sometimes outright crazy) things to lock in a core group of die-hard supporters before worrying about the general populace of voters.

This brings us to one of the most fascinating presidential primaries and general elections in recent history, that of U.S. president Donald Trump. The question on everyone's mind, whether they agree or disagree is: is President Trump simply mad? Well, let's have a look.

The Curious Case of President Trump

As I write this, Donald Trump currently sits as the forty-fifth president of the United States, and this book likely will be released just as the 2020 presidential election cycle gets under way. At the outset, let me note how difficult it is to render any kind of accurate judgment of a political figure in real time. Even historically, this can be difficult. Beloved figures during their own times sometimes become villains in history and vice versa. The same is true for assessing the mental health of a public figure. Psychologists, psychiatrists, and other mental health professionals are often biased by their own political beliefs, and it's too easy for a "diagnosis" to be a political smear. Thus I hope to examine this issue as cautiously as possible with an aim of discussing how our society has gone a little bit mad in the era of Donald Trump as much as I aim to discuss the man himself.

It's worth noting that psychiatrists (but not psychologists) are bound by something called the Goldwater Rule. This rule has its origin in the 1964 presidential election when a magazine surveyed thousands of psychiatrists to ask whether conservative candidate Barry Goldwater was fit for the office of presidency. Only about 10 percent of psychiatrists responded to the survey and, of these, about half said Goldwater was unfit for service. However, the magazine spun this into a damning critique of Goldwater, portraying him as a paranoid, delusional lunatic. Goldwater lost the election (what role the magazine article specifically played is hard to say) but then successfully sued the magazine for libel, which is quite rare for public figures. Several years later the American Psychiatric Association instituted the Goldwater Rule, which bars members from rendering public diagnoses of individuals for whom they have not conducted an actual assessment. Of course, there's a catch-22 built into this, for psychiatrists also would be bound by confidentiality regarding anyone they *did* conduct an assessment on unless that individual waived confidentiality. This effectively hamstrung psychiatrists from speaking publicly about political figures.[24] Apparently expecting a wave of comments about Donald Trump, the American Psychiatric Association strengthened the rule in 2017. The American Psychological Association doesn't have an equivalent rule, although psychologists are cautioned to speak within their expertise and without implying that they have a professional relationship with the subject of their statements. Fair enough: for the record I do not have a professional relationship with Donald Trump (nor Caligula, Marie Antoinette, or anyone else appearing in this book), nor have I conducted a psychological assessment on him.

The Goldwater Rule does make some sense. It prevents rogue psychiatrists from turning their political views into scientific sounding but ad hominem rubbish political attacks. "Don't vote for Matilda for school board as her views on string theory *clearly* indicate latent schizophrenia!" But some folks don't care much for the Goldwater Rule, saying it goes too far and prevents psychiatrists from engaging in a duty to warn the public when a figure becomes clearly unhinged. Some have suggested a compromise wherein psychologists and psychiatrists could render judgments, particularly for political figures, on evidence for mental health without making judgments about political fitness. This is particularly true given how common mental illness has been among U.S. presidents and other political figures, thus establishing that mental illness, in and of itself, does not render an individual unfit for public service.[25]

On the other end of the spectrum is a group of psychiatrists and other mental health experts who argue for a "duty to warn," asserting that mental health experts have an obligation to, in essence, break the Goldwater Rule when the mental status of a world leader places the world, or at least many lives, in significant jeopardy. Probably the best-known argument along these lines is a book of essays by prominent mental health experts compiled by psychiatrist Brandy Lee. At its best, the book does a sophisticated job of arguing the pros and cons of the Goldwater Rule. At its worst, the authors seem to do rhetorical calisthenics to diagnose Trump as a malignant and potentially delusional narcissist without ever mentioning a formal diagnosis such as narcissistic personality disorder so as to stay narrowly within the confines of the Goldwater Rule. As such, there's quite a bit of winking and nudging in the essays.[26]

That all out of the way, let's look at Trump and the Trump phenomenon. Honestly, compared to some of the other folks in this book, I don't find Trump all that interesting, other than the fact that he happened to become president and in so doing pushed the world over the precipice it was already dangling into full-throated paranoid nuttiness.

Trump's background is well established both in memoirs/biographies he contributed to[27] and those he did not.[28] Trump was born into a life of considerable privilege and wealth, attending private schools and demonstrating a large personality from childhood on. His relationship with his father, like many of those in this book, were arguably strained,[29] with his father coming across as considerably demanding. Trump's brother, Fred Jr., ultimately would die in his early forties from complications of alcoholism, which some attribute to his inability to live up to the elder Trump's demands.[30] Trump has married three times, each time to a glamorous model or actress (including current First Lady Melania Trump). Trump's extra-marital affairs have been fodder for the tabloid press, including accusations of affairs while married to current wife Melania. Trump has five children from his marriages, and if we are to imply Trump has sometimes been callous in his relations with his wives, it is worth noting that his children appear to be among his closest confidants, even if his approach to child-rearing wasn't stereotypically warm and snuggly. Again, Trump always has been known as something of a large personality, involved in aggressive business practices, high-risk deals that have brought him both enormous successes and spectacular failures, and sometimes sketchy fraud-like enter-prises such as the failed Trump University. Some of his businesses ended in bankruptcy, though Trump himself appears not to have personally suf-fered in terms of wealth. As noted, Trump's personal life has been a thing for the tabloids, including an infamous 2005 *Access Hollywood* mic tape in which he bragged about groping women without their consent.[31] Trump's public persona has mixed brash egoism, a sense of humor that can straddle the line between bullying and (just being fair to both sides here) honestly kind of funny when it's not too mean-spirited (which too often it is), and a weird charm that served him well as a reality TV star.

Trump had dipped a toe into presidential politics as early as 2000, though he switched parties from Democrat to Reform to Republican, suggesting a lack of ideological conviction. He achieved notoriety begin-ning in 2011 with his endorsements of the "birther" conspiracy suggest-ing then-president Barack Obama was not a U.S. citizen. This particular tinfoil-hat theory would represent one of the most audacious cases of resume padding in history were it true. Mainly, his presidential ambitions were treated more as publicity stunts than serious efforts.

In June 2015 Trump lumbered into the 2016 presidential primary with an unusually downbeat speech that implied the United States was amid a serious crisis and achieved notoriety for suggesting Mexican im-migrants were mainly criminals, drug abusers, and rapists.[32] Available data suggests that criminal perpetration among immigrants, legal or illegal, are lower than for native U.S. citizens.[33] However, there are some nuances in the data, such as showing higher incarceration rates among illegal His-panic immigrants than native whites but not native African Americans, among whom incarceration is much higher.[34] Nonetheless, such a bluntly misleading and racist statement would have been the end to most presi-

President Trump.

dential ambitions. However, whether strategic or not, Trump's crude language attracted the allegiance of a disaffected segment of the Republican Party and he was able to swat aside each of his primary opponents, most of whom were career politicians.

Trump continued to engage in many public statements and behaviors that were highly polarizing, so his nomination for the Republic ticket in the 2016 election appeared to be a gift to the Democratic Party. All it needed to do was avoid nominating a deeply unpopular and polarizing candidate of their own. So, ignoring good sense and arguably with the Democrat Party leadership's thumb on the scale, it nominated Hillary Clinton. Although Clinton had considerable expertise as senator and secretary of state, she also carried extensive baggage from her husband Bill's presidency, as well as her own missteps over the years. And people were probably a little tired of seeing the same two families, Clinton and Bush,[35] return to the White House so often. Fair or not, many people simply didn't care for her, which was hardly a news flash in 2016. Her nomination was, in turn, a gift to the Republican Party. Despite polls showing her winning, she lost, making Trump the forty-fifth president.

As I write this, Trump has been president for roughly two and a half years. One thing we can say is that he hasn't broken the world, at least so far, which the previous Republican president, George W. Bush, was handily on the path to doing by the same point. Most of the past two years, policy wise, have been the typical low taxes for the rich, deregulation, high defense-spending stuff that Republicans tend to like. But the Trump presidency has been a swirling tempest of angry tweets, high staff turnover, impulsivity, and chaos. It certainly hasn't looked like a normal presidency. Whether that is an asset or a bug depends on one's perspective.

Is Trump mad? Destructiveness is a key element of the madness as defined for this book. Whatever Trump is, arguably it served him well until he assumed the presidency. At the moment, destructiveness is hard to gauge. Other than the matter of U.S. prestige, Trump's wilder impulses appear not to have seen purchase in actual policy. Whether this is because Trump has some grand, clever strategy in mind, or the checks-and-balances system of U.S. government, including the bureaucracy of it all, is actually working is hard to say, although I suspect the latter is having a nontrivial influence. In other words, Trump may be mad, but assessing it could be difficult if bureaucrats, his White House staff, the opposing political party in Congress,[36] the press, and others are impeding his worst impulses. Indeed, the Mueller Report, investigating charges of collusion with the Russians in the 2016 election and obstruction of justice, was released in 2019. Though finding no evidence that Trump worked with the Russians to defeat Clinton in 2016, the report claimed Trump's clumsy efforts to obstruct justice were mainly thwarted by his own aides who refused to carry out his orders.

What appears to be beyond much question is the presence of narcissism. Trump's penchant for engaging in petulant Twitter wars with those who anger him suggests the kind of thin skin we see among what are called "vulnerable narcissists," or those who feel the need to lash out against those who threaten their self-image.[37] Beyond that, the case for other diagnoses is, I feel, weaker. I've seen speculations about psychosis or dementia and of course it's possible that Trump may have such issues and we don't know it, but from his public behavior I think the case for such disorders is harder to substantiate. Narcissism is hardly rare among politicians of all stripes. Among career politicians, it may be that the more vulnerable types tend to be weeded out somewhat over time, given their tendency to lash out and create enemies. But Trump came to influence via an unusual pathway, having no prior significant government expertise. Indeed, based on the Mueller Report, he often seems more bull in the china shop than shrewd intriguer.

What is interesting is not that Trump is mad (and he probably is, a little, at least), but that his madness is probably one element that draws at least some of his fans to him. In this sense, Trump is a symptom, not a cause, and the disease is a kind of madness that has overtaken elements of our society.

Trump Derangement Syndrome

One of the features of the Trump era is the significant degree of anger that people on both sides of the political spectrum express toward each other. Politics has always been a touchy subject of conversation but ever more so today. Unfortunately, public discussions tend to be dominated by the largest and loudest voices and although I'm generally reluctant to blame technology for most of society's ills, social media has likely amplified the reach of some of the most extreme voices. In this case I look at the "right" and the "left"[38] as quasi-tribal units fighting for political dominance with increased aggression, both sides employing ideological litmus tests and bullying members to avoid any hint of compromise.

It helps to remember again that many of our decisions or attitudes are not based on facts or cognitions but rather on emotions or, related, on tribal identity. Take global warming, for instance. Generally, folks on the right are more skeptical of claims of human involvement in climate change than folks on the left. Given the weight of evidence from science currently supporting climate change, folks on the left may thus assume that they are more informed than people on the right. But this would be an erroneous judgment. Most of us are completely uninformed about climate science other than what we read in the newspapers, if that. Instead, people on the right are skeptical of global warming because that's what people on the right do. People on the left accept global warming because that's what people on the left do, not because they are actually any more informed. The fact that science suggests the left happens to be correct is largely coincidental.

In fairness, the same can be said of the left related to topics that they don't like. For instance, many on the left may continue to deny the existence of biologically determined differences in male and female behavior, despite the presence of strong evidence for the same. Put simply, both liberals and conservatives engage in science denialism when the science conflicts with the ideological views.[39] In this sense, a kind of cultural tribalism ends up becoming a powerful influence on beliefs, and this can make belief systems highly polarized since those with different beliefs are tribal enemies.[40] This isn't to say that everyone falls neatly into a tribe, and things like science curiosity can counteract this kind of reflexive myside bias.[41]

Thus, when we look at many folks who voted for Trump, they may not have been entirely enthused with his crassness but perhaps viewed it as a necessary counterbalance to the weaponization of terms like racism and sexism against any challenge to progressive ideals. In this sense, many individuals are concerned not with maintaining cultural dominance but with being excluded from the dialogue altogether because they don't share a preset approved list of progressive values. In this sense, the left and the right may have difficulty dialoguing because extreme voices on the left characterize any divergence from ideological purity as "white supremacy," whereas some extreme voices on the right actually express white supremacist views, reinforcing the ideology of the leftist ideologues. Most people are simply caught in the middle, trying to avoid being sucked into a big mud fight and are simply sick of it all, not unreasonably so. This is not to say the election of Trump is a rational outcome, but rather that extreme voices on both left and right contribute to a culture of hostility that makes the election of madness to the White House on either side more probable.

A few examples can highlight this issue. One concern that has emerged regarding the extreme left has been its censoriousness and bullying in regard to positions that do not conform to an ideological purity on issues such as race and gender. In January 2019, author Amélie Wen Zhao pulled her debut novel *Blood Heir* from publication following hostile Twitter reactions from some loud voices that were concerned the book was racist toward African Americans. These concerns emerged despite the fact that no African Americans appear in the book, which takes place in an entirely fictional world. In this case a small number of "influencers" appear to have convinced or bullied the author into canceling or delaying publication despite the accusations being, at very least, a subjective interpretation.[42] Appealing to the ideological purity of a few has resulted in *no one* being able to read the book (at least in original form) and make up their own minds. That many folks look upon incidents such as this as corrosive to free speech is hardly surprising.

This enforcement of "sensitivity" can also appear hypocritical when some on the left appear to feel free to express racist or sexist views, so long as these are limited to whites or males. For instance, in August 2018, *New York Times* columnist Sarah Jeong attracted controversy when it was revealed that over several years, she had released a series of anti-white and anti-male tweets such as "white men are bullshit," "oh man it's kind of sick how much joy I get out of being cruel to old white men," or "dumbass fucking white people marking up the internet with their opinions like dogs pissing on fire hydrants." Sure, perhaps it's goofy aggressive trolling, but try replacing "white" with "black" or "Hispanic" and the problem becomes readily apparent. Some on the left defended Jeong by claiming it's impossible to be racist toward whites, but this confuses institutional racism with individual racism.[43] It's also hypocritical and, rather than bringing people together and fostering racial harmony and cooperation, simply reshuffles the racist deck of which races (or genders) are "good" and "bad." The argument that Trump is racist (or at least uses racism strategically) is, I believe, supportable based on his public behavior. But to not apply that same metric to a person of color such as Sarah Jeong creates a self-sabotaging double standard.

A set of clinical guidelines by the American Psychological Association on treatment for boys and men also came under fire for using language that many perceived as disparaging, particularly of more traditional males, potentially sexist toward men, and likely to discourage rather than encourage men from seeking therapy.[44] Although the guidelines had some decent ideas, many seemed devoted to pushing feminist and intersectional theories onto male patients, whatever their reason for seeking therapy.[45] I am skeptical that the out-of-work coal miner struggling to pay his bills and support his family is likely to benefit from a discussion of his privilege. I sat on the APA's Council of Representatives at the time and wrote a review noting that the guidelines lacked scientific merit and were likely to provoke a strong negative response. Unfortunately, I was not heeded.

I had my own run-in with ideological purity once. I belong to a listserve of video game scholars. Following the New Zealand Christchurch shooting in 2019, when the shooter made a few offhand references to video games and technology, which may have been purposeful trolling by him, several scholars suggested the need to examine the toxic aspects of gamer culture. I inquired whether, using this logic, these same scholars would argue that we ought to examine the "toxic" (to use their word) elements of other cultures among which some individuals have committed shootings. For instance, I inquired, since some shooters have proclaimed allegiance to Islamist terror groups, should we evaluate Islam? Or because the IRA perpetrated terrorist bombings in the 1970s and 1980s, should we examine toxic elements of Irish culture? Naturally, I was advocating no such thing, merely pointing out the hypocritical irrationality of targeting entire groups on account of the behavior or a tiny minority of individuals. Nonetheless a handful of scholars seized the opportunity to signal virtue and deplore my "dog whistles"[46] regarding Islam (nobody, it turned out, was particularly concerned about the Irish). As a tenured faculty member, I was surprised but unfazed by what seemed like clear bullying behavior of a few. Others on the listserve spoke to my defense; however, I could only imagine the impact on open dialogue for untenured scholars or students, who saw a question meant to challenge a hypocritical political position mischaracterized and met with significant aggression. Naturally, the behavior of a few don't characterize the whole listserve but that's rather my point. The extreme behavior of only a few outliers can have a major impact on the culture at large.

Of course, it works both ways, with plenty of jerks, bullies, and real racists and misogynists on the right. I've picked on the left a bit, but I should note that the right can also try to silence those with whom it disagrees. Once[47] I wrote an essay for CNN suggesting that convicted felons being able to print workable handguns on a 3-D printer maybe wasn't the best idea. One irate gun rights advocate filed an ethics complaint against me alleging that I had abused my power as a member of CNN's editorial board. My promotion from occasional columnist was news to me and the complaint didn't go far. The problem is when we mix up Nazis marching through Charlottesville with the attitudes of the average Caucasian American. Or if we assume that every act of violence by a movement like ANTIFA reflects the attitudes of everyone concerned about disadvantaged groups.

The example of *Blood Heir* also points to two other related concerns. One is that by giving into bullies, whether on right or left, we ultimately reinforce the bullying behavior and actually make things worse. Second, by fostering a victimhood mentality, those who consider themselves victims may come to view their aggression toward others as justified by their own victimhood. And this can work in an ongoing cycle among both the right and the left.

In this sense, the Trump administration is a symptom rather than a cause of a creeping madness within our sociopolitical culture in which people with different views become the enemy and must be defeated or humiliated at all costs. This does not mean that there isn't madness within the Trump administration or that we should regard the Trump administration as merely the expected costs of our own tumultuous society. Indeed, though it is hard to gauge history from the present, it is difficult to imagine that the judgment of history on this stage of U.S. politics will be positive. Again, this is because of the tendency to lurch to extremes, at which the Trump administration has been tragically adroit.

As only one example, the United States certainly has the right to set a pragmatic, humane immigration policy that is of value to the country. There is little evidence that, overall, the U.S. immigration policy is particularly draconian.[48] However, the Trump administration lost any sense of reason by cruelly separating illegal immigrant children from their families at the border, allegedly losing track of the children in some cases.[49] Certainly, the United States has the right to detain those illegally crossing the border, but it shouldn't be controversial to suggest detention facilities be as humane and comfortable as possible, with careful attention to due process and to reasonable requests for asylum for those who can demonstrate need. Children should not be separated from their parents under these circumstances and asking the government to warehouse them is a recipe for disaster. Even if the obvious human rights and due process issues are ignored, the practical issues of the public relations catastrophe for the United States should be more than obvious.

It is the failure of the administration to foresee the sensible backlash to harmful policies such as this and numerous others that leads me to suggest that, in the end, my best guess is that Trump will go down as one of the maddest presidents in U.S. history.

MADNESS IN THE FUTURE

In March 2019 a twenty-eight-year-old Australian man opened fire at two mosques in Christchurch New Zealand, perpetrating one of the worst massacres in that country's history. The shooter brought with him multiple firearms and a helmet camera with which he livestreamed the violence. Much of the shooting was carried live on Facebook and later spread through the internet. At the door of the first mosque, the shooter was greeted by a religious attendee with a polite "Hello brother" before he began to open fire, indiscriminately killing men, women, and children. After the first shooting, he traveled to another mosque where he killed worshippers there before being stopped by police. All told, he killed fifty people and wounded many more.

The shooting was inspired by a growing fringe-right movement dedicated to racial and religious hate and predicated on the notion that whites must defend themselves from immigrants from other nations, particularly Muslims. Like the perpetrator of a 2011 Norwegian attack that killed seventy-seven people, mostly teens at a summer camp, the Christchurch shooter left behind a cockamamie manifesto filled with paranoid fantasies of new crusades against Islam. He also trolled readers with silly statements about social media and video games that seemed calculated to set the usual moral panickers off on the wrong track.

This shooting set off a fresh round of soul-searching among many industrialized countries. Is a wave of madness gripping the populace, whether in the form of right-wing nationalism, radical Islam extremism, or just disaffected young men who hate everyone? Is social media becoming a dangerous medium through which madness or even just mad ideas spread like wildfire? Are we on the precipice of a global cultural catastrophe spread by the madness of the masses?

During the last years of the twenty-first century's second decade, a wave of lunacy appeared to sweep the industrialized world. Nativism, authoritarianism, and nationalism seems on the rise from the United States and United Kingdom to the European mainland and much of the rest of the industrialized world. No doubt this tide is fueled by legitimate concerns: income inequality, illegal immigration, terroristic violence directed at the industrialized world, and the sense that industrialized nations are losing influence to new powers such as China. And, as I noted in the previous chapter, loud and extreme voices on both right and left have probably done much to stoke tensions. Will this period mark the end of a historical phase in which liberal democracies had been on the rise?

Honestly, I tend to be more optimistic. First, we must remember that there are always negative voices forecasting doom. In the 1980s people lived in fear of an inevitable nuclear war; in the 1990s the United States and Europe appeared on the verge of being eclipsed by Japan economically; in the 2000s fears of Middle Eastern terrorism gripped the world. This is not to say we needn't be alert to creeping madness in our political systems, but rather that it helps to take stock of all the data. Today both the right and the left worry that we have lost our place in the world (if American) or that the world has gone mad (pretty much everywhere else).

Sometimes it helps to take stock. We have to remember that by most indices, the world today looks better behaviorally, medically, and economically, than it ever has.[1] This isn't to make light of the real challenges human society faces, whether global warning, human migration patterns, or authoritarian governments in some parts of the world. But if we've been decrying the end of society for as long as we can remember, perhaps we can breathe and start from an assumption that, whatever challenges we face, we're not wobbling on the precipice of disaster.

Doing so can help us remain less emotional about the issues that face us. And, let's remember, emotional decision making in its extreme can lead to political madness and make those real challenges into bigger problems. At present, the difficulties we have in escaping societal madness involve the pressing feelings of political polarization and the amplifications of more extreme voices through new media and technology platforms. How do we retain our sanity when the mad can scream the loudest?

Some Thoughts on Historical Sanity

Much of this book I spent looking at what went wrong. Even for the few success stories such as Alexander the Great, the cost of madness, societally and personally, was enormous. Assuming we (whichever group we mean by "we") don't want to invade the rest of the world, naming cities and towns after ourselves (one or two Fergusonvilles would be enough for me, I think), it can be illustrative to consider how societies sometimes pulled back from madness and set themselves on a productive path. How did people like Abraham Lincoln, Marcus Aurelius, Tang Taizong,[2] or Emmeline Pankhurst[3] manage to project sanity during times in which madness appeared ready to reign?[4]

This, of course, requires a great person to come to our rescue. And perhaps that might happen, though looking at our available slate of politicians cross-nationally, I wonder if we have time to wait. Yet sanity at a societal level is something we can all participate in to a small degree.

It seems any book such as this one should end with an optimistic note and a few suggestions. It's probably just something psychologists do. But let me start by saying that advice is always easier given than taken. I am no angel. There are moments when I have disparaged others who thought differently that I did, when I contributed to polarized debates, when I made decisions out of anger and fear, and where I have undoubtedly said *something* that offended *someone* to their core beliefs. Thus, my advice comes from a place where I consider what *I* could do better, not simply lecturing others about how *they* could do better.

Part of it comes in realizing that it is doubtful that we are inherently better people than those who hold disparate worldviews from our own. This is a tricky balancing act for the current historical moment. On one hand, people often feel pressured to engage in "virtue signaling," which involves demonstrations of allegiance to the ideological values of a political tribe, often by public condemnation of those who hold opposing values. On the other, people may also feel forced into public self-criticism, in which individuals must express either regret for past ideological failings or reduced worth as a consequence of not belonging to particularly valued identity groups.

Progress also comes from recognizing that the things we see that make it to news media (or our social media streams) are not representative of how the world is. Usually, that which is brought to our attention is the *worst* of the world. As news consumers, we are drawn to the spectacle of the disaster. Though perhaps not the most flattering feature of the human condition, it does mean we tend to get a distorted view of our current moment in history. Further, we can filter this information through our preexisting worldviews and political tribal identities to reinforce our own prejudices about the world. Thus, for the person on the political right who sees mass shootings and bombings perpetrated by some who claim allegiance to Islamist terrorist organizations, those from other parts of the world can seem inordinately threatening. By contrast, the same mass shootings and bombings viewed through the lens of the progressive can seem to be the fault of white men.[5] Nonetheless, things are actually better than they may seem and, for the most part, other people just want to get by and have their place in the world. To be sure, there are a few who are hopeless, the loudest, craziest voices intent on sowing mayhem, who can't help but sort the world into good and evil (mainly with themselves on the side of good, of course). Those people have always been with us; we just didn't listen to them quite so much as we do now.

Looking through the cases in this book, madness appears to be empowered through three main paths. First are societies in which individuals were elevated to systems of power for reasons other than their merit. This is the case for monarchies, which often lacked clear means of shifting power from the mad to those with better abilities to lead. The second situation is that in which ambitious individuals seized upon moments of chaos, weakness, or fear in a subject population. This is the case of the authoritarian strongman such as Idi Amin or Saddam Hussein. Last is the situation in which the populace itself gave way to madness and made decisions based on fear or anger. Such was the case for Athens, and notes of its downfall can be seen in the modern era. Not every case neatly fits this pattern, of course. For instance, the fall of the Roman Republic has elements of both the strongman and democratic chaos models and transpired gradually over many generations. This, too, is something to learn from. Although we may decry the apparent rise of authoritarian executives in many countries, certainly in some cases, such as the United States, power has been shifting toward the executive slowly for years and under multiple parties in power.

Shared Purpose

In Athens, the democracy was driven to madness by perceived threats from outside as the Peloponnesian War progressed in ways that threatened the citizenry. During the current age, modern democracies often feel pressure from without, whether due to terrorism, threatening actions of authoritarian nations, or uncontrolled immigration. However, much of the strife comes from within. Our enemies are no longer fascists or communists from other regimes but our neighbors who hold different beliefs than we do and who, we are led to believe, would corrupt our own cultures in horrid and unforgiveable ways. I suspect this is one factor that leads to our present sense of madness and that leads our governments, as democracies, into worse and worse decisions. So how do we overcome this level of strife within our societies?

Humans appear to have a natural sense of division, readily looking for differences between themselves and others, and tend to interpret these in hostile ways. We can see this in our own current political and social conflicts in which people don't just disagree but assume that those with whom they disagree are essentially *evil* and must be excised from public life forever. Few things give us a shared purpose with our in-group than an out-group to demonize. Tearing apart the moral decrepitude of an out-group also gives us an opportunity to signal our virtue to our own tribe. This might even make sense to the degree that groups historically competed for scarce resources and may have been evolutionarily adaptive in the past. Instinctive suspiciousness of strangers among an aggressive species is obviously something that would be selected for.

However, our tribes have gotten larger and more diverse and hostility within those megatribes can lead to an inability to compromise, movement toward more extreme (and unwise) policy positions, and breakdown of the social fabric that holds a community together in shared purpose. How do we restore that sense of purpose?

One consistent finding in psychological research concerns how groups come to loathe each other and also how they can find opportunities to cooperate. A famous study called the Robbers Cave experiment brought boys together in a summer camp and divided them randomly into separate social groups. At first, the groups didn't know of each other's existence. Group cohesion was fostered in these randomly assigned groups of kids to give them a social identity. One group became the Rattlers, the other the Eagles (not to be confused with the "Hotel California"–singing rock band). Then these groups of kids were brought into contact with each other.

As you might expect, this phase of contact didn't go well, particularly as the experimenters gave them competitive tasks to fight over. One group always won at the other's expense. Verbal taunts began, each group developed negative stereotypes of the other as weak, stupid, or mean, and they began to steal or vandalize each other's property. This doesn't sound too different from Twitter these days! Basically, when the two groups were placed in a situation in which each was competing against and frustrating the other's goals, hostility intensified quickly.

In the third phase of the study, the two groups were forced to cooperate toward a mutual goal, in this case, securing access to a water tank. This shared or superordinate goal reduced tension and prejudice between the groups. This led the authors to conclude that finding common goals can reduce intergroup tension.[6]

To be fair, psychology tends to wrap its coolest experiments up with a neat bow. This experiment has sometimes been criticized because the experimenters intervened too much, possibly influencing the results. Others critique the ethics of purposefully bringing boys into aggressive conflict with each other, but pfft, ethics, smethics. This was the 1950s. Other experiments have supported at least the broad outlines of the Robbers Cave experiment[7] and even playing action-oriented video games cooperatively can reduce outgroup tensions.[8] So there's probably something to this. Historically, we could see it after 9/11, when most of the country, left and right, united behind President George W. Bush unquestioningly. Sure, that led to a string of disasters, so it's possible to go *too* far with group cohesion, too.

So too much discord can lead to madness but so can too much conformity. This suggests that perhaps there's some kind of ideal balance between conflict and conformity that we should strive for. If the obsessive flag-waving of the early 2000s was too far in one direction, surely today's social media callout culture is too far in the other.

Now, finding a sense of shared purpose is particularly challeng-ing. Whenever a pressing social issue develops, one side seems to rush to one conclusion with the other then taking the opposing conclusion with irrational glee, each side proclaiming that working toward middle ground would amount to treason. We could name any number of social issues: Should we have no gun control at all or work to remove every weapon from every law-abiding citizen? Do we eliminate all abortions or allow women the opportunity to engage elective abortions right up through the third trimester? Do black, blue, or all lives matter? Do we look upon all nonwhite immigrants with suspicion or open our borders to all comers? I don't mean to suggest that the middle-ground solution is *always* the best answer, either. But I do mean to say it would be helpful to find ways to remember that we're all in the rowboat together and we can disagree, even fundamentally, on certain issues while still respecting each other's basic worth.

This is a choice we can each make individually. That means finding ways to communicate to those we disagree with that we still respect them. It means withholding the satisfaction of that awesome zinger or show-ing off for those in our own tribe how well we can smash the enemy. It also means acknowledging when one's opponent has a fair point, even if we still disagree with the larger position. It also means knowing when to respectfully disengage from an argument that has become unproductive. This is a largely dying artform but employing it can diffuse arguments and also reduce stress.

Shared purpose doesn't necessarily mean choosing a problem and literally working together toward a solution, although it certainly can. Rather, we all need to reaffirm that we belong to a larger community of in-dividuals, including those with whom we disagree or are different. Shared community need not mean shared opinions or ideology nor even shared values, at least not always, but rather a willingness to respect a process of compromise and negotiation as a road forward to resolving differences with an aim toward a mutual good.

Don't Speak from Frustration

When we think about what angers us most in the social arena, it seldom involves positions that are absurd. For instance, an individual espousing the view that Western countries should adopt a Soviet-style Communism would elicit little more than disinterest or eye rolls. Such a view is obviously a crazed minority one with little influence to impede most people's goals of self-improvement and fulfillment. By contrast, views expressed by a significant proportion of a population can be threatening and frustrating for those with opposing outlooks. Take the immigration debate, for instance. Recommending open borders or even just a lax immigration system of amnesty, sanctuary cities, opposition to assimilation, and so forth can be frustrating to those who believe immigration should be strategic, limited, and focused on cultural assimilation. By contrast, recommending border walls, caps on legal immigration and asylum, and an end to family sponsorship frustrate those who advocate a compassionate, broad immigration system or who worry about discrimination in immigration. *Both sides have fair points.* Yet in arguing from frustration, they not only miss opportunities for compromise, but also find themselves taking more extreme positions, almost with the intent of further frustrating the opposition, who then take more extreme positions in return, contributing to evident madness. Thus border walls and open immigration become valuable less because they solve the problem of immigration but more because they piss off the other tribe. This is a bad way to address societal problems.[9]

When we develop a vision of a future world and begin working toward it, it's natural to perceive others working toward a different vision of a future world to be a major source of frustration. To the extent that they are working toward something we *don't* want (reduced regulation of industry, higher taxes, decreased immigration, more abortion freedoms, vegan burgers, a reboot of *The Brady Bunch*, whatever), we can find that we dislike them often without ever meeting them. This in turn can lead us to saying things that, with reflection, might sound extreme even to us, "I'd rather *die* than eat a vegan burger!"[10] Taking a moment or two to remember that (A) this other person has the right to a differing opinion, however stupid, and (B) screaming rarely convinces anyone of anything aside from our own madness can help us to walk back our emotions a bit.

If readers remember nothing else from this book, I hope it is this: calling someone an asshole seldom succeeds in encouraging anyone to listen more. Frustration only causes us to dig in further on our ideologies, seek allies, and ignore critics. In this sense, even people who are dead-on right can contribute to awful outcomes by being right in the wrongest possible way. The vaccine debate is an excellent example. I'm no vaccine researcher, but I accept that the evidence is quite clear that vaccines are not, except perhaps for the extremely rare one-in-ten-million exception, involved in autism or other cognitive impairments. Even being generous, we can say that any vaccination risks are far less than the diseases they prevent. But I also cringe whenever I see folks make derogatory statements about the anti-vaccine movement. Not because the anti-vaccine movement is right on the science, but by missing an opportunity to affirm their concerns and address them through dialogue, we merely drive them further into their ideology. The vaccine debate has been going on for more than twenty years. Perhaps it's time to try something aside from public ridicule? To be sure, convincing people is hard, but it can be done. One of the most astounding examples has been public support for gay rights. As with any movement, advocacy for gay rights includes a mixture of approaches, but I firmly believe that (as with desegregation in the mid-twentieth century) a commitment to be the adults in the room was instrumental in winning the hearts and minds of the majority. There's a whole body of psychological literature on persuasion, most of which acknowledges it is a hard business. But rationality is part of this and, increasingly, debates about policy have lost any semblance of rationality.

Internet as Usual

Technology gets blamed for a lot of things, most of which it probably does not do. Lost to history, there was undoubtedly a Cro-Magnon debate about the deleterious effects of the wheel on youth development. "Carrying stuff by hand was good enough when I was a young ape, and it should be good enough for my kid, too!" There *were* verifiable debates about the written word, Greek plays, translating the Bible from Latin, the theater, locomotives,[11] the radio, comic books, television, microwave ovens,[12] video games, Dungeons and Dragons, Harry Potter, and pretty much any other cool new thing one can think of. It does *not* appear, for instance, that using the internet or social media causes suicide in young people, despite excessive hand-wringing among some.[13]

But let's not give social media a total pass just yet. For the moment I'll ignore the considerable privacy concerns and cynical use of our personal data by big tech companies.[14] Of concern is the way we often behave on social media. That is to say: like jerks. Now don't get me wrong, plenty of people are jerks in real life, too, believe me, I've met plenty. And although there's much talk about the anonymity of the internet, which is part of the issue, I've also seen plenty of people behave like boors with their names in full view. I suspect two issues contribute to bad internet behavior. First, the immediate gratification of the internet. Second, the lack of face-to-face connection.

I want to be clear: I am not advocating the notion that the internet makes us into tossers. Rather I suggest the internet makes it easier for us to be the dicks we already are. Going back to my earlier point about frustration, the internet makes it easy to toss off a comment out of irritation or snideness toward another human being without much thought. I'm just going to put it out there: I've done it, and I'm sure most readers have, too, aside from those who live in proverbial caves.[15] Compare that to years past, when an aggressive response required a *strongly worded note* sent to the editor of a newspaper, an exercise in time and effort that would allow most of us to come to our senses before investing. Joe Biden creepily sniffing someone's hair[16] might have gotten some news attention twenty years ago (or maybe not), but today we can spend weeks online parsing it all out, getting angry with each other when we don't engage the "right" response. Is it good enough for him to laugh it off[17] and promise not to do it again, or does he require public flogging with a scourge dipped in vinegar? I look forward to the tweets and emails I'll get for even bringing this issue up.

I generally don't like the way folks in the humanities and sociology use the word "performance" to indicate that our public behavior is generally directed toward pleasing some kind of social master. I doubt, for the most part, that we *perform* gender, for instance, with gender largely residing in the hypothalamus, not as a social construct (see chapter 4). But I think sociology has a point in this context.[18] I suspect part of the internet's appeal, particularly once we got beyond looking up our old high school chums to see if they are fatter and balder than us (for me, at least, they are—sorry guys!), is that it gives us an immediate opportunity to signal our virtue to our tribe. How else do we explain why any number of person hours were burned, on both sides I may point out, arguing whether Sesame Street characters Bert and Ernie were gay?[19] They're *Muppets!* Let it go. Everyone.

There seems to be few easier ways to indicate what a good, moral human being one is than to laugh at how immoral someone else is. More difficult is to acknowledge our own moral failings (though this does not require a Cultural Revolution–like public humiliation) while being generous to the faults of others. Let our internet presence be one of kindness and rational arguments rather than snark and callouts. For most of us this isn't something we can just turn off and turn on. Indeed, I shudder to think when my last moment of internet snark was—probably sometime during a break between writing the paragraphs of this chapter. But for every decision we make *not* to add to callout culture on the internet, we can individually help pull back on our societal madness just a little bit.

Don't Let the Bastards Grind You Down

With everyone being outraged, our culture can become something akin to a sea of drowning people, each trying to scramble atop the others to breathe but, in the process, simply dragging one another down. If you put an idea out there into public space, inevitably someone will try to smash it in order to enhance his or her own worth. The more successful you become, the greater will be the passion and persistence of your detractors. It's easy to get mired in negativity if you're not careful.

Becoming part of the social madness isn't just a matter of resisting the urge to scream into the hurricane with everyone else. It also does require a measure of standing firm. This, too, can be difficult to manage.

In the last chapter we discussed the controversy over the young adult novel *Blood Heir*, which the author Amélie Wen Zhao cancelled after a Twitter campaign complaining it was insensitive to racial issues.[20] Probably there's a more complex story behind it. But whatever the reason, canceling the book was almost certainly the wrong decision. I don't mean to be critical of Zhao and undoubtedly her publisher and agent played some role in the decision. However, I do believe that public figures who come under critique have some obligation to stand firm when those critiques are unreasonable. Sure, that's a subjective line. Saying a mean-spirited thing certainly warrants an apology. But by the time we've gotten to *Blood Heir*, we're at a point where art and literature are being censored (and it's still censorship if the author is bullied into it) in the name of ideological purity.

Books and art should be provocative and points for discussion. The notion that all such material that does not fit within a particular worldview should be eliminated is outright dangerous. It was bad when the right argued *Harry Potter* was going to turn our children into little witches and it's bad when the left argued *Blood Heir* is going to turn our children into racists. *It's the same argument.*

To be sure, standing firm in the Twitter storm requires fortitude and courage. But it can be done. It involves remembering that the loudest voices do not represent a societal consensus. Worse, by giving in to the maddest voices in our society, we only encourage them in their madness. A fundamental component of behavioral research is that behaviors that are rewarded occur with greater frequency. If we don't want the angriest people on social media to hold sway over our society, we have to stop giving them what they want, plain and simple. That means standing up to bullies, politely and firmly to be sure, but we've got to make the decision to do it. So put unpopular but good-faith ideas out there if you've got the stomach for it, but politely remain firm in the face of craziness. Don't engage with those who hurl insults. Remember, as they say, never get into a mud fight with a pig. Everybody comes out dirty, but only the pig has fun.

Remember Basic Civic Principles

Finally, we would do well to remember two basic principles that are easily forgotten. Those are free speech and due process. We all think we want these things, but usually only when they benefit us and not when they benefit those we do not like.

Most of us would agree that free speech and due process are fundamental components of any functioning democracy. Yet we often become surprisingly willing to jettison these values when people we think are awful would benefit from them. As we've seen at other points in the book, politicians even in republics and democracies have been willing to degrade free speech principles when it has suited them. As I write this, our current U.S. president often uses language contemptuous of free speech, and free speech protections in other countries have eroded more directly as authoritarian leaders have taken charge.

Surveys of college students often reveal some confusion and ambivalence around the issue of free speech. For instance, college students overwhelmingly support free speech and to a greater degree than do older adults. At the same time, significant proportions of students also express willingness to shut down speech they see as "hate" speech, although the borders of this are not always clearly defined.[21] This is an age-old struggle, not one invented by college students in the most recent generation: what to do with speech that is constitutionally protected (which in the United States includes hate speech so long as it doesn't directly incite violence) but loathsome by the standards of the average person? Nobody is eager to have a group of Nazis march down the central street of his or her town (well, except the Nazis, I suppose), but how do we appropriately challenge them while supporting their right to be schlongs? The answer is generally to challenge bad speech with good speech, but this requires a certain degree of tolerance and, given our emotional nature, we're not always good at tolerance. Heck, we're not great at tolerating good-faith divergences of viewpoint, let alone actual hateful speech. Words like "racist," "white supremacy," and "sexist" have been so broadly applied in recent years they've begun to lose their bite. To be sure, the best speech is that which is rationally grounded and offered in good faith under civil norms of engagement. Yet we can't be sure to protect that unless we also protect the worst things people say. This doesn't mean we need to condone such speech, but we can protect it even as we challenge it.

We discussed due process in chapter 7. As with free speech, presumably everybody thinks it's important until it's time to offer it to someone we don't like. Then it's not so important anymore. And as with free speech it's not just a set of laws but a value system that both informs those laws and extends beyond them. Without being willing to offer due process to the people we personally suspect are guilty, there's no way to protect it for the people we think are innocent.

Some Concluding Thoughts

Are we living in a time of great madness? I remain optimistic. To be sure, we are looking at significant challenges. Many of our world leaders seem at least a little bit mad, and our societal discourse is beginning to reflect some of the same. Yet for all our discontents, things continue to mostly look up. Sure, nothing is forever, and global calamity may set in the very moment this book goes to print (heck, maybe because of it). But I don't think so.

But staying off the path of madness will require a choice on each of our parts as individuals not to contribute to it. None of us are perfect, but with every decision not to contribute to the chaos of our present age, I believe we can help make the world we live in just a little bit less mad. And by remaining stalwart in the face of madness we can give it just a bit less power. Mainly my advice to the world boils down to this: we all need to mellow out a little bit. And keep our fingers crossed that in one hundred years somebody won't be writing a book just like this one about us.

NOTES

Chapter 1. Introduction: Mad as a Hatter

1. See Joshua Shenk, "Lincoln's Great Depression," *Atlantic Monthly*, October 2005, www.theatlantic.com/magazine/archive/2005/10/lincoln-apos-s-great-de pression/4247/# (accessed September 24, 2018). Also, Douglas Wilson, *Honor's Voice: The Transformation of Abraham Lincoln* (New York: Vintage, 1999).

2. George McGovern, *Grassroots: The Autobiography of George McGovern* (New York: Random House, 1977).

3. Jonathan Davidson, Kathryn Connor, and Marvin Swartz, "Mental Illness in U.S. Presidents between 1776 and 1974: A Review of Biographical Sources," *Journal of Nervous and Mental Disease* 194 (2006): 47–51.

4. The most well-known ancient biographies of Alexander include Plutarch's *The Age of Alexander* and Arrian's *The Age of Alexander*. Even these were written long after his death and debate continues regarding which are more accurate. See A. B. Bosworth, "Errors in Arrian," *The Classical Quarterly* 26 (1976): 117–39. Bosworth contends Arrian relied too heavily on the narrative of Alexander's general Ptolemy, who, after Alexander's death, may have been more concerned about the various axes he had to grind rather than 100 percent historical accuracy.

5. Plutarch, in fact, appears to blame the snakes-in-bed thing for cooling of the marital ardor between Philip and Olympias, saying, "At another time a snake was seen stretched out at Olympias' side as she slept, and it was this more than anything else, we are told, which weakened Philip's passion and cooled his affection for her, so that from that time on he seldom came to sleep with her. The reason for this may either have been that he was afraid she would cast some evil spell or charm upon him or else that he recoiled from her embrace because he believed that she was the consort of some higher being." Usually both parties in a

marriage contribute to discord but, in this case, who can blame Philip? Plutarch, *The Age of Alexander* (New York: Penguin Classics, 2012).

6. Guy Rogers, *Alexander: The Ambiguity of Greatness* (New York: Random House, 2005).

7. Hermann Bengtson and Edmund Bloedow, *History of Greece: From the Beginning to the Byzantine Era* (Ottowa: University of Ottawa Press, 1997).

8. This appears to be particularly true during the last months of his life upon his return to Persia after his conquests in India. One can credit him with navigating a near mutiny of his Macedonian troops precipitated by an unintended humiliation of them by Alexander (by retiring some older veterans, he implied they were no longer wanted or needed). Plutarch describes Alexander's state of mind this way: "Alexander had become overwrought and terrified in his own mind, and now abandoned himself to superstition. He interpreted every strange or unusual occurrence, no matter how trivial, as a prodigy or a portent, with the result that the palace was filled with soothsayers, sacrificers, purifiers and prognosticators. Thus, disbelief or contempt for the power of the gods is a terrible thing, but superstition is also terrible; like water, it constantly gravitates to a lower level. So unreasoning dread filled Alexander 's mind with foolish misgivings, once he had become a slave to his fears." Clearly, this serves as a lesson: immense power does not always bring reciprocal happiness.

9. This is by almost any measure, whether examining homicides, war deaths, rapes, and so forth. See Steven Pinker, *The Better Angels of Our Nature: Why Violence Has Declined* (New York: Viking, 2011).

10. Grant McCall and Nancy Shields, "Examining the Evidence from Small-Scale Societies and Early Prehistory and Implications for Modern Theories of Aggression and Violence," *Aggression and Violent Behavior* 13 (2008): 1–9. The myth that humans once lived in an idyllic society that was lost as cultures evolved into modern societies is arguably one of the most enduring.

11. Francis Fukuyama, *The End of History and the Last Man* (New York: Free Press, 2006).

12. Steven Pinker, *Enlightenment Now: The Case for Reason, Science, Humanism and Progress* (New York: Viking, 2018).

13. Freedom House, *Freedom in the World: Democracy in Crisis*, 2018, https://freedomhouse.org/report/freedom-world/freedom-world-2018 (accessed September 24, 2018).

14. Pinker, *Enlightenment Now.*

15. Centers for Disease Control, *Suicide Rising across the US*, 2018, www.cdc .gov/vitalsigns/suicide/ (accessed September 24, 2018).

16. Michael Lofchie, "The Uganda Coup: Class Action by the Military," *Journal of Modern African Studies* 10 (1972): 19–35.

17. Richard Ullman, "Human Rights and Economic Power: The United States versus Idi Amin," *Foreign Affairs*, April 1978, www.foreignaffairs.com/articles/uganda/1978-04-01/human-rights-and-economic-power-united-states-versus-idi-amin (accessed September 24, 2018).

18. Emma Boyle, "Was Idi Amin's Government a Terrorist Regime?" *Terrorism and Political Violence* 29 (2017): 593–609.

19. Chibiuke Uche, "The British government, Idi Amin and the Expulsion of British Asians from Uganda," *Interventions: International Journal of Postcolonial Studies* 19 (2017): 818–36.

20. Saul David, *Operation Thunderbolt* (New York: Little, Brown, 2015).

21. Michael Kaufman, "Idi Amin, Murderous and Erratic Ruler of Uganda in the 70s Dies in Exile," *New York Times*, August 2003, www.nytimes.com/2003/08/17/world/idi-amin-murderous-and-erratic-ruler-of-uganda-in-the-70-s-dies-in-exile.html (accessed September 24, 2018).

22. Daniel Kalinaki, "Entebbe Raid Humiliated Amin, Nearly Caused East African War," *Daily Nation*, July, 2016, www.nation.co.ke/news/Entebbe-raid-embarrassed-Amin—nearly-caused-East-African-war/1056-3277804-1327oaiz/index.html (accessed September 24, 2018).

23. Ian Morris, *Why the West Rules—For Now: The Patterns of History, and What They Reveal about the Future* (New York: Farrar, Straus and Giroux, 2010).

24. Jared Diamond, *Guns, Germs and Steel: A Short History of Everybody for the Last 13,000 Years* (London: Vintage, 1997).

25. It is worth noting that the writing of history seldom occurs in a moral vacuum and historical texts often contain underlying moral messages. Throughout much of the European Enlightenment, history focused on the apparent superiority of European culture over other cultures in ways that argued for both cultural and biological superiority. Obviously, such narratives were Eurocentric and racist. More recent history, which focuses on exogenous variables to explain cultures' successes, at times may seem to attempt to level the moral, cultural, and biological playing field. Like the texts that came before, this too has a point to make when speaking of history. I note the improbability that all cultures are of inherently equal moral worth as well as that biological differences are negligible across peoples from distinct regions (we need only look to skin color, skeletal structure, body shape, etc., to see the influence of genetics across diverse peoples). This does not mean the Europeans were right to assert their superiority (after all, Europe was a lesser player for much of human history), only that we must always be alert for the morality tale of historical texts. Only this book is truly objective!

26. Without clear boundaries, scientific support, or conceptual value, the term "toxic masculinity" is arguably rubbish. Like many pseudoscientific terms, it is based in gender politics and virtue signaling rather than in commentary that

delineates our understanding of gender. Like many such terms, it likely does more to foment polarization than it does understanding—indeed, increasing society's madness more than promoting rational thought. Men certainly have been overrepresented in physical violence throughout history, but boiling this down to a "bad" masculinity (evidenced by such things as enjoying football or action-oriented video games) that could be replaced by a "good" masculinity (typically involving traits valued by the progressive left) is a gross oversimplification and moralization of this issue. See Christopher Ferguson, "How 'Toxic Masculinity' Is Hurting Boys," *Houston Chronicle*, March 2018, www.houstonchronicle.com/local/gray-matters/article/toxic-masculinity-gender-norms-harmful-boys-12782202.php (accessed September 25, 2018).

27. Leslie Carroll, *Royal Pains: A Rogue's Gallery of Brats, Brutes and Bad Seeds* (New York: Penguin, 2011). This is something of a reminder of the value of humanism, briefly put, the belief that human lives have intrinsic value whatever their place in society. Modern humanism (which we now take for granted in the West) arose during the European Enlightenment but had not yet taken hold in Bathory's time, undoubtedly leading to relative indifference to her actions so long as she targeted those who were perceived lesser human beings.

28. It is worth noting that a counter-narrative is sometimes advanced that Bathory was the victim of a show trial and mistaken impressions. This line of thought suggests that Bathory's attempts to provide medical services to sick individuals were mistaken as torture, and natural deaths in the area—including some bodies hastily buried on her premises—due to disease misattributed as homicides. Coupled with a show trial designed to benefit Bathory's main investigator, Palatine György Thurzó, Bathory was a victim of the widespread misogyny of the time. This argument is interesting, although overall I do not find it persuasive. Painful medical procedures were common at the time and not typically misattributed to sexualized torture, and presumably disease outbreaks would not have struck mainly young women. That Elizabeth was so unfortunate as to have an assistant healer who clumsily hid bodies of disease victims around her castle for investigators to find and attribute to violence would have to be a remarkable stroke of bad luck for Elizabeth. Trials at that time certainly were nothing like the admittedly still-flawed due process of the modern age, but the trials of Bathory's accomplices would have had to have been masterfully fixed in order for the setup to escape mention in the popular narrative. Finally, the accusations against Bathory arguably constituted a major scandal for the nobility, and it is unclear who benefited from them (even Thurzó, usually presumed the main beneficiary, appears to have been slow to investigate initial complaints of Bathory's behavior, and it is unclear that he benefited from her arrest). It's not evident that Thurzó was the originator of the accusations against Bathory. Undoubtedly there have

been embellishments to Bathory's crimes, but it is likely that the basic accusation that she murdered multiple young girls is true. Nonetheless, I invite readers to evaluate a counter-narrative and decide for themselves. See Irma Szádeczky-Kardoss, "The Bloody Countess: An Examination of the Life and Trial of Erzsébet Báthory," *Life and Science*, September 2005, https://notesonhungary.word press.com/2014/05/31/the-bloody-countess/ (accessed September 25, 2018).

29. David Daniel, "Eastern Europe," in *Women in Reformation and Counter-Reformation Europe*, ed. Sherrin Marshall (Indianapolis: Indiana University Press, 1989).

30. László Kürti, "The Symbolic Construction of the Monstrous: The Elizabeth Bathory Story," *Journal of Ethnology and Folklore Research* 46, no. 1 (2009): 133–59.

31. Andreas Hill, Niels Habermann, Wolfgang Berner, and Peer Briken, "Sexual Sadism and Sadistic Personality Disorder in Sexual Homicide," *Journal of Personality Disorders* 20, no. 6 (2006): 671–84. It should be noted that the diagnosis of sadistic personality disorder is controversial. It is not in the American Psychiatric Association's *DSM-V*, although some scholars advocate for its inclusion nonetheless.

Chapter 2. Madness, Mental Illness, and Insanity

1. Kimberly Leach was, in fact, one of his youngest victims.

2. Ann Rule, *The Stranger Beside Me* (New York: Pocket Books, 2008).

3. Bundy's trick of posing as an injured person to lure helpful and unsuspecting women was reportedly one inspiration for the Buffalo Bill character in *Silence of the Lambs*. "Silence of the Lambs: Trivia," Internet Movie Database, www .imdb.com/title/tt0102926/trivia (accessed October 5, 2018).

4. Richard Gray, "Psychopathy and Will to Power: Ted Bundy and Dennis Rader," in *Serial Killers: Being and Killing*, ed. S. Waller, 191–205 (New York: Wiley-Blackwell, 2010).

5. Robert Whitaker, *Mad in America* (Philadelphia: Basic Books, 2002).

6. Alex Alfieri, Christian Strauss, Harald Meller, Pawel Tacik, and Silvio Brandt, "The Woman of Pritschoena: An Example of the German Neolithic Neurosurgery in Saxony-Anhalt," *Journal of the History of the Neurosciences* 21 (2012): 139–46.

7. Miguel Faria, "Violence, Mental Illness, and the Brain—A Brief History of Psychosurgery: Part 1—From Trephination to Lobotomy," *Surgical Neurology International* 4 (2013), www.ncbi.nlm.nih.gov/pmc/articles/PMC3640229/ (accessed October 13, 2018).

8. Tomislav Breitenfeld, M. J. Jurasic, and D. Breitenfeld, "Hippocrates: The Forefather of Neurology," *Neurological Sciences* 35 (2014): 1349–52.

9. How the four humors interacted in the body were quite complex according to Hippocrates, and yellow and black bile were not as abundant as the others. Although Hippocrates does not make such a clear allusion, it is tempting nonetheless to entertain the notion that pee and poop may have been at least unconsciously on his mind with these latter two.

10. A. Roback, "Graeco-Roman Psychiatry," in *History of Psychology and Psychiatry*, 202–11 (Secaucus, NJ: Citadel Press, 1961).

11. In fairness, scientific medicine wasn't fully interrupted, and nontrivial advances were made in the Muslim world during the medieval period, even as European medicine largely languished in bleedings, potions, and exorcisms.

12. After getting one's arm amputated, one also might get a nice shave and haircut. The modern barber's pole originates from the bloody rags wrapped around a pole for advertising. Lars Himmelmann, "From Barber to Surgeon—The Process of Professionalization," *Svensk Medicinhistorisk Tidskrift* 11 (2007): 69–87.

13. J. Kroll and B. Bachrach, "Sin and Mental Illness in the Middle Ages," *Psychological Medicine* 14 (1984): 507–14.

14. Heinrich Kramer and Sprenger Jacob, *Malleus Maleficarum* (1487).

15. Beatriz Quintanilla, "Witchcraft or Mental Illness?" *Psychiatric Times*, June 21, 2010, www.psychiatrictimes.com/schizoaffective/witchcraft-or-mental-illness (accessed October 14, 2018).

16. And yes, I have a copy.

17. Albert Roberts and Linda Kurtz, "Historical Perspectives on the Care and Treatment of the Mentally Ill," *Journal of Sociology and Social Welfare* 14 (1987): 75–94.

18. Roberts and Kurtz, "Historical Perspectives on the Care and Treatment of the Mentally Ill."

19. Psychology professor Brent Robbins suggests that the medical profession has come too often to view patients as, in effect, corpses-to-be, reducing empathy in medical practice. Brent Robbins, *The Medicalized Body and Anesthetic Culture* (New York: Palgrave Macmillan, 2018).

20. Whitaker, *Mad in America*.

21. Whitaker, *Mad in America*.

22. American Psychological Association, *Clinical Practice Guideline for the Treatment of Posttraumatic Stress Disorder (PTSD)*, 2017, www.apa.org/ptsd-guideline/ (accessed October 6, 2018).

23. Christiane Steinert, Thomas Munder, Sven Rabung, Jürgen Hoyer, and Falk Leichsenring, "Psychodynamic Therapy: As Efficacious as Other Empirically Supported Treatments? A Meta-Analysis Testing Equivalence of Outcomes," *American Journal of Psychiatry* 174 (2017): 943–53. Also, Joseph Carpenter, Leigh A. Andrews, Sara M. Witcraft, Mark B. Powers, Jasper A. J.

Smits, and Stefan G. Hofmann, "Cognitive Behavioral Therapy for Anxiety and Related Disorders: A Meta-Analysis of Randomized Placebo-Controlled Trials," *Depression and Anxiety* (forthcoming). While serving as a volunteer on the APA's Council of Representatives, I informed them, in fact, of the Carpenter meta-analysis, but the APA expressed no interest in considering it or revising their clinical guidelines accordingly.

24. American Psychological Association, *Timeline of APA Policies & Actions Related to Detainee Welfare and Professional Ethics in the Context of Interrogation and National Security*, 2018, www.apa.org/news/press/statements/interrogations .aspx (accessed October 6, 2018). It should be noted that the APA's problems did not end with accusations of complicity in torture. After its internal report (the "Hoffman Report") came out, the organization was accused of failing to provide due process to many individuals named in the report and, at the time of this writing, has been sued for libel. The APA is now in a no-win situation in which it is clear to me that its approach to ethics is cynical, predatory, and focused on the welfare of the organization itself rather than the general public. Hopefully this will change in the future.

25. David Rosenhan, "On Being Sane in Insane Places," *Science* 179 (1973): 250–58.

26. In all fairness, a book just came out challenging the validity of this experiment. See https://www.nature.com/articles/d41586-019-03268-y.

27. Jack Drescher, "Queer Diagnoses Revisited: The Past and Future of Homosexuality and Gender Diagnoses in *DSM* and *ICD*," *International Review of Psychiatry* 27 (2015): 386–95.

28. Aniko Maraz, Róbert Urbán, Mark Damian Griffiths, and Zsolt Demetrovics, "An Empirical Investigation of Dance Addiction," *PLoS ONE* 10 (2015), http://journals.plos.org/plosone/article?id=10.1371/journal.pone.0125988 (accessed October 5, 2018).

29. News Media, Public Education and Public Policy Committee, *An Official Division 46 Statement on the WHO Proposal to Include Gaming Related Disorders in ICD-11*, 2018. https://div46amplifier.com/2018/06/21/an-official-division -46-statement-on-the-who-proposal-to-include-gaming-related-disorders-in -icd-11/ (accessed October 5, 2018).

30. Anthony Bean, Rune K. L. Nielsen, Antonius J. van Rooij, and Christopher J. Ferguson, "Video Game Addiction: The Push to Pathologize Video Games," *Professional Psychology: Research and Practice* 48 (2017): 378–89.

31. In fairness, some clinicians view this positively, arguing that it allows individuals to get treatment rather than being excluded if depressive symptoms are a reaction to grief. See, for example, Ronald Pies, "How the *DSM-5* Got Grief, Bereavement Right," *PsychCentral* (2013), https://psychcentral.com/blog/

how-the-dsm-5-got-grief-bereavement-right/ (accessed October 5, 2018). This argument makes fair points, but overall I suspect the potential for abuse is considerable and further dilutes our conceptualization of mental illness.

32. Kevin Douglas, Laura Guy, and Stephen Hart, "Psychosis as a Risk Factor for Violence to Others: A Meta-Analysis," *Psychological Bulletin* 135 (2009): 679–706.

33. Christopher J. Ferguson, "Video Games and Youth Violence: A Prospective Analysis in Adolescents," *Journal of Youth and Adolescence* 40 (2011): 377–91.

34. Eric Hickey, *Serial Murderers and Their Victims* (New York: Cengage, 2015).

35. It is worth noting that some scholars contend that psychopathy is a subclass of antisocial personality disorder (APD) that is more prone to violence. This perspective is arguable, although it has not made its way to diagnostic systems like the *DSM*. See Robert Hare, *Without Conscience: The Disturbing World of the Psychopath among Us* (New York: Guilford Press, 1999). In the past, the use of terms such as psychopathy and sociopathy tended to reflect ideological positions about the disorder, whether it was biologically (psychopathy) or learning (sociopathy) based. The *DSM*, attempting to dodge these ideological debates on cause, adopted the APD label. However, this label admittedly causes some confusion because, to the layperson, it tends to suggest individuals who avoid others, which is not typically the case for APD.

36. Thus, providing fair warning that adoption of a statement by such groups provides little evidentiary value of the truthfulness of such statements. Professional guilds and governmental bodies tend to endorse positions seen as beneficial to those organizations, not necessarily those that are "true" in an objective, scientific sense.

37. David Adams, S. Barnett, N. Bechtereva, Bonnie Carter, Jose Delgado, José-Luis Díaz, Andrzej Eliasz, Santiago Genoves, Benson Ginsburg, Jo Groebel, Samir-Kumar Ghosh, Robert Hinde, Richard Leakey, Taha Malasi, J. Ramirez, Federico Zaragoza, Diana Mendoza, Ashis Nandy, John Scott, and Riitta Wahlstrom, "The Seville Statement on Violence," *American Psychologist* 45 (1990): 1167–68.

38. Frans de Waal, "Aggression as a Well-Integrated Part of Primate Social Relationships: A Critique of the Seville Statement on Violence," in *Aggression and Peacefulness in Humans and Other Primates*, ed. James Silverberg and J. Patrick Gray, 37–56. (New York: Oxford University Press, 1992). It is the time-honored tradition of "consensus statements" to form such consensuses by simply not inviting anyone to weigh in who might be expected to disagree with the desired consensus.

39. Soo Rhee and Irwin D. Waldman, "Genetic and Environmental Influences on Antisocial Behavior: A Meta-Analysis of Twin and Adoption Studies,"

Psychological Bulletin 128 (2002): 490–529; Christopher J. Ferguson, "Genetic Contributions to Antisocial Personality and Behavior: A Meta-Analytic Review from an Evolutionary Perspective," *Journal of Social Psychology* 150 (2010): 160–80.

40. Kevin Beaver, Joseph A. Schwartz, and Jamie M. Gajos, "A Review of the Genetic and Gene-Environment Interplay Contributors to Antisocial Phenotypes," in *The Development of Criminal and Antisocial Behavior: Theory, Research and Practical Applications*, ed. Julien Morizot and Lila Kazemian, 109–22 (New York: Springer, 2010).

41. Elizabeth Moes, "Ted Bundy: A Case of Schizoid Necrophilia," *Melanie Klein & Object Relations* 9 (1991): 54–72.

42. Jess Wakefield, "Wonderful Tonight: How Old Is Eric Clapton, What Happened to His Son, What Are the 'Tears in Heaven' Singer's Biggest Songs and Who Is His Wife?" *Sun*, June 30, 2018, www.thesun.co.uk/tvandshow biz/6657776/eric-clapton-son-hit-songs-wife/ (accessed October 6, 2018).

43. Many of the commissioners were anti-porn crusaders themselves, a rather obvious conflict of interest. As a result, the commission appeared to have cherry-picked and distorted scientific findings to support an anti-porn agenda. See Daniel Linz, Edward Donnerstein, and Steven Penrod, "The Findings and Recommendations of the Attorney General's Commission on Pornography: Do the Psychological 'Facts' Fit the Political Fury?" *American Psychologist* 42 (1987): 946–53.

44. Christopher J. Ferguson and Richard D. Hartley, "The Pleasure Is Momentary . . . the Expense Damnable? The Influence of Pornography on Rape and Sexual Assault," *Aggression and Violent Behavior* 14 (2009): 323–29.

45. Taylor Kohut, Jodie L. Baer, and Brendan Watts, "Is Pornography Really about 'Making Hate to Women'? Pornography Users Hold More Gender Egalitarian Attitudes than Nonusers in a Representative American Sample," *Journal of Sex Research* 53 (2016): 1–11.

46. Understanding the minds and motives of those who are drawn to famous killers—hardly unique to the case of Bundy—would make for fascinating psychological study.

47. Stanley Milgram, "Behavioral Study of Obedience," *Journal of Abnormal and Social Psychology* 67 (1963): 371–78.

48. Philip Zimbardo, *The Lucifer Effect: Understanding How Good People Turn Evil* (New York: Random House, 2007).

49. Stephen Reicher and S. Alexander Haslam, "Rethinking the Psychology of Tyranny: The BBC Prison Study," *British Journal of Social Psychology* 45 (2006): 1–40.

50. Peter Gray, "Why Zimbardo's Prison Experiment Isn't in My Textbook," *Psychology Today*, October 19, 2013, www.psychologytoday.com/us/

blog/freedom-learn/201310/why-zimbardo-s-prison-experiment-isn-t-in-my -textbook (accessed October 15, 2018); Greg Toppo, "Time to Dismiss the Stanford Prison Experiment?" *Inside Higher Ed*, June 20, 2018, www.inside highered.com/news/2018/06/20/new-stanford-prison-experiment-revelations -question-findings (accessed October 15, 2018).

51. Matthew M. Hollander and Jason Turowetz, "Normalizing Trust: Participants' Immediately Post-hoc Explanations of Behaviour in Milgram's 'Obedience' Experiments," *British Journal of Social Psychology* 56 (2017): 655–74.

52. Gina Perry, *Behind the Shock Machine: The Untold Story of the Notorious Milgram Psychology Experiments* (New York: New Press, 2012).

53. Wendy Lower, *Hitler's Furies: German Women in the Nazi Killing Fields* (New York: Houghton Mifflin Harcourt, 2013).

54. Tom Clark, *The Beautiful Beast: Why Was Irma Grese Evil?* www.academia .edu/2183067/The_beautiful_beast_Why_was_Irma_Grese_evil (accessed October 15, 2018).

55. In fairness, even to this day, history continues to be rewritten through the lens of contemporary mores.

56. Suetonius, *The Life of Caligula*, https://facultystaff.richmond .edu/~wstevens/history331texts/caligula.html.

57. The Praetorians were an elite military unit who served as guardians of the emperor. They also killed emperors a lot whenever they got tired of them. Go figure.

58. Philo, *On the Embassy to Gaius*, www.earlychristianwritings.com/yonge/ book40.html.

59. See, for example, Aloys Winterling, *Caligula: A Biography* (Oakland: University of California Press, 2009).

60. Anthony Barrett, *Caligula: The Corruption of Power* (New Haven, CT: Yale University Press: 1990).

61. José León-Carrión and Francisco Javier Chacartegui-Ramos, "Brain Injuries and Violent Crime," in *Violent Crime: Clinical and Social Implications*, ed. Christopher J. Ferguson, 99–118 (Thousand Oaks, CA: Sage Publications, 2010).

62. Barrett, *Caligula*.

63. Dio, *Roman History*, www.loebclassics.com/view/LCL083/1917/volume .xml.

64. Caligula died before managing to actually do it, if he really had the intention.

65. Barrett, *Caligula*.

66. Then again, looking at Congress, how much worse could a horse do?

67. Nicholas H. Taylor, "Popular Opposition to Caligula in Jewish Palestine," *Journal for the Study of Judaism* 32 (2001): 54–70.

Chapter 3. Deviance of the Personality

1. Previous versions of the *DSM* made this more explicit by placing personality disorders, along with intellectual disabilities (or "mental retardation" as it was called until 2013), under their own classification or "axis." Presumably the distinction between disorders on this axis and other mental conditions involved the essential core nature and permanency of these conditions.

2. Indeed, individuals with schizophrenia often enjoy perfectly normal childhoods with symptoms beginning only in their teens or early adulthood.

3. Not to be confused with obsessive-compulsive disorder (OCD), an anxiety disorder. Obsessive-compulsive personality disorder (OCPD) is similar to popular concepts of "type A" or "anal retentive" personalities focused on cleanliness, order, and the "proper" way of doing things, often foisted aggressively onto others. If you've ever argued vehemently about the "proper" way to fold towels, you may have OCPD. One can have fun with individuals with OCPD by refolding their laundry in the most absurd ways possible (rolling towels into tubes, for instance). By contrast, OCD is marked by excessive anxiety and intrusive, unpleasant thoughts (obsessions). Compulsive behaviors such as counting, checking locks, washing hands, and so forth are adopted as rituals to reduce the anxiety. Individuals with OCD are neither particularly neat and orderly, nor particularly worried about the "proper" way of doing things, at least not in the sense of foisting a kind of moral supremacy onto others.

4. For instance, more than once in my own practice I have been hired by parents who wanted me to "fix" teens with unusual interests, often Goth kids who adopted unusual styles of dress or taste in art. In such cases, helping parents to understand and appreciate their unique children (often experiencing schizotypal or histrionic personality disorders) and to accept and love them for who they are rather than hoping for the miracle of conversion to "normal" kids is more constructive than trying to reshape an established personality. To be clear, most Goth individuals do not have personality disorders, although individuals with certain personality disorders may gravitate toward more exotic lifestyles.

5. And no small number within academia, one observes.

6. From my clinical experience, borderline personality disorder is often misdiagnosed as bipolar disorder, despite being far more common. With borderline personality disorder, the mood swings are not delusional in nature, can shift very rapidly, and tend to be extreme overreactions to real-life events. By contrast, the manic and depressive phases tend to be long lasting for bipolar disorder (one week for manic episodes, two weeks or more for depressive episodes) and often include delusional components during the manic phases such as the belief that one's touch can heal the sick, that one has a secret stash of millions of dollars, or that one can fly.

7. Yana Weinstein, Marci E. J. Gleason, and Thomas F. Oltmanns, "Borderline but Not Antisocial Personality Disorder Symptoms Are Related to Self-Reported Partner Aggression in Late Middle-Age," *Journal of Abnormal Psychology* 121 (2012): 692–98.

8. Sarah L. Desmarais, Andrea Gibas, and Tonia L. Nicholls, "Beyond Violence against Women: Gender Inclusiveness in Domestic Violence Research, Policy, and Practice," in *Violent Crime: Clinical and Social Implications*, edited by Christopher J. Ferguson, 184–206 (Thousand Oaks, CA: Sage, 2010).

9. Nadia Cattane, Roberta Rossi, Mariangela Lanfredi, and Annamaria Cattaneo, "Borderline Personality Disorder and Childhood Trauma: Exploring the Affected Biological Systems and Mechanisms." *BMC Psychiatry* 17 (2017), https://bmcpsychiatry.biomedcentral.com/articles/10.1186/s12888-017-1383-2 (accessed November 16, 2018).

10. Narcissism was the center of a dubious claim that the millennial generation experienced a "narcissism epidemic." Promoted by some psychologists such as Jean Twenge, such claims were later largely debunked. See, for example, Eunike Wetzel, Anna Brown, Patrick L. Hill, Joanne M. Chung, Richard W. Robins, and Brent W. Roberts, "The Narcissism Epidemic Is Dead; Long Live the Narcissism Epidemic," *Psychological Science* 28 (2017): 1833–47. This proves that books disparaging younger generations tend to sell rather well to grumpy old people, perhaps a lesson I should have learned better than I have.

11. Adrian Furnham, Steven C. Richards, and Delroy L. Paulhus, "The Dark Triad of Personality: A 10 Year Review," *Social and Personality Psychology Compass* 7 (2013): 199–216.

12. Alan Bullock, *Hitler and Stalin* (New York: Alfred A. Knopf, 1992).

13. Bullock, *Hitler and Stalin*.

14. The casebook of Walter Langer presents more lurid hypotheses about Hitler's sexuality. Langer wrote during the war and successfully predicted some outcomes, such as Hitler's suicide. Other elements of the book appear somewhat psychoanalytically anachronistic, but it is an interesting example of how contemporary American war leaders sought to understand the mind of Hitler. Walter Langer, *The Mind of Adolf Hitler: The Secret Wartime Report* (New York: New American Library, 1972).

15. Leonard Heston and Renate Heston, *The Medical Casebook of Adolf Hitler* (Briarcliff Manor, NY: Stein & Day, 1979).

16. The myth that Hitler or other Nazi leaders were devoid of significant mental pathology is often promulgated by sources that should know better. For instance, sometimes even psychology textbooks claim Hitler had "high self-esteem," a clumsy observation that is insidiously misleading. See Uli Shimmack, "Auditing Social Psychology Textbooks: Hitler Had High Self-Esteem,"

Replicability Index (2018), https://replicationindex.wordpress.com/2018/12/28/socpsytextbookch2self/?fbclid=IwAR3R8FOoFZRggEdaoAWqcI7g73OK6HptlHXIbcGDIArG_xmTTQDagAQrN10 (accessed December 26, 2018).

17. Susan C. South, Robert F. Krueger, Gun Peggy Knudsen, Eivind Ystrom, Nikolai Czajkowski, Steven H. Aggen, Michael C. Neale, Nathan A. Gillespie, Kenneth S. Kendler, and Ted Reichborn-Kjennerud, "A Population Based Twin Study of *DSM–5* Maladaptive Personality Domains," *Personality Disorders: Theory, Research, and Treatment* 8 (2017): 366–75.

18. A little discussed fact is that Poland, ultimately the victim of Nazi aggression that started World War II in the European theater, invaded and annexed part of Czechoslovakia when that nation fell apart under Nazi pressure. One interesting counterfactual to consider is whether Germany might have rallied much of Eastern Europe, including Poland, against the Soviet Union. Alas, that was not to be, as World War II in Europe began with the invasion of Poland in 1939. Obviously just as well, since a Nazi win for World War II is horrible to consider.

19. For a detailed history, see David Faber, *Munich, 1938* (New York: Simon & Schuster, 2009).

20. Though why anyone would want this to have been the case is, obviously, less clear.

21. Historical analyses suggest Stalin planned to invade Germany in 1942. See Constantine Pleshakov, *Stalin's Folly: The Tragic First Ten Days of WWII on the Eastern Front* (New York: Houghton Mifflin, 2005).

22. The Ukraine suffered particularly under Stalin's agricultural policies in the 1930s, when he took most of their grain away, allowing perhaps a quarter of the population to starve to death.

23. Though Hitler was not particularly inclined toward war with the United Kingdom, avenging the dishonor of defeat in World War I was surely on his mind vis-à-vis France.

24. Germany ended the war with far better tanks—including the Panzer IV, Panther, and Tiger tanks, as well as with excellent assault guns, particularly once bugs due to rushed production had been worked out of them—than most of its enemies (aside from the admittedly excellent Russian tanks). By 1944, Germany had jet fighters, cruise missiles, guided bombs, ballistic missiles, advanced submarines, and a mass-produced assault rifle (the Sturmgewehr 44). Germany could have used extra time to design an effective strategic bomber, which it lacked, a decent long-range escort fighter, and a surface navy.

25. See Ervin Staub, *The Roots of Evil* (Cambridge: Cambridge University Press, 1992) for a comprehensive theory of how genocides occur from a social perspective.

26. These same college students, well in the cups, also set forth an interesting moral dilemma: if such time-traveling assassinations were possible, is it more evil to assassinate a baby who has, as of that moment, committed no evil act, or to allow that baby to live, knowing the suffering he or she will inflict on countless millions of others? Fortunately, we do not place our time machines into the care of young adults under the influence of curious substances.

27. Hence the term *compatibilism*. For an interesting debate, see Daniel Dennett and Gregg Caruso, "Just Deserts," *Aeon*, October 4, 2018, https://aeon.co/essays/on-free-will-daniel-dennett-and-gregg-caruso-go-head-to-head (accessed November 22, 2018).

28. John A. Bargh, Mark Chen, and Lara Burrows, "Automaticity of Social Behavior: Direct Effects of Trait Construct and Stereotype Activation on Action," *Journal of Personality and Social Psychology* 71 (1996): 230–44.

29. Stéphane Doyen, Olivier Klein, Cora-Lise Pichon, and Axel Cleeremans, "Behavioral Priming: It's All in the Mind, but Whose Mind?" *PLoS ONE* 7 (2012), https://journals.plos.org/plosone/article?id=10.1371/journal.pone.0029081#pone.0029081.s001 (accessed November 24, 2018).

30. Open Science Collaboration, "Estimating the Reproducibility of Psychological Science," *Science*, 349 (2015): 1–8; Colin Camerer, Anna Dreber, Felix Holzmeister, Teck-Hua Ho, Jürgen Huber, Magnus Johannesson, Michael Kirchler, Gideon Nave, Brian A. Nosek, Thomas Pfeiffer, Adam Altmejd, Nick Buttrick, Taizan Chan, Yiling Chen, Eskil Forsell, Anup Gampa, Emma Heikensten, Lily Hummer, Taisuke Imai, Siri Isaksson, Dylan Manfredi, Julia Rose, Eric-Jan Wagenmakers, and Hang Wu, "Evaluating the Replicability of Social Science Experiments in Nature and Science between 2010 and 2015," *Nature Human Behavior* 2 (2018): 637–44.

31. Rafi Letzter, "Scientists Are Furious after a Famous Psychologist Accused Her Peers of 'Methodological Terrorism,'" *Business Insider UK*, http://uk.businessinsider.com/susan-fiske-methodological-terrorism-2016-9?r=US&IR=T (accessed November 24, 2018).

32. Joseph F. Rychlak, "In Search and Proof of Human Beings, Not Machines," *Journal of Personality Assessment* 85 (2005): 239–56.

33. See, for example, Mikkel C. Vinding, Mads Jensen, and Morten Overgaard, "Distinct Electrophysiological Potentials for Intention in Action and Prior Intention for Action," *Cortex: A Journal Devoted to the Study of the Nervous System and Behavior* 50 (2014): 86–99; Also J. Miller and W. Schwartz, "Brain Signals Do Not Demonstrate Unconscious Decision Making: An Interpretation Based on Graded Conscious Awareness," *Consciousness and Cognition* 24 (2014): 12–21.

34. Roy F. Baumeister, "Constructing a Scientific Theory of Free Will," in *Moral Psychology*, vol 4: *Free Will and Moral Responsibility*, ed. Walter Sinnott-Armstrong, 235–55 (Cambridge, MA: MIT Press, 2014).

35. This precept, named after French philosopher Charles Renouvier, bears an obvious resemblance to Pascal's wager, which suggests that it is best to believe in God *just in case* since there are no eternal rewards for being correct about atheism.

36. Susan Hatters Friedman and Renée Sorrentino, "Postpartum Psychosis, Infanticide, and Insanity—Implications for Forensic Psychiatry," *Journal of the American Academy of Psychiatry and the Law* 40 (2012): 326–32.

37. Patricia Pearson, *When She Was Bad* (New York: Penguin, 1997).

38. S. Fernando Rodriguez, Theodore R. Curry, and Gang Lee, "Gender Differences in Criminal Sentencing: Do Effects Vary across Violent, Property, and Drug Offenses?" *Social Science Quarterly* 87 (2006): 318–39.

39. See Patrick T. Galligan, *Report on Certain Matters Related to Karla Homolka*, https://drive.google.com/file/d/0B3ORC8Ev2VnnaDg5LWVWVjJzUGM/view (accessed November 25, 2018).

40. Anne McGillivray, "'A Moral Vacuity in Her Which Is difficult if Not Impossible to Explain': Law, Psychiatry and the Remaking of Karla Homolka," *International Journal of the Legal Profession* 5 (1998): 255–88.

41. Pearson, *When She Was Bad*, 46. The discrepancy in the psychological evaluations also likely speaks to the unreliability of such evaluations and how they, too, can be the product of stereotypes and preconceptions.

42. "Homolka's Psychiatric Report Released," *Globe and Mail*, June 5, 2005, www.theglobeandmail.com/news/national/homolkas-psychiatric-report-released/article20422606/ (accessed November 25, 2018).

43. Particularly Pearson, *When She Was Bad*.

44. Tania Kohut, "Convicted Killer Karla Homolka Volunteers at Her Children's Montreal School: Reports," *Global News*, May 31, 2017, https://globalnews.ca/news/3491735/karla-homolka-school-montreal/ (accessed November 25, 2018).

45. Oeindrila Dube and S. P. Harish, *Queens*, NBER Working Paper No. 23337 (April 2017), www.nber.org/papers/w23337.pdf (accessed November 25, 2018).

46. Barnaby Rogerson, *The Last Crusades* (New York: Overlook, 2009).

47. The Turks would eventually win but not until 1669, long after Ibrahim was dead.

48. Jason Goodwin, *Lords of the Horizons* (New York: Henry Holt, 1998).

49. One of Ibrahim's concubines who survived his reign, Turhan Hatice Sultan, became a regent of the Ottoman Empire, one of the most powerful women

in its history. It was rumored she had her mother-in-law, Ibrahim's mother, Kösem Sultan, murdered as part of her ascent to power. Life was rough in the Ottoman Empire.

Chapter 4. Madness of the Monarch

1. I shared the video with a biologist colleague at Stetson University who surmised the other male may have been an older male who'd lost status. That might also explain the alpha male's particular hostility toward him.

2. Studies suggest that alpha males, in fact, have more stress than "betas"—high- but not top-ranked males. See Laurence Gesquiere, Niki Learn, M. Carolina Simao, Patrick O. Onyango, Susan C. Alberts, and Jeanne Altmann, "Life at the Top: Rank and Stress in Wild Male Baboons," *Science* 333 (2011): 357–60.

3. T. Nishida, "Alpha Status and Agonistic Alliance in Wild Chimpanzees (Pan Troglodytes Schweinfurthii)," *Primates* 24 (1983): 318–36. Also Nicholas E. Newton-Fisher, "Hierarchy and Social Status in Budongo Chimpanzees," *Primates* 45 (2004): 81–87.

4. Thomas Hobbes, *Leviathan*, 1651.

5. Grant McCall and Nancy Shields, "Examining the Evidence from Small-Scale Societies and Early Prehistory and Implications for Modern Theories of Aggression and Violence," *Aggression and Violent Behavior*, 13 (2008): 1–9.

6. Nicole Hess, Courtney Helfrecht, Edward Hagen, Aaron Sell, and Barry Hewlett, "Interpersonal Aggression among Aka Hunter-Gatherers of the Central African Republic: Assessing the Effects of Sex, Strength, and Anger," *Human Nature* 21 (2010): 330–54.

7. Ian Armit, "Violence and Society in the Deep Human Past," *British Journal of Criminology* 51 (2011): 499–517.

8. Steven Pinker, *The Better Angels of Our Nature: Why Violence Has Declined* (New York: Viking, 2011). Fear of crime is often characterized as more common among the elderly. Interestingly, research suggests this is not true. See Derek Chadee and Jason Ditton, "Are Older People Most Afraid of Crime? Revisiting Ferraro and LaGrange in Trinidad," *British Journal of Criminology* 43 (2003): 417–33.

9. This includes the slaughter of infants. Chimpanzees, like humans, can be horrible creatures. Jane Goodall, "Infant-Killing and Cannibalism in Free-Living Chimpanzees," *Folia Primatologica* 28 (1977): 259–82 and "Life and Death at Gombe," *National Geographic* 155 (1979): 595–621.

10. This does not make it right, of course, it only helps us to understand how this may have come to be.

11. Which of course led the Ottomans to the logical if brutal solution of fratricide as discussed in chapter 3.

12. Dio, *Roman History*, www.loebclassics.com/view/LCL083/1917/volume .xml.

13. Herodian, *History of the Roman Empire since the Death of Marcus Aurelius*.

14. Elagabalus also had himself circumcised, apparently publicly, which was not a thing among the Romans.

15. Whether the vestal virgin in question, Julia Aquilia Severa, had much say in any of this, or as to her ultimate fate, is left unclear. The penalty for breaking the vow of chastity for vestal virgins was typically execution.

16. Andrew Flores, Jody Herman, Gary Gates, and Taylor Brown, *How Many Adults Identify as Transgender in the United States?* (Los Angeles: Williams Institute, 2016). In this study, the number of transsexual individuals who didn't identify as one gender or the other (either definitively male or female) was so few it couldn't be reliably measured.

17. See for instance, C. Roselli, "Neurobiology of Gender Identity and Sexual Orientation," *Journal of Neuroendocrinology* 30 (2018): 1–8, or Dick Swaab and E. Fliers, "A Sexually Dimorphic Nucleus in the Human Brain," *Science* 228 (1985): 1112–15, among many others who clearly indicate a sexually dimorphic nucleus in the hypothalamus that appears to determine one's sense of maleness or femaleness. Even for a small number of individuals who don't identify as either male or female, this gender fluidity still probably results from this region of the brain. So have your boys play with dolls all you like, and it's not going to make one whit of difference to their gender identity (they're more likely to bend the doll over and make a gun out of it).

18. Dick Swaab and Alicia Garcia-Falgueras, "Sexual Differentiation of the Human Brain in Relation to Gender Identity and Sexual Orientation," *Functional Neurology* 24 (2009): 17–28.

19. Bonnie Auyeung, Simon Baron-Cohen, Emma Ashwin, Rebecca Knickmeyer, Kevin Taylor, Gerald Hackett, and Melissa Hines, "Fetal Testosterone Predicts Sexually Differentiated Childhood Behavior in Girls and in Boys," *Psychological Science* 20 (2009): 144–48. To be sure, parents often do treat biological boys and girls differently in anticipation of fairly predictable sex and gender differences that are biologically determined. However, such socialization behaviors appear to have little actual causal impact on gender identity. On the other hand, they can cause further dysphoria in those individuals whose gender identity do not match their biological sex. Unfortunately, in pursuit of the admirable goal of greater sensitivity and inclusivity for individuals whose gendered behaviors don't meet societal expectations, some advocates created a myth that gender identity is divorced from biological factors and can be shaped powerfully by socialization alone.

20. Milton Diamond, "Sexual Identity, Monozygotic Twins Reared in Discordant Sex Roles and a BBC Follow-Up," *Archives of Sexual Behavior* 11 (1982): 181–86.

21. Associated Press, "David Reimer, 38, Subject of John/Joan Case," *New York Times*, May 12, 2004, www.nytimes.com/2004/05/12/us/david-reimer -38-subject-of-the-john-joan-case.html (accessed December 7, 2018).

22. But we all know it's really a miniskirt. No judgment here.

23. Isabella's marriage to Ferdinand of Aragon united the kingdoms of Castile and Aragon, an uneasy union that still ripples with an independence movement by some in modern Aragon (Catalan) to the present day.

24. Whether Columbus might be called a madman himself is a matter of continual dispute. His reputation has waxed and waned depending on whether historians focus on his remarkable persistence and achievements or his stubbornness in thinking he'd achieved a route to India and the genocidal impact of his arrival on the natives of the region.

25. Barnaby Rogerson, *The Last Crusaders* (New York: Overlook Press, 2009).

26. Mary Erickson, "Rethinking Oedipus: An Evolutionary Perspective of Incest Avoidance," *American Journal of Psychiatry* 150 (1993): 411–16; Liqun Luo, "Is There a Sensitive Period in Human Incest Avoidance?" *Evolutionary Psychology* 9 (2011): 285–95.

27. I herein limit my discussion to consenting adult incestuous relationships. Nonconsenting incest, such that occurs in the context of child sexual abuse or sibling rape, naturally brings with it a whole host of other emotional, health, and legal issues.

28. Robin Bennett, Arno Mutulsky, Alan Bittles, Louanne Hudgins, Stefanie Uhrich, Debra Lochner Doyle, Kerry Silvey, C. Ronald Scott, Edith Cheng, Barbara McGillivray, Robert D. Steiner, Debra Olson, "Genetic Counseling and Screening of Consanguineous Couples and Their Offspring: Recommendations of the National Society of Genetic Counselors," *Journal of Genetic Counseling* 11 (2002): 97–119.

29. This was actively promoted, for instance, by Queen Victoria, who had relatives in many nations' royal families and, of course, had a love match with her first cousin Prince Albert. These familial ties did not stop the outbreak of World War I.

30. Who, unlike their Spanish cousins, would be cast from power only after World War I.

31. Marie Antoinette, a Habsburg I discuss in a future chapter, was said to have a touch of it, giving her a pouting lower lip.

32. As is the case with inherited diseases, not all Habsburgs had the Habsburg jaw. Females of the family seemed to be spared the worst consequences of this feature, though whether they were spared other elements of inbreeding is less certain.

33. Gonzalo Alvarez, Francisco Ceballos, and Celsa Quintiero, "The Role of Inbreeding in the Extinction of a European Royal Dynasty," *PLoS One 4* (2009): https://journals.plos.org/plosone/article?id=10.1371/journal.pone.0005174 (accessed December 9, 2018).

34. J. H. Elliot, *Imperial Spain 1469–1716* (New York: Penguin: 2002).

35. Alvarez, Ceballos, and Quintiero, "The Role of Inbreeding in the Extinction of a European Royal Dynasty."

36. Anne had somewhere around seventeen pregnancies, only five of which resulted in live births and only one child who survived infancy. He died at age eleven.

37. Technically this occurred in 1701, some years after James II's ouster, given that the last Protestant Stuarts failed to produce any heirs.

38. A slide rule might help to keep track.

39. And thus lost the opportunity to break up an absurdly long line of Georges.

40. His chief prime minister during the war, Lord North, tried to resign several times citing his own inability to manage the war, but George III declined his efforts.

41. Barbara Tuchman, *March of Folly* (New York: Random House, 1985).

42. Janice Hadlow, *A Royal Experiment: The Private Life of King George III* (New York: Henry Holt, 2014).

43. Hadlow, *A Royal Experiment.*

44. Francis Willis and his treatment of King George III is the focus of the famous play and movie *The Madness of King George*, although it's unlikely that Willis's treatment was as helpful as the film implies.

45. Technically, he was the prince of Wales while George III was still alive.

46. Hadlow, *A Royal Experiment.*

47. This symptom likely helped create a rubbish belief that porphyria might be related to vampire myths.

48. Ida Macalpine and Richard Hunter, "The 'Insanity' of King George III: A Classic Case of Porphyria," *British Medical Journal* 1 (1966): 65–71.

49. Timothy Peters and Allan Beveridge, "The Madness of King George III: A Psychiatric Re-Assessment," *History of Psychiatry* 21 (2010): 20–37.

50. Elementary schoolkids, by contrast, would find it cool.

51. In fairness, there is speculation regarding an earlier potential bout of illness in 1765, although few medical records survive and it is unclear whether mental health symptoms were involved.

52. See also Dean Keith Simonton, "Mad King George: The Impact of Personal and Political Stress on Mental and Physical Health," *Journal of Personality* 66 (1998): 443–66.

53. Timothy Cox, Nicola Jack, Simon Lofthouse, John Watling, Janice Haines, and Martin J Warren, "King George III and Porphyria: An Elemental Hypothesis and Investigation," *The Lancet* 366 (2005): 332–35.

54. Doses of arsenic, despite being well known as a poison, were sometimes mixed with other medicines purposefully or accidentally. Whoops.

55. Vassiliki Rentoumi, Timothy Peters, Jonathan Conlin, and Peter Garrard, "The Acute Mania of King George III: A Computational Linguistic Analysis," *PLoS ONE* 12 (2017), www.ncbi.nlm.nih.gov/pmc/articles/PMC5362044/ (accessed December 13, 2018).

56. John O'Farrell, *An Utterly Impartial History of Britain* (London: Transworld Publishers, 2007).

57. Which was just as well for the United Kingdom, which had to expend resources defending the German principality with which it had little in common other than the shared monarch.

Chapter 5. When God Speaks: Madness and Faith

1. Karen McComb, Lucy Baker, and Cynthia Moss, "African Elephants Show High Levels of Interest in the Skulls and Ivory of Their Own Species," *Biology Letters* 2 (2006): 26–28. They do not, however, build graveyards or conduct seances. Exactly what the elephants might be thinking or feeling remains unknown as elephants rarely consent to participate in survey research.

2. Ian Tattersall, "Once We Were Not Alone," *Scientific American*, January 2000 www.ucd.ie/artspgs/langevo/earlyhominids.pdf (accessed December 15, 2018).

3. Meaning that there is no evidentiary basis upon which to disprove such beliefs. The question of whether some form of afterlife awaits us is simply beyond the reach of science to inform us. An experiment could be developed, although the participants, quite inconveniently, would be unable to report back. This of course means that atheists are just as guilty as religious individuals in asserting their beliefs as fact when they cannot be answered by science.

4. John A. Terrizzi, "Is Religion an Evolutionarily Evoked Disease-Avoidance Strategy?" *Religion, Brain & Behavior* 7 (2017): 328–30.

5. Ara Norenzayan, Azim F. Shariff, Will M. Gervais, Aiyana K. Willard, Rita A. McNamara, Edward Slingerland, and Joseph Henrich, "The Cultural Evolution of Prosocial Religions," *Behavioral and Brain Sciences* 39 (December 2014).

6. Ara Norenzayan and Azim F. Shariff, "The Origin and Evolution of Religious Prosociality," *Science* 322 (2008): 58–62.

7. Lee A. Kirkpatrick, "Toward an Evolutionary Psychology of Religion and Personality," *Journal of Personality* 67 (1999): 921–52.

8. Dominic Johnson and Jesse Bering, "Hand of God, Mind of Man: Punishment and Cognition in the Evolution of Cooperation," *Evolutionary Psychology* 4 (2006): 219–33.

9. Andrea M. Yetzer, Tom Pyszczynski, and Jeff Greenberg, "A Stairway to Heaven: A Terror Management Theory Perspective on Morality," in *Atlas of Moral Psychology*, ed. Kurt Gray and Jesse Graham, 241–51 (New York: Guilford Press, 2018).

10. Hardly a unique human trait. The natural world is vicious, cruel, and brutal even within species.

11. Typically 85 percent of minimum body weight is used as a guideline, though the most recent *DSM-5* removed the specific number. AN should not be mistaken for other forms of anorexia brought on by medical conditions such as chemotherapy or stomach cancer.

12. Christopher J. Ferguson, "The Devil Wears Stata: Thin-Ideal Media's Minimal Contribution to Our Understanding of Body Dissatisfaction and Eating Disorders," *Archives of Scientific Psychology* 6 (2018): 70–79.

13. Michael B. King and Gillian Mezey, "Eating Behaviour of Male Racing Jockeys," *Psychological Medicine* 17 (1987): 249–53.

14. Sorry jockeys!

15. Fernando Espi Forcen and Carlos Espi Forcen, "The Practice of Holy Fasting in the Late Middle Ages: A Psychiatric Approach," *Journal of Nervous and Mental Disease* 203 (2015): 650–53.

16. Catherine is reported to have carried on quite a bit, shaving her head, wearing a veil, and enduring the menial labor required of her in punishment for disobeying her parents. Kids today with their Christ and their hair!

17. Isabella Sukkar, Madeleine Gagan, and Warren Kealy-Bateman, "The 14th Century Religious Women Margery Kempe and Catherine of Siena Can Still Teach Us Lessons about Eating Disorders Today," *Journal of Eating Disorders* 5 (July 2017), https://jeatdisord.biomedcentral.com/articles/10.1186/s40337-017-0151-5 (accessed December 18, 2018).

18. R. Bianucci, P. Charlier, P. Evans, and O. Appenzeller, "Temporal Lobe Epilepsy and Anorexia Nervosa in St. Catherine of Siena (1347–1380)," *Journal of the Neurological Sciences* 379 (2017): 122–23.

19. Bianucci, Charlier, Evans, and Appenzeller, "Temporal Lobe Epilepsy and Anorexia Nervosa in St. Catherine of Siena."

20. Sukkar, Gagan, and Kealy-Bateman, "The 14th Century Religious Women."

21. Francesco M. Galassi, Nicole Bender, Michael E. Habicht, Emanuele Armocida, Fabrizio Toscano, David A. Menassa, and Matteo Cerri. "St. Catherine of Siena (1347–1380 AD): One of the Earliest Historic Cases of Altered Gustatory Perception in Anorexia Mirabilis," *Neurological Sciences* (forthcoming).

22. Albert Rothenberg, "Eating Disorder as a Modern Obsessive-Compulsive Syndrome," *Psychiatry: Interpersonal and Biological Processes* 49 (1986): 45–53. See also Joy D. Humphreys, James R. Clopton, and Darcy A. Reich, "Disordered Eating Behavior and Obsessive Compulsive Symptoms in College Students: Cognitive and Affective Similarities," *Eating Disorders: The Journal of Treatment & Prevention* 15 (2007): 247–59.

23. Felicity Ng, "The Interface between Religion and Psychosis," *Australasian Psychiatry* 15 (2007): 62–66.

24. Dominiek D. Coates, "'Cult Commitment' from the Perspective of Former Members: Direct Rewards of Membership versus Dependency Inducing Practices," *Deviant Behavior* 33 (2012): 168–84.

25. Wendy Gale Robinson, "Heaven's Gate: The End?" *Journal of Computer-Mediated Communication* 3 (1997), https://academic.oup.com/jcmc/article/3/3/JCMC334/4584381 (accessed December 21, 2018). The cult was also known for its androgynous appearance, including castration for many of the men (zounds!) and identical clothing.

26. His given name was Vernon Howell; he renamed himself David Koresh to assume a name with Biblical reference.

27. William L. Pitts, "Davidians and Branch Davidians," *Handbook of Texas Online*, Texas State Historical Association, 2010, https://tshaonline.org/handbook/online/articles/ird01 (accessed December 22, 2018).

28. Robert R. Agne, "Reframing Practices in Moral Conflict: Interaction Problems in the Negotiation Standoff at Waco," *Discourse & Society* 18 (2007): 549–78.

29. U.S. Department of Justice, *Report to the Deputy Attorney General on the Events at Waco, Texas* (Washington, DC: U.S. Department of Justice, 1993), www.justice.gov/archives/publications/waco/report-deputy-attorney-general-events-waco-texas (accessed December 22, 2018).

30. Simultaneously, the Texas Rangers began investigating whether there had been a leak of the ATF's raid to the Branch Davidians.

31. Committee on Government Reform, *The Tragedy at Waco: New Evidence Examined* (Washington, DC: Government Printing Office, 2000), www.congress.gov/106/crpt/hrpt1037/CRPT-106hrpt1037.pdf (accessed December 22, 2018).

32. Robert R. Agne, "Reframing Practices in Moral Conflict: Interaction Problems in the Negotiation Standoff at Waco," *Discourse & Society* 18 (2007): 549–78.

33. Dick Reavis, *Ashes of Waco: An Investigation* (Syracuse, NY: Syracuse University Press, 1998).

34. A. Adityanjee, "Jauhar: Mass Suicide by Self-Immolation in Waco, Texas," *Journal of Nervous and Mental Disease* 182 (1994): 727–28.

35. David Holley, "Japanese Guru: A Youthful Bully's Quest for Power," *Los Angeles Times*, March 27, 1995, http://articles.latimes.com/1995-03-27/news/mn-47649_1_japanese-guru (accessed December 23, 2018).

36. Alexander E. Raevskiy, "Psychological Aspects of the Aum Shinrikyo Affair," *Psychology in Russia: State of the Art* 7 (2014): 34–39.

37. Robert Jay Lifton, "Aum Shinrikyo: The Threshold Crossed," *Journal of Aggression, Maltreatment & Trauma* 9 (2004): 57–66.

38. Lifton, "Aum Shinrikyo."

39. Ian Reader, "Scholarship, Aum Shinrikyô, and Academic Integrity," *Nova Religio* 3 (2000): 368–82.

40. William Rosenau, "Aum Shinrikyo's Biological Weapons Program: Why Did It Fail?" *Studies in Conflict & Terrorism* 24 (2001): 289–301.

41. Lifton, "Aum Shinrikyo."

42. Benjamin Beit-Hallahmi, "Apocalyptic Dreams and Religious Ideologies: Losing and Saving Self and World," *Psychoanalytic Review* 90 (2003): 403–39.

43. Kyle B. Olson, "Aum Shinrikyo: Once and Future Threat?" *Emerging Infectuous Diseases* 4 (1999): 513–16, www.ncbi.nlm.nih.gov/pmc/articles/PMC2627754/pdf/10458955.pdf (accessed December 24, 2018).

44. Olson, "Aum Shinrikyo."

45. "Tokyo Sarin Attack: Aum Shinrikyo Cult Leaders Executed," BBC News, July 6, 2018, www.bbc.com/news/world-asia-43395483 (accessed December 24, 2018).

46. I use this term to indicate those brought up in a vaguely Christian majority culture but who may exhibit varying degrees of actual faith ranging from fundamentalism to atheism.

47. U.S. Government Accountability Office, *Countering Violent Extremism* (Washington, DC: United States Government Accountability Office, 2017), www.gao.gov/assets/690/683984.pdf (accessed December 26, 2018).

48. Adam Lankford, "A Comparative Analysis of Suicide Terrorists and Rampage, Workplace, and School Shooters in the United States from 1990 to 2010," *Homicide Studies: An Interdisciplinary & International Journal* 17 (2013): 255–74.

49. Inspectors General of the Intelligence Community, Central Intelligence Agency, Department of Justice, and Department of Homeland Security,

Unclassified Summary of Information Handling and Sharing Prior to the April 15, 2013 Boston Marathon Bombings (Washington, DC: Office of Inspectors General, 2014), https://oig.justice.gov/reports/2014/s1404.pdf (accessed December 26, 2018).

50. Phillip Martin, "Is the Waltham Triple Murder Investigation at a Dead End?" WGBH, April 12, 2018, www.wgbh.org/news/2018/04/12/news/waltham-triple-murder-investigation-dead-end (accessed December 26, 2018).

51. Massachusetts Emergency Management Agency, *After Action Report for the Response to the 2013 Boston Marathon Bombings*, December 2014, www.mass.gov/files/documents/2016/09/uz/after-action-report-for-the-response-to-the-2013-boston-marathon-bombings.pdf (accessed December 26, 2018).

52. Ann O'Neill, "Boston Marathon Bomber Dzhokhar Tsarnaev Sentenced to Death," CNN, May 15, 2015, www.cnn.com/2015/05/15/us/boston-bombing-tsarnaev-sentence/index.html (accessed December 26, 2018).

53. O'Neill, "Boston Marathon Bomber Dzhokhar Tsarnaev Sentenced to Death."

54. Saeed Ahmed, "Who Were Rizwan Farook and Tashfeen Malik?" CNN, December 3, 2015, www.cnn.com/2015/12/03/us/syed-farook-tashfeen-malik-mass-shooting-profile/index.html (accessed December 30, 2018).

Chapter 6. Madness on the Commune

1. Trying to describe Communism succinctly in a few sentences is, of course, a fraught undertaking. Communism is a complex political philosophy with many threads, though those seeking to understand it thoroughly might start by reading Marx and Engels *Communist Manifesto*. It is not long and conveniently available online for budding revolutionaries everywhere. Karl Marx and Freidrich Engels, *Communist Manifesto*, (1948), www.slp.org/pdf/marx/comm_man.pdf (accessed January 1, 2019).

2. The case of Nicholas and Alexandra were a close call for inclusion in this book, given their personal neuroses and the disasters caused by the same. Nicholas generally comes across history as a decent husband and father but a lousy tsar. Mainly because it just kinda wasn't his thing. He might have been a perfectly reasonable accountant or dentist. But tsar? No. He and Alexandra genuinely loved one another, but their son was born with hemophilia, a painful, fatal, and untreatable condition at the time. Her son's illness created significant neuroses in Alexandra, eventually involving her with the notorious charlatan Rasputin. Certainly, the chaos Alexandra and Rasputin created in the government of St. Petersburg, the capital, can't be blamed entirely for the fall of the tsarist govern-

ment, but it certainly didn't help. Alexandra's neuroses and how they contributed to revolution in Russia certainly are interesting to consider.

3. Robert K. Massie, *The Romanovs: The Final Chapter* (New York: Random House, 2012).

4. Russia's enemy Germany helped, bless them.

5. Stalin was a nickname he assumed in later life meaning "man of steel." This was, of course, pre-Superman. One also notes rather shameless self-aggrandizement in choosing such a nickname.

6. The date is given as either 1878 or 1879.

7. Alan Bullock, *Hitler and Stalin* (New York: Alfred A. Knopf, 1992).

8. One scholar uses the term "excrement-soaked sausages" to describe swaddled infant babies of the time. See Stephanie Shakhireva, "Swaddled Nation: Modern Mother Russia and a Psychohistorical Reassessment of Stalin." *Journal of Psychohistory* 35 (2007): 34–60.

9. Shakhireva, "Swaddled Nation."

10. Stephen Kontin, *Stalin: Paradoxes of Power, 1878–1928* (New York: Penguin, 2015).

11. At this juncture I will stop feeding exotic-sounding Russian names into this particular meat grinder. Suffice to say, by the time World War II broke out, most of the high-ranking men who had been Stalin's comrades during Lenin's time and erstwhile allies in the years after Lenin's death were dead on Stalin's orders.

12. The distinction between what is meant by "peasant" or "serf" is, admittedly, unsatisfyingly vague.

13. This number roughly doubles the number of Jews estimated to have died during the Nazi Holocaust.

14. Alan Bullock, *Hitler and Stalin*.

15. Perhaps the most famous was Konstantin Rokossovsky, who went on to become one of the most celebrated Soviet commanders in the war against Germany after his release from prison.

16. A precursor to the KGB.

17. Michael Ellman, "Soviet Repression Statistics: Some Comments," *Europe-Asia Studies* 54 (2002): 1151–72.

18. They had not yet signed the Tripartite Pact.

19. Bullock, *Hitler and Stalin*.

20. Constantine Pleshakov, *Stalin's Folly: The Tragic First Ten Days of WWII on the Eastern Front* (New York: Houghton Mifflin, 2005).

21. Viktor Suvorov, *The Chief Culprit: Stalin's Grand Design to Start World War II* (Annapolis, MD: Naval Institute Press, 2013).

22. David Glantz, *Stumbling Colossus* (Lawrence: University Press of Kansas, 1998).

23. Pleshakov, *Stalin's Folly*.

24. An excellent summary of the evidence on all sides of this debate is by Ia. S. Drabkin, "'Hitler's War' or 'Stalin's War'?" *Journal of Russian and East European Psychology* 40 (2002): 5–30.

25. Jonathan Fenby, *Alliance: The Inside Story of How Roosevelt, Stalin and Churchill Won One War and Began Another* (New York: Simon & Schuster, 2008).

26. Sting's "Russians" is my personal favorite.

27. Vtadimir Hachinski, "Stalin's Last Years: Delusions or Dementia?" *European Journal of Neurology* 6 (1999): 129–32.

28. Hachinski, "Stalin's Last Years."

29. Hachinski, "Stalin's Last Years."

30. See, for example, Lee Feigon, *Mao: A Reinterpretation* (Chicago: Ivan R. Dee, 2002), for a much more positive interpretation of Mao than you're about to get here.

31. A former Red Guard, or militant pro-Mao youth, whose family was ultimately hounded by the communist regime after rejecting its violence.

32. Jung Chang and Jon Halliday, *Mao: The Unknown Story* (New York: Alfred A. Knopf, 2005).

33. Gregor Benton and Lin Chun, *Was Mao Really a Monster? The Academic Response to Chang and Halliday's "Mao: The Unknown Story"* (Abingdon, UK: Routledge, 2010).

34. Delia Devin, "Dark Tales of Mao the Merciless," in *Was Mao Really a Monster? The Academic Response to Chang and Halliday's "Mao: The Unknown Story,"* ed. Gregor Benton and Lin Chun, 15–20 (Abingdon, UK: Routledge, 2010). The editors of the book, in their introduction, appear to be among those who see famine deaths under Mao as accidental rather than due to purposeful or callous indifference, likening it to other avoidable famines. This highlights the confusion about whether Mao's actions should be compared to, say, Stalin's callous and purposeful initiation of the starvation of Ukrainians in the 1930s, or perhaps the bureaucratic incompetence and indifference with which the United Kingdom treated the Irish during the potato famines of the 1800s, which were also avoidable. To the degree any of these famines persisted for years without correction in efforts or concern for the dying and dead, this feels like splitting hairs to me. To say the United Kingdom is also responsible for atrocities against others (which is true) does little to excuse Mao's culpability in the deaths of his own citizens. This is classic "whataboutism."

35. And this, curiously, does seem to be more consistent for the men than the women.

36. Alexander V. Pantsov and Steven L. Levine, *Mao: The Real Story* (New York: Simon and Schuster, 2013).

37. The last Qing emperor, the boy-emperor Pu Yi, has a fascinating story of his own, subject of the film *The Last Emperor*. Pu Yi, at heart an ordinary man shielded from normal development in his early life, became the puppet emperor of the Japanese in Manchuria during World War II. That obviously didn't work out for him long term, but after the war he was rehabilitated by the Chinese communists as a kind of propaganda tool. Somewhat surprisingly, for someone ping-ponged between China, Japan, and Russia, he died of natural causes in 1967.

38. Edgar Snow, *Red Star over China* (New York: Grove Press, 1938).

39. Chang and Halliday, *Mao: The Unknown Story*.

40. Barbara W. Tuchman, *Stilwell and the American Experience in China: 1911–1945* (New York: Random House, 2017).

41. Andrew Jacobs, "China Is Wordless on Traumas of Communists' Rise," *New York Times*, October 1, 2009, www.nytimes.com/2009/10/02/world/asia/02anniversary.html (accessed January 13, 2019).

42. Mao Yushi, "Lessons from China's Great Famine," *CATO Journal* 34 (2014): 483–90.

43. Frank Dikötter, *Mao's Great Famine: The History of China's Most Devastating Catastrophe, 1958–62* (New York: Walker, 2010).

44. David Lester, "Suicide and the Chinese Cultural Revolution," *Archives of Suicide Research* 9 (2005): 99–104.

45. Chang and Halliday, *Mao: The Unknown Story*.

46. Stephen Uhalley Jr. and Jin Qiu, "The Lin Biao Incident: More Than Twenty Years Later," *Pacific Affairs* 66 (1993): 386–98.

47. Nicholas D. Kristof, "Suicide of Jiang Qing, Mao's Widow, Is Reported," *New York Times*, June 5, 1991, www.nytimes.com/1991/06/05/obituaries/suicide-of-jiang-qing-mao-s-widow-is-reported.html (accessed January 14, 2019).

48. See Derek Watkins, "What China Has Been Building in the South China Sea," *New York Times*, October 27, 2015, www.nytimes.com/interactive/2015/07/30/world/asia/what-china-has-been-building-in-the-south-china-sea.html (accessed January 14, 2019). The islands are being used by China to dominate control of waterways in this area, which it claims despite counterclaims by neighboring countries such as Vietnam and the Philippines. If they make a tropical island for me, maybe I'll write more sympathetic biographies of Mao in the future.

49. Steve Jackson, "Papers Reveal Mao's View of Women," BBC News, February 13, 2008, http://news.bbc.co.uk/2/hi/asia-pacific/7243500.stm (accessed January 14, 2019).

50. Zing-yang Kuo and Yut-hang Lam, "Chinese Religious Behavior and the Deification of Mao Tse-Tung," *The Psychological Record* 18 (1968): 455–68.

51. Who, being an overachiever, murdered nearly one-quarter to one-third of the population of his country.

52. A vacation? Sure. Although after this biography of Mao, we'll see if I can get a visa.

53. Herbert E. Krugman, "The Role of Hostility in the Appeal of Communism in the United States," *Psychiatry: Journal for the Study of Interpersonal Processes* 16 (1953): 253–61. Being from the 1950s, the paper wraps this up in some psychoanalytic mumbo jumbo, so take it for what it's worth.

54. George Windholz, "Karl Marx's Paranoid Ideation in the Communist Manifesto," *Imagination, Cognition and Personality* 20 (2000): 257–73.

55. H. J. Eysenck and Thelma T. Coulter, "The Personality and Attitudes of Working-Class British Communists and Fascists," *Journal of Social Psychology* 87 (1972): 59–73.

Chapter 7. Madness among the 1 Percent

1. I here include the Byzantine Empire as the final third of Rome's history even though the city of Rome itself, for most of Byzantium's existence, was not part of that empire. However, the Byzantine Empire was simply the surviving half of the Roman Empire after the western half fell in the fifth century ACE.

2. It is interesting that some of the most famous names from the Roman Republic's history were, in fact, enemies of the republic. Pyrrhus would be another example, the fellow from whom we get the term "Pyrrhic victory," meaning a victory so costly that it likely results in the loss of the larger war.

3. Usually the go-to rationalization for insidious moral agendas.

4. In case you think I am being polemic, this is more or less what happened to Socrates. Granted, it probably didn't happen a lot.

5. Livy, *The History of Rome*, http://mcadams.posc.mu.edu/txt/ah/Livy/.

6. Anthony Everitt, *The Rise of Rome* (New York: Random House, 2013).

7. Everitt, *The Rise of Rome*.

8. Socialism comes to Rome!

9. As the story goes, during one confrontation Tiberius pointed toward his head, a traditional signal that he was in trouble, but the Senate, somewhat nonsensically, interpreted this as his seeking a crown.

10. Plutarch, *Lives*, https://oll.libertyfund.org/pages/plutarch-s-parallel-lives.

11. Plutarch, *Lives*.

12. Plutarch, *Lives*.

13. Suetonius, *The Lives of the Twelve Caesars*, www.perseus.tufts.edu/hopper/text?doc=Perseus:text:1999.02.0132.

14. Kit Morrell, "Cato and the Courts in 54 B.C.," *Classical Quarterly* 64 (2014): 669–81.

15. The French sure did like their Louises.

16. Antonia Fraser, *Marie Antoinette: The Journey* (New York: Anchor Books, 2001).

17. Evelyn Farr, *I Love You Madly: Marie-Antoinette and Count Fersen: The Secret Letters* (London: Peter Owen, 2016).

18. Nancy Barker, "Let Them Eat Cake: The Mythical Marie Antoinette and the French Revolution," *The Historian* 55 (1993): 709–24.

19. From whom, indeed, we get the term "mesmerize."

20. Daniel Ricciuto, "Anton Mesmer and Mesmerization: Past and Present," *Historical Review* 83 (2005): 135–37.

21. Ryan Fogg and Stephen A. Boorjian, "The Sexual Dysfunction of Louis XVI: A Consequence of International Politics, Anatomy, or Naïveté?" *BJU International* 106 (2010): 457–59.

22. Evelyne Lever, *Marie Antoinette: The Last Queen of France* (New York: St. Martin's Griffon, 2000).

23. For this look at Steve Jobs, except where otherwise noted, I relied on two main biographies. These included the official biography of Walter Isaacson, *Steve Jobs* (New York: Simon and Schuster, 2011). The other was the crisp but lively narrative by Karen Blumenthal, *Steve Jobs: The Man Who Thought Different* (New York: Feiwel and Friends, 2012). The latter is good for those who want a quick read or for younger readers, whereas the Isaacson biography is a far more in-depth tome.

24. See Katy Waldman, "'Small Fry,' Reviewed: Lisa Brennan-Jobs's Mesmerizing, Discomfiting Memoir," *New Yorker*, September 2018, www.newyorker .com/books/page-turner/small-fry-reviewed-lisa-brennan-jobss-mesmerizing -discomfiting-memoir (accessed February 2, 2019). Jordan Valinsky, "Laurene Powell Jobs Pushes Back on her Stepdaughter's Memoir," CNN, August 28, 2018, https://money.cnn.com/2018/08/28/technology/laurene-powell-jobs -statement/index.html (accessed February 2, 2019).

25. Jodi Kantor and David Streitfeld, "Inside Amazon: Wrestling Big Ideas in a Bruising Workplace," *New York Times*, August 16, 2015, www.nytimes .com/2015/08/16/technology/inside-amazon-wrestling-big-ideas-in-a-bruising -workplace.html?_r=0 (accessed February 2, 2019).

26. Carolyn Johnson, "Elizabeth Holmes, Founder of Blood-Testing Company Theranos, Indicted on Wire Fraud Charges," *Washington Post*, June 15, 2018, www.washingtonpost.com/business/economy/elizabeth-holmes-founder -of-blood-testing-company-theranos-indicted-on-wire-fraud-federal-authorities

-announce/2018/06/15/8779f538-70df-11e8-bd50-b80389a4e569_story.html?utm_term=.d49a72ece5bf (accessed February 2, 2019).

27. Jim Ruttenberg, "A Long-Delayed Reckoning of the Cost of Silence on Abuse," *New York Times*, October 22, 2017, www.nytimes.com/2017/10/22/business/media/a-long-delayed-reckoning-of-the-cost-of-silence-on-abuse.html (accessed February 3, 2019).

28. Ronan Farrow, "From Aggressive Overtures to Sexual Assault: Harvey Weinstein's Accusers Tell Their Stories," *New Yorker*, October 10, 2017, www.newyorker.com/news/news-desk/from-aggressive-overtures-to-sexual-assault-harvey-weinsteins-accusers-tell-their-stories (accessed February 3, 2019).

29. Graham Bowley and Joe Coscarelli, "Bill Cosby, once a Model of Fatherhood, Sentenced to Prison," *New York Times*, September 25, 2018, www.nytimes.com/2018/09/25/arts/television/bill-cosby-sentencing.html (accessed February 3, 2019).

30. Stephanie Pappas, "Bill Cosby Deposition: What Is Somnophilia?" LiveScience, www.livescience.com/51562-what-is-somnophilia.html (accessed February 3, 2019).

31. Christopher J. Ferguson and D. Cricket Meehan, "An Analysis of Females Convicted of Sex Crimes in the State of Florida," *Journal of Child Sexual Abuse: Research, Treatment, & Program Innovations for Victims, Survivors, & Offenders* 14 (2005): 75–89.

32. Randy Thornhill and Craig T. Palmer, *A Natural History of Rape: Biological Bases of Sexual Coercion* (Cambridge, MA: MIT Press, 2000).

33. Richard Prum, *The Evolution of Beauty: How Darwin's Forgotten Theory of Mate Choice Shapes the Animal World—and Us* (New York: Doubleday, 2017).

34. Martin Gottschalk and Lee Ellis, "Evolutionary and Genetic Explanations of Violent Crime," in *Violent Crime: Clinical and Social Implications*, ed. Christopher J. Ferguson, 57–74 (Thousand Oaks, CA: Sage, 2010).

35. Cathy Young, "Feminists Treat Men Badly: It's Bad for Feminism," *Washington Post*, June 30, 2016, www.washingtonpost.com/posteverything/wp/2016/06/30/feminists-treat-men-badly-its-bad-for-feminism/?utm_term=.4e730c10da1e 2/3/19; Leslie Knight, "Enough with the Male-Bashing," *Forbes*, April 26, 2011, www.forbes.com/2011/04/26/enough-with-the-male-bashing.html#58b005ed6e5c (accessed February 3, 2019).

36. Maria Puente, "Asia Argento Shock: Could #MeToo Be Damaged by Statutory Rape Allegation against Her?" *USA Today*, August 20, 2018, www.usatoday.com/story/life/people/2018/08/20/metoo-damaged-rape-allegation-against-leader-asia-argento/1042473002/ (accessed February 7, 2019).

37. Grace Panetta, "Sen. Dianne Feinstein Denies Withholding Christine Blasey Ford's Allegations against Brett Kavanaugh for Political Reasons,"

Business Insider, September 2018, www.businessinsider.com/dianne-feinstein -refutes-accusations-she-withheld-ford-allegations-political-ploy-2018-9 (accessed February 6, 2019).

38. Christal Hayes, "'I Was Angry and I Sent It': Another Kavanaugh Accuser Referred to FBI after Recanting," *USA Today*, November 2, 2018, www.usatoday .com/story/news/politics/2018/11/02/brett-kavanaugh-accuser-referred-fbi-doj -investigation/1863210002/ (accessed February 8, 2018).

39. Perhaps the most famous of these in recent years was the Duke lacrosse rape case from 2006. In this case three white students were accused of rape by an African American student at another university who also worked as a stripper. Despite inconsistencies in her reports, prosecutors moved forward with the case and many academics signed a letter presuming the guilt of the accused. Eventually, the charges were dropped and the lacrosse players exonerated. The prosecutor in the case was disbarred for misconduct. The accuser in this case was convicted of murdering a boyfriend several years later.

40. Greg Hampikian, Emily West, and Olga Askelrod, "The Genetics of Innocence: Analysis of 194 U.S. DNA Exonerations," *Annual Review of Genomics and Human Genetics* 12 (2011): 97–120.

41. Lara Bazelon and Jennifer Thompson, "Christine Blasey Ford's Memory of Her Assault Isn't a Case of Mistaken Identity," *Slate*, October 2018, https:// slate.com/news-and-politics/2018/10/brett-kavanaugh-christine-blasey-ford -mistaken-identity.html (accessed February 9, 2019).

42. Elizabeth Loftus, "Memory Faults and Fixes," *Issues in Science and Technology* 18 (2002): 41–50.

Chapter 8. When the Mind Goes: Dementia among the Ruling Class

1. Louisa Lim, "Who Murdered China's Emperor 100 Years Ago?" NPR, November 2008, www.npr.org/templates/story/story.php?storyId=96993694 (accessed February 13, 2019).

2. Seriously. Swallow your embarrassment and get your penicillin shot.

3. Ruth A. Sibbett, Tom C. Russ, Alison Pattie, John M. Starr, and Ian J. Deary, "Does Incipient Dementia Explain Normal Cognitive Decline Determinants? Lothian Birth Cohort 1921," *Psychology and Aging* 33 (2018): 674–84.

4. I unfortunately can't remember who said it but remember reading it some years ago. Sadly, this particular quote will have to go uncredited.

5. Although the following study also includes the case of a dwarf circus clown who had been injured multiple times as part of a "dwarf throwing" routine in

which he was repeatedly knocked unconscious. And you think you've got a tough job. Ann McKee, Robert Cantu, Christopher Nowinkski, E. Tessa Hedley-Whyte, Brandon E. Gavett, Andrew E. Budson, Veronica E. Santini, Hyo-Soon Lee, Caroline A. Kubilus, and Robert A. Stern, "Chronic Traumatic Encephalopathy in Athletes: Progressive Tauopathy Following Repetitive Head Injury," *Journal of Neuropathology and Experimental Neurology* 68 (2009): 709–35.

6. Dietrich Blumer, "The Illness of Vincent van Gogh," *American Journal of Psychiatry* 159 (2002): 519–26.

7. Dirk Lachenmeier, David Nathan-Maister, Theodore Breaux, Eva-Maria Sohnius, Kerstin Schoeberl, Thomas Kuballa, "Chemical Composition of Vintage Preban Absinthe with Special Reference to Thujone, Fenchone, Pinocamphone, Methanol, Copper, and Antimony Concentrations," *Journal of Agriculture and Food Chemistry* 56 (2008): 3073–81.

8. Presumably, supply and demand play a role in this. The death of an artist necessarily limits supply, increasing the value of individual pieces of art. Granted, this is no panacea for the unappreciated scribbler. Plenty of painters go to their graves with their works effectively tossed into the casket with them.

9. Although alcohol consumption can directly cause some loss of brain tissue, most of the damage comes from thiamine deficiency brought on by chronic alcohol consumption.

10. Germany tried to convince Mexico to launch an invasion of the southern United States, so fair enough.

11. M. Dennis, "Looking Backward: Woodrow Wilson, the New South, and the Question of Race," *American Nineteenth Century History* 3 (2002): 77–104.

12. H. W. Brands, *Woodrow Wilson* (New York: Henry Holt, 2003).

13. A decent enough fellow who had the misfortune of being sandwiched between Teddy Roosevelt and Woodrow Wilson, such that no one remembers him.

14. Though it must be said that in those days, Democrats weren't necessarily liberals as is often assumed today.

15. And thank you cable and internet television for rescuing us.

16. Technically all his-es as of this writing, but the 2020 election season looms with a bevy of female candidates.

17. A. Scott Berg, *Wilson* (New York: G. P. Putman's Sons, 2013).

18. I'm obvious summarizing a lot of complex history rather quickly here. For more reading, I'd recommend Barbara Tuchman, *The Guns of August* (New York: Random House, 1994) and Robert K. Massie, *Dreadnought* (New York: Random House, 1991).

19. Matthew White, *Atrocities: The 100 Deadliest Episodes in Human History* (New York: W. W. Norton, 2012).

20. This was actually one source of tension that led to the war. Ironically, the Germans were shy about testing out their new fleet, largely keeping it mothballed during the war. The one time they let it ride out to battle during the Battle of Jutland in 1916, the German fleet arguably performed better than the British. The Germans probably won the battle on points (more enemy ships sunk) but got skittish and returned their ships to port, where they remained for the rest of the war. This made the battle a British strategic victory despite their higher losses.

21. The Irish would rebel against the British in 1916 during the Easter Rising. Though militarily unsuccessful, it led to support for Irish independence both in Ireland and the United Kingdom.

22. Even less realistically, Germany fantasized that Japan might join in, too. It didn't.

23. Before the war, Italy had been allied with the Central Powers but stayed out of the initial conflicts and then switched sides in 1915.

24. Brands, *Woodrow Wilson*.

25. He actually considered it anyway, despite his stroke.

26. Lou Cannon, *President Reagan: The Role of a Lifetime* (New York: Public Affairs, 2000).

27. Robert E. Gilbert, "Ronald Reagan's Presidency: The Impact of an Alcoholic Parent," *Political Psychology* 29 (2008): 737–65.

28. Patti Davis, *The Way I See It* (New York: Putnam, 1992).

29. Not to make light of the incident, but the joke is rather on Hinkley, since Foster later acknowledged being gay.

30. 100th Congress, *Senate Report #216: Iran Contra Investigation Report*, 1987, https://archive.org/stream/reportofcongress87unit#page/n7/mode/2up (accessed February 24, 2019).

31. Seymour M. Hersh, "The Iran-Contra Committees: Did They Protect Reagan?" *New York Times*, April 29, 1990, www.nytimes.com/1990/04/29/mag azine/the-iran-contra-committees-did-they-protect-reagan.html?pagewanted= all&src=pm (accessed February 24, 2019).

32. L. Backman, S. Jones, A. Berger, E. Laukka, and B. Small, "Multiple Cognitive Deficits during the Transition to Alzheimer's Disease," *Journal of Internal Medicine* 256 (2004): 195–204.

33. Craig Shirley, *Last Act: The Final Years and Emerging Legacy of Ronald Reagan* (Nashville, TN: Nelson Books, 2015).

34. Lawrence K. Altman, "A Recollection of Early Questions about Reagan's Health," *New York Times*, June 15, 2004, www.nytimes.com/2004/06/15/health/the-doctor-s-world-a-recollection-of-early-questions-about-reagan-s-health.html (accessed February 24, 2019).

35. Alex Spillius, "Ronald Reagan Had Alzheimer's 'While in White House' His Son Claims," *Telegraph*, www.telegraph.co.uk/news/worldnews/us -politics/8262924/Ronald-Reagan-had-Alzheimers-while-in-White-House-his -son-claims.html (accessed February 25, 2019).

36. Visar Berisha, Shuai Wang, Amy LaCross, and Julie Liss, "Tracking Discourse Complexity Preceding Alzheimer's Disease Diagnosis: A Case Study Comparing the Press Conferences of Presidents Ronald Reagan and George Herbert Walker Bush," *Journal of Alzheimer's Disease* 45 (2015): 959–63.

37. Francois Boller and Margaret Forbes, "History of Dementia and Dementia in History: An Overview," *Journal of the Neurological Sciences* 158 (1998): 125–33.

38. One of the earliest descriptions comes from China. See Jia Liu, Lu-ning Wang, and Jin-zhou Tian, "Recognition of Dementia in Early China," *Neurobiology of Aging* 33 (2012): 2948.e11–2948.e13

39. P. Stride and K. Lopes Floro, "Henry VIII, McLeod Syndrome and Jacquetta's Curse," *Journal of the Royal College of Physicians, Edinburg* 43 (2013): 353–60.

40. And, for the record, Alzheimer's disease runs in my own family, so I know of what I speak.

Chapter 9. Madness as a Political Football

1. Gary Greenberg, *The Book of Woe* (New York: Blue Rider Press, 2013).

2. There is, I am sure, a very special place in hell for Samuel Cartwright.

3. S. B. Hunt, "Dr. Cartwright on 'Drapetomania,'" *Buffalo Medical Journal* 10 (1855): 438–42, https://books.google.com/books?id=coBYAAAAMAAJ&pg=P A438#v=onepage&q&f=false (accessed March 2, 2019).

4. Madness, on the other hand, has *always* been a feature of politics.

5. Terms like these, now quite pejorative, were actually considered fairly technical during the nineteenth century. I take this particular quote from Edward Wakefield, who was actually a concerned reformer. Edward Wakefield, "Plan of an Asylum for Lunatics," *The Philanthropist* 2 (1812): 226–29.

6. Most governments were still largely centralized monarchies. To the extent such governments had a few bucks laying around, which wasn't as often as you might think, these monarchs had the obvious choice of funding services for the mentally ill or, say, buying a new pony. One need only tour the grand palaces of the world to see which choice the royalty usually made.

7. Maybe not the huge loss we might think, as we see in a bit.

8. Ian McMillan, "Insight into Bedlam: One Hospital's History," *Journal of Psychosocial Nursing and Mental Health Services* 35 (1997): 28–34.

9. Laura Wright, "Syntactic Structure of Witnesses' Narratives from the 16th-Century Court Minute Books of the Royal Hospitals of Bridewell and Bedlam," *Neuphilologische Mitteilungen* 96 (1995): 93–105.

10. "Virgin" queen and all, you know.

11. McMillan, "Insight into Bedlam."

12. Presumably he and Samuel Cartwright are bunkmates in hell.

13. Legal protections for confined mentally ill individuals have improved since most of Bedlam's history.

14. James Gilligan, "The Last Mental Health Hospital," *Psychiatric Quarterly* 72 (2001): 45–61.

15. And thank you, dear reader, for helping with that.

16. Gilligan, "The Last Mental Health Hospital."

17. Lawrence French, "Victimization of the Mentally Ill: An Unintended Consequence of Deinstitutionalization," *Social Work* (November–December 1987): 502–5.

18. Joni Lee Pow, Alan A. Baumeister, Mike F. Hawkins, Alex S. Cohen, and James C. Garand, "Deinstitutionalization of American Public Hospitals for the Mentally Ill before and after the Introduction of Antipsychotic Medications," *Harvard Review of Psychiatry* 23 (2015): 176–87.

19. Good figures on homelessness is tricky, as one might imagine. Estimates vary among sources and the frame of measurement. The 500,000 rough estimate is for any given night and was reported for 2017 by the U.S. government. If we look at how many people experienced homelessness for any time period during a given year, that number could be several times higher.

20. Pow, Baumeister, Hawkins, Cohen, and Garand, "Deinstitutionalization of American Public Hospitals."

21. Gilligan, "The Last Mental Health Hospital."

22. Pow, Baumeister, Hawkins, Cohen, and Garand, "Deinstitutionalization of American Public Hospitals."

23. Pow, Baumeister, Hawkins, Cohen, and Garand, "Deinstitutionalization of American Public Hospitals."

24. Pow, Baumeister, Hawkins, Cohen, and Garand, "Deinstitutionalization of American Public Hospitals."

25. Such rifles are commonly referred to as "assault rifles," but this terminology is technically incorrect.

26. In recent years criminologists have argued against using the names of mass homicide perpetrators. The argument is that some (though certainly not all) shooters seek fame, and not using their names is one means of reducing this incentive. My own read of the data is that although some shooters certainly do

express an interest in fame, this is by no means universal among shooters, and when it occurs, is likely only a small part of their motivation. Thus, I am skeptical that name withholding will play a major role in reducing mass shootings. Nonetheless, there's little lost by doing so, so I will follow this convention and refer to the perpetrator simply as the Sandy Hook shooter.

27. Christopher J. Ferguson, Mark Coulson, and Jane Barnett, "Psychological Profiles of School Shooters: Positive Directions and One Big Wrong Turn," *Journal of Police Crisis Negotiations* 11(2011): 141–58.

28. State's Attorney for the Judicial District of Danbury, *Report of the State's Attorney for the Judicial District of Danbury on the Shootings at Sandy Hook Elementary School and 36 Yogananda Street, Newtown, Connecticut on December 14, 2012*, 2013.

29. The term "violent video game" is largely meaningless. It has little scientific value, mainly being an emotionally evocative term. After all, we don't talk about "violent books" much, though of course such things exist and include many religious texts.

30. Christopher J. Ferguson, "Do Angry Birds Make for Angry Children? A Meta-Analysis of Video Game Influences on Children's and Adolescents' Aggression, Mental Health, Prosocial Behavior, and Academic Performance," *Perspectives on Psychological Science* 10 (2015): 646–66.

31. S. Fazel and M. Grann, "The Population Impact of Severe Mental Illness on Violent Crime," *American Journal of Psychiatry* 163 (2006): 1397–1403.

32. Kevin S. Douglas, Laura S. Guy, and Stephen D. Hart, "Psychosis as a Risk Factor for Violence to Others: A Meta-Analysis," *Psychological Bulletin* 135 (2009): 679–706.

33. Christopher J. Ferguson. "Video Games and Youth Violence: A Prospective Analysis in Adolescents," *Journal of Youth and Adolescence* 40 (2011): 377–91.

34. Greenberg, *The Book of Woe*.

35. Robert L. Spitzer and Joseph L. Fleiss, "A Re-Analysis of the Reliability of Psychiatric Diagnosis," *British Journal of Psychiatry* 125 (1974): 341–47.

36. Thomas S. Szasz, "The Myth of Mental Illness," *American Psychologist* 15 (1960): 113–18.

37. Brett J. Deacon, "The Biomedical Model of Mental Disorder: A Critical Analysis of Its Validity, Utility, and Effects on Psychotherapy Research," *Clinical Psychology Review* 33 (2013): 846–61.

38. Greenberg, *The Book of Woe*.

39. Michael B. First, "The Importance of Developmental Field Trials in the Revision of Psychiatric Classifications," *Lancet Psychiatry* 3 (2016): 579–84.

40. Many of these disorders have their advocates for inclusion in the *DSM* or *ICD*, but they're not official diagnoses as of this time.

41. Presumably they got tired explaining that V was *not* for Vendetta.

42. For a full and intriguing account of this, see Gary Greenberg, *The Book of Woe: The* DSM *and the Unmaking of Psychiatry* (New York: Blue Rider Press, 2013).

43. Allen Frances, "The British Psychological Society Condemns *DSM-5*," *Psychology Today*, July 2011, www.psychiatrictimes.com/dsm-5/british-psycholog ical-society-condemns-dsm-5 (accessed March 16, 2019).

Chapter 10. Madness of the Masses

1. Thomas Allen, *Tories: Fighting for the King in America's First Civil War* (New York: Harper Paperbacks, 2011).

2. Usually credited to Winston Churchill, although it doesn't seem to have originated with him.

3. Thucydides, *The Complete Writings of Thucydides*, trans. R. Crawley (New York: Random House, 1934).

4. In essence, Socrates was executed for being a stubborn pain-in-the-ass gadfly, but corruption of youth and encouraging delinquency were among the charges.

5. The name for the running event comes from this battle and the legendary story of a Greek hoplite who ran from the battle site back to Athens to announce the victory before promptly falling dead from exhaustion. A lovely story, but it appears to be a mishmash, at best, of actual events.

6. Donald Kagan, *The Outbreak of the Peloponnesian War* (Ithaca, NY: Cornell University Press, 1969).

7. Sparta probably won on points.

8. As in the Corinthians from Paul's letter in the Bible.

9. Things are always worse when relatives are involved, aren't they?

10. I initially mistyped this as "democrazy" and thought perhaps I should let it stay as such.

11. Peter Green, *Armada from Athens: The Failure of the Sicilian Expedition, 415–413* (London: Holder and Stoughton, 1970).

12. Green, *Armada from Athens*.

13. Xenophon. *Hellenica*, www.perseus.tufts.edu/hopper/text?doc=Xen.%20 Hell.

14. Xenophon, *Hellenica*.

15. In fairness, we might consider the long Byzantine Empire mainly a Greek-run enterprise, but this was mainly focused on Constantinople, not so much Athens, Sparta, Corinth, or Thebes. Athens remained important and finally regained its status as capital of newly independent Greece in the nineteenth century.

16. Indeed, Thucydides mainly stops mentioning Epidamnus after the initial stages of the war.

17. For instance, having worked on college campuses for years, I can say, sure, there definitely are some ideologues filling kids' heads with ugly nonsense, most of which is left wing. But most university faculty are more concerned with teaching chemistry, math, or psychology than getting students to vote for any particular presidential candidate.

18. Elaine Kamarack, Alexander Podkul, and Nick Zeppos, *Political Polarization and Voters in the 2016 Congressional Primaries*, Brookings Center for Effective Public Management, 2017, www.brookings.edu/wp-content/uploads/2017/01/primaries-paper-ii.pdf (accessed March 27, 2019).

19. John Sides, Chris Tausanovich, and Christopher Warshaw, "On the Representativeness of Primary Electorates," *British Journal of Political Science* (in press).

20. David Brady, Hahrie Han, and Jeremy Pope, "Primary Elections and Candidate Ideology: Out of Step with the Primary Electorate?" *Legislative Studies Quarterly* 32 (2007): 79–105.

21. Michael Rogin, "Politics, Emotion, and the Wallace Vote," *British Journal of Sociology* 20 (1969): 27–49.

22. Shigeo Hirano, James M. Snyder Jr., and Michael M. Ting, "Distributive Politics with Primaries," *Journal of Politics* 71 (2009): 1467–80.

23. Michael D. Henderson, Sunshine Hillygus, and Trevor Tompson, "'Sour Grapes' or Rational Voting? Voter Decision Making among Thwarted Primary Voters in 2008," *Public Opinion Quarterly* 74 (2010): 499–529.

24. Scott O. Lilienfeld, Joshua D. Miller, and Donald R. Lynam, "The Goldwater Rule: Perspectives from, and Implications for, Psychological Science," *Perspectives on Psychological Science* 13, no. 1 (January 2018): 3–27.

25. Lilienfeld, Miller, and Lynam, "The Goldwater Rule."

26. Brandy X. Lee, *The Dangerous Case of Donald Trump: 27 Psychiatrists and Mental Health Experts Assess a President* (New York: Thomas Dunne Books, 2017). Curiously, for a book in which the diagnosis of narcissist is made fairly frequently, the editor and contributors have their own moments, such as when the author boasts of five major publishing houses fighting over the book.

27. Donald J. Trump and Tony Schwartz, *The Art of the Deal* (New York: Random House, 1987).

28. Michael Kranish and Marc Fisher, *Trump Revealed: An American Journey of Ambition, Ego, Money, and Power* (New York: Scribner, 2016). Developed by the *Washington Post*, this book makes little pretext of being unbiased, opening with a fairly snarky prologue.

29. Granted it's not clear Trump views it this way, as he tends not to express much regret regarding his father's demands.

30. Kranish and Fisher, *Trump Revealed.*

31. When brought up during the 2016 presidential election, Trump pointed out that his opponent Hilary Clinton's husband, former president Bill Clinton, had been accused by multiple women of sexual assault and largely gotten a pass.

32. *Washington Post* Staff, "Full Text: Donald Trump Announces a Presidential Bid," *Washington Post*, June 16, 2015, www.washingtonpost.com/news/post-politics/wp/2015/06/16/full-text-donald-trump-announces-a-presidential-bid/?utm_term=.e8b9aaee886f (accessed April 1, 2019).

33. Michael T. Light and Ty Miller, "Does Undocumented Immigration Increase Violent Crime?" *Criminology* 56 (2018): 370–401.

34. Michelangelo Landgrave and Alex Nowrasteh, *Incarcerated Immigrants in 2016: Their Numbers, Demographics, and Countries of Origin*, The Cato Institute, 2018, www.cato.org/publications/immigration-research-policy-brief/their-numbers-demographics-countries-origin (accessed April 1, 2019).

35. Jeb Bush ran against Trump in the Republican primary and lost. Had he been elected president, he would have been the third Bush in the White House during my lifetime and I'm not *that* old.

36. The Republicans, as of now, have largely marched to Trump's tune.

37. Drew M. Parton and Michael R. Ent, "Vulnerable Narcissism Predicts Greater Spiteful Punishment of a Third-Party Transgressor," *Journal of Research in Personality* 76 (2018): 150–53.

38. With the understanding that these are both very broad terms.

39. Anthony N. Washburn and Linda J. Skitka, "Science Denial across the Political Divide: Liberals and Conservatives Are Similarly Motivated to Deny Attitude-Inconsistent Science," *Social Psychological and Personality Science* (in press).

40. Donald Braman, Dan M. Kahan, and James Grimmelmann, "Modeling Facts, Culture, and Cognition in the Gun Debate," *Social Justice Research* 18 (2005): 283–304.

41. Dan M. Kahan, Asheley Landrum, Katie Carpenter, Laura Helft, and Kathleen Hall Jamieson, "Science Curiosity and Political Information Processing," *Political Psychology* 38 (2017): 179–99.

42. Aja Hoggart, "An Author Canceled Her Own YA Novel over Accusations of Racism. But Is It Really Anti-Black?" *Slate*, January, 2019, https://slate.com/culture/2019/01/blood-heir-ya-book-twitter-controversy.html (accessed April 1, 2019). In full disclosure I haven't read *Blood Heir* because, you know—it got canceled.

43. Andrew Sullivan, "When Racism Is Fit to Print," *New York Magazine*, August 2018, http://nymag.com/intelligencer/2018/08/sarah-jeong-new-york-times-anti-white-racism.html (accessed April 1, 2019).

44. American Psychological Association, *APA Guidelines for Psychological Practice with Boys and Men*, August 2018, www.apa.org/about/policy/boys-men-practice-guidelines.pdf (accessed April 3, 2019).

45. This is the reverse of how therapy is usually done, with therapists trying to understand a patient's perspective rather than the opposite. In one exchange I had with one of the developers, he acknowledged that feminist and intersectional theories were a foundation of the guidelines. I am not saying such theories are without value, but they may not have been the correct starting point for understanding the mental health of men.

46. By this point "dog whistle" is itself a dog whistle for the left.

47. Indeed, during my lifetime, censorship was advocated more often from the right. It is disappointing to see the left abrogate that moral high ground more recently.

48. Indeed, I can say firsthand that other countries, including Mexico, which is often the bête noire of current U.S. immigration debates, have more rigid immigration policies. I once had my own run-in with being denied a visa to enter Australia. Fortunately, after non-trivial time and money, I managed to convince the Australians that I'm not a convicted felon.

49. Alex Lockie, "Conclusive Proof That It Is Trump's Policy to Separate Children from Their Families at the Border," *Business Insider*, June 2018, www.businessinsider.com/trump-administration-policy-separating-children-border-cbp-dhs-2018-6 (accessed April 3, 2019).

Chapter 11. Madness in the Future

1. Steven Pinker, *Enlightenment Now: The Case for Reason, Science, Humanism and Progress* (New York: Viking, 2018).

2. Generally regarded as one of the wisest Chinese emperors.

3. A founder of the women's enfranchisement movement in the United Kingdom. I had the honor of once staying in a house owned by her son.

4. It is worth noting that to be free of mental illness was not a criterion. Mental illness has been known to be present in many great rulers including Lincoln and Winston Churchill, both of whom experienced nontrivial depression.

5. In fact, the ethnic distribution of mass homicide perpetrators is roughly equivalent to the national populations from which they come. Nor, of course, are the vast majority of Muslims supporters of mass casualty attacks against civilians.

6. Muzafer Sherif, "Superordinate Goals in the Reduction of Intergroup Conflict," in *Intergroup Relations: Essential Readings*, ed. Michael A. Hogg and Dominic Abrams, 64–70 (New York: Psychology Press, 2001).

7. Lutfy N. Diab, "A Study of Intragroup and Intergroup Relations among Experimentally Produced Small Groups," *Genetic Psychology Monographs* 82 (1970): 49–82.

8. Paul J. C. Adachi, Gordon Hodson, Teena Willoughby, Carolyn Blank, and Alexandra Ha, "From Outgroups to Allied Forces: Effect of Intergroup Cooperation in Violent and Nonviolent Video Games on Boosting Favorable Outgroup Attitudes," *Journal of Experimental Psychology: General* 145 (2016): 259–65.

9. I look forward to my honorary degree in political science for pointing this out.

10. Though my attitude isn't too far from this. I believe in vegetable rights.

11. It was thought that high speeds would either smash human bodies or suck air from their lungs.

12. We still talk about "nuking" our food, which comes from early concerns about microwave ovens.

13. Amy Orben and Andrew Przybylski, "The Association between Adolescent Well-Being and Digital Technology Use," *Nature: Human Behavior* 3 (2019): 173–82.

14. That's a subject for another book I'm sure somebody has written already.

15. And, to be clear, I in no way intend that as a derogatory statement toward cave dwellers.

16. I met Joe Biden once. He did not sniff my hair.

17. Whether morally right or wrong, I suspect this was strategically brilliant to separate himself from a Democratic Party that, as of this writing, appears to be on a perpetual apology tour.

18. As they say, even a stopped clock is right twice a day.

19. Snopes.com, "Are Bert and Ernie Gay?" www.snopes.com/fact-check/open-sesame/ (accessed April 14, 2019).

20. The last I heard, as of this writing, was that an edited version has been rescheduled for forthcoming release. Nonetheless, the self-appointed censors won.

21. The Knight Foundation, *Free Expression on Campus: A Survey of U.S. College Students and U.S. Adults*, 2016, www.knightfoundation.org/media/uploads/publication_pdfs/FreeSpeech_campus.pdf (accessed April 14, 2019).

BIBLIOGRAPHY

100th Congress. *Senate Report #216: Iran Contra Investigation Report.* 1987. https://archive.org/stream/reportofcongress87unit#page/n7/mode/2up. Accessed February 24, 2019.

Adachi, Paul J. C., Gordon Hodson, Teena Willoughby, Carolyn Blank, and Alexandra Ha. "From Outgroups to Allied Forces: Effect of Intergroup Cooperation in Violent and Nonviolent Video Games on Boosting Favorable Outgroup Attitudes." *Journal of Experimental Psychology: General* 145 (2016): 259–65.

Adams, David, S. Barnett, N. Bechtereva, Bonnie Carter, Jose Delgado, José-Luis Díaz, Andrzej Eliasz, Santiago Genoves, Benson Ginsburg, Jo Groebel, Samir-Kumar Ghosh, Robert Hinde, Richard Leakey, Taha Malasi, J. Ramirez, Federico Zaragoza, Diana Mendoza, Ashis Nandy, John Scott, and Riitta Wahlstrom. "The Seville Statement on Violence." *American Psychologist* 45 (1990): 1167–68.

Adityanjee. "Jauhar: Mass Suicide by Self-Immolation in Waco, Texas." *Journal of Nervous and Mental Disease* 182 (1994): 727–28.

Agne, Robert R. "Reframing Practices in Moral Conflict: Interaction Problems in the Negotiation Standoff at Waco." *Discourse & Society* 18 (2007): 549–78.

Ahmed, Saeed. "Who Were Rizwan Farook and Tashfeen Malik?" CNN, December 3, 2015. www.cnn.com/2015/12/03/us/syed-farook-tashfeen-malik-mass-shooting-profile/index.html. Accessed December 30, 2018.

Alfieri, Alex, Christian Strauss, Harald Meller, Pawel Tacik, and Silvio Brandt. "The Woman of Pritschoena: An Example of the German Neolithic Neurosurgery in Saxony-Anhalt." *Journal of the History of the Neurosciences* 21 (2012): 139–46.

BIBLIOGRAPHY

Allen, Thomas. *Tories: Fighting for the King in America's First Civil War*. New York: Harper, 2011.

Altman, Lawrence K. "A Recollection of Early Questions about Reagan's Health." *New York Times*, June 15, 2004. www.nytimes.com/2004/06/15/health/the-doctor-s-world-a-recollection-of-early-questions-about-reagan-s-health.html. Accessed February 24, 2019.

Alvarez, Gonzalo, Francisco Ceballos, and Celsa Quintiero. "The Role of Inbreeding in the Extinction of a European Royal Dynasty." *PLoS One 4* (2009). https://journals.plos.org/plosone/article?id=10.1371/journal.pone.0005174. Accessed December 9, 2018.

American Psychological Association. *APA Guidelines for Psychological Practice with Boys and Men*. August 2018. www.apa.org/about/policy/boys-men-practice-guidelines.pdf. Accessed April 3, 2019.

———. *Clinical Practice Guideline for the Treatment of Posttraumatic Stress Disorder (PTSD)*. 2017. www.apa.org/ptsd-guideline/. Accessed October 6, 2018.

———. *Timeline of APA Policies & Actions Related to Detainee Welfare and Professional Ethics in the Context of Interrogation and National Security*. 2018. www.apa.org/news/press/statements/interrogations.aspx. Accessed October 6, 2018.

Armit, Ian. "Violence and Society in the Deep Human Past." *British Journal of Criminology* 51 (2011): 499–517.

Associated Press. "David Reimer, 38, Subject of John/Joan Case." *New York Times*, May 12, 2004. www.nytimes.com/2004/05/12/us/david-reimer-38-subject-of-the-john-joan-case.html. Accessed December 7, 2018.

Auyeung, Bonnie, Simon Baron-Cohen, Emma Ashwin, Rebecca Knickmeyer, Kevin Taylor, Gerald Hackett, and Melissa Hines. "Fetal Testosterone Predicts Sexually Differentiated Childhood Behavior in Girls and in Boys." *Psychological Science* 20 (2009): 144–48.

Backman, L., S. Jones, A. Berger, E. Laukka, and B. Small. "Multiple Cognitive Deficits during the Transition to Alzheimer's Disease." *Journal of Internal Medicine* 256 (2004): 195–204.

Bargh, John A., Mark Chen, and Lara Burrows. "Automaticity of Social Behavior: Direct Effects of Trait Construct and Stereotype Activation on Action." *Journal of Personality and Social Psychology* 71 (1996): 230–44.

Barker, Nancy. "Let Them Eat Cake: The Mythical Marie Antoinette and the French Revolution." *The Historian* 55 (1993): 709–24.

Barrett, Anthony. *Caligula: The Corruption of Power*. New Haven: Yale University Press, 1990.

Baumeister, Roy F. "Constructing a Scientific Theory of Free Will." In *Moral Psychology*, Vol. 4: *Free Will and Moral Responsibility*. Edited by Walter Sinnott-Armstrong, 235–55. Cambridge, MA: MIT Press, 2014.

Bazelon, Lara, and Jennifer Thompson. "Christine Blasey Ford's Memory of Her Assault Isn't a Case of Mistaken Identity." *Slate*, October 2018. https://slate.com/news-and-politics/2018/10/brett-kavanaugh-christine-blasey-ford-mistaken-identity.html. Accessed February 9, 2019.

BBC News. "Tokyo Sarin Attack: Aum Shinrikyo Cult Leaders Executed." BBC, July 6, 2018. www.bbc.com/news/world-asia-43395483. Accessed December 24, 2018.

Bean, Anthony, Rune K. L. Nielsen, Antonius J. van Rooij, and Christopher J. Ferguson. "Video Game Addiction: The Push to Pathologize Video Games." *Professional Psychology: Research and Practice* 48 (2017): 378–89.

Beaver, Kevin, Joseph A. Schwartz, and Jamie M. Gajos. "A Review of the Genetic and Gene-Environment Interplay Contributors to Antisocial Phenotypes." In *The Development of Criminal and Antisocial Behavior: Theory, Research and Practical Applications*. Edited by Julien Morizot and Lila Kazemian, 109–22. New York: Springer, 2010.

Beit-Hallahmi, Benjamin. "Apocalyptic Dreams and Religious Ideologies: Losing and Saving Self and World." *Psychoanalytic Review* 90 (2003): 403–39.

Bengtson, Hermann, and Edmund Bloedow. *History of Greece: From the Beginning to the Byzantine Era*. Ottowa: University of Ottawa Press, 1997.

Bennett, Robin, Arno Mutulsky, Alan Bittles, Louanne Hudgins, Stefanie Uhrich, Debra Lochner Doyle, Kerry Silvey, C. Ronald Scott, Edith Cheng, Barbara McGillivray, Robert D. Steiner, and Debra Olson. "Genetic Counseling and Screening of Consanguineous Couples and Their Offspring: Recommendations of the National Society of Genetic Counselors." *Journal of Genetic Counseling* 11 (2002): 97–119.

Berg, A. Scott. *Wilson*. New York: G. P. Putman's Sons, 2013.

Berisha, Visar, Shuai Wang, Amy LaCross, and Julie Liss. "Tracking Discourse Complexity Preceding Alzheimer's Disease Diagnosis: A Case Study Comparing the Press Conferences of Presidents Ronald Reagan and George Herbert Walker Bush." *Journal of Alzheimer's Disease* 45 (2015): 959–63.

Bianucci, R., P. Charlier, P. Evans, and O. Appenzeller. "Temporal Lobe Epilepsy and Anorexia Nervosa in St. Catherine of Siena (1347–1380)." *Journal of the Neurological Sciences* 379 (2017): 122–23.

Blumenthal, Karen. *Steve Jobs: The Man Who Thought Different*. New York: Feiwel and Friends, 2012.

Blumer, Dietrich. "The Illness of Vincent van Gogh." *American Journal of Psychiatry* 159 (2002): 519–26.

Boller, Francois, and Margaret Forbes. "History of Dementia and Dementia in History: An Overview." *Journal of the Neurological Sciences* 158 (1998): 125–33.

Bosworth, A. B. "Errors in Arrian." *The Classical Quarterly* 26 (1976): 117–39.

Bowley, Graham, and Joe Coscarelli. "Bill Cosby, once a Model of Fatherhood, Sentenced to Prison." *New York Times*, September 25, 2018. www.nytimes .com/2018/09/25/arts/television/bill-cosby-sentencing.html. Accessed February 3, 2019.

Boyle, Emma. "Was Idi Amin's Government a Terrorist Regime?" *Terrorism and Political Violence* 29, (2017): 593–609.

Brady, David, Hahrie Han, and Jeremy Pope. "Primary Elections and Candidate Ideology: Out of Step with the Primary Electorate?" *Legislative Studies Quarterly* 32 (2007): 79–105.

Braman, Donald, Dan M. Kahan, and James Grimmelmann. "Modeling Facts, Culture, and Cognition in the Gun Debate." *Social Justice Research* 18, (2005): 283–304.

Brands, H.W. *Woodrow Wilson*. New York: Henry Holt, 2003.

Breitenfeld, Tomislav, M. J. Jurasic, and D. Breitenfeld. "Hippocrates: The Forefather of Neurology." *Neurological Sciences* 35 (2014): 1349–52.

Bullock, Alan. *Hitler and Stalin*. New York: Alfred A. Knopf, 1992.

Camerer, Colin, Anna Dreber, Felix Holzmeister, Teck-Hua Ho, Jürgen Huber, Magnus Johannesson, Michael Kirchler, Gideon Nave, Brian A. Nosek, Thomas Pfeiffer, Adam Altmejd, Nick Buttrick, Taizan Chan, Yiling Chen, Eskil Forsell, Anup Gampa, Emma Heikensten, Lily Hummer, Taisuke Imai, Siri Isaksson, Dylan Manfredi, Julia Rose, Eric-Jan Wagenmakers, and Hang Wu. "Evaluating the Replicability of Social Science Experiments in Nature and Science between 2010 and 2015." *Nature Human Behavior* 2 (2018): 637–44.

Cannon, Lou. *President Reagan: The Role of a Lifetime*. New York: Public Affairs, 2000.

Carpenter, Joseph K., Leigh A. Andrews, Sara M. Witcraft, Mark B. Powers, Jasper A. J. Smits, and Stefan G. Hofmann. "Cognitive Behavioral Therapy for Anxiety and Related Disorders: A Meta-Analysis of Randomized Placebo-Controlled Trials." *Depression and Anxiety* (forthcoming).

Carroll, Leslie. *Royal Pains: A Rogue's Gallery of Brats, Brutes and Bad Seeds*. New York: Penguin, 2011.

Cattane, Nadia, Roberta Rossi, Mariangela Lanfredi, and Annamaria Cattaneo. "Borderline Personality Disorder and Childhood Trauma: Exploring the Affected Biological Systems and Mechanisms." *BMC Psychiatry* 17 (2017). https://bmcpsychiatry.biomedcentral.com/articles/10.1186/s12888-017-1383 -2. Accessed November 16, 2018.

Centers for Disease Control. *Suicide Rising across the US.* (2018). www.cdc.gov/vitalsigns/suicide/. Accessed September 24, 2018.

Chadee, Derek, and Jason Ditton. "Are Older People Most Afraid of Crime? Revisiting Ferraro and LaGrange in Trinidad." *British Journal of Criminology* 43 (2003): 417–33.

Clark, Tom. *The Beautiful Beast: Why Was Irma Grese Evil?* www.academia.edu/2183067/The_beautiful_beast_Why_was_Irma_Grese_evil. Accessed October 15, 2018.

Coates, Dominiek D. "'Cult Commitment' from the Perspective of Former Members: Direct Rewards of Membership versus Dependency Inducing Practices." *Deviant Behavior* 33 (2012): 168–84.

Committee on Government Reform. *The Tragedy at Waco: New Evidence Examined.* Washington, DC: Government Printing Office, 2000. www.congress.gov/106/crpt/hrpt1037/CRPT-106hrpt1037.pdf. Accessed December 22, 2018.

Cox, Timothy, Nicola Jack, Simon Lofthouse, John Watling, Janice Haines, and Martin J. Warren. "King George III and Porphyria: An Elemental Hypothesis and Investigation." *The Lancet* 366 (2005): 332–35.

Daniel, David. "Eastern Europe." In *Women in Reformation and Counter-Reformation Europe.* Edited by Sherrin Marshall. Indianapolis: Indiana University Press, 1989.

David, Saul. *Operation Thunderbolt.* New York: Little, Brown, 2015.

Davidson, Jonathan, Kathryn Connor, and Marvin Swartz. "Mental Illness in U.S. Presidents between 1776 and 1974: A Review of Biographical Sources." *Journal of Nervous And Mental Disease* 194 (2006): 47–51.

Davis, Patti. *The Way I See It.* New York: Putnam, 1992.

Deacon, Brett J. "The Biomedical Model of Mental Disorder: A Critical Analysis of Its Validity, Utility, and Effects on Psychotherapy Research." *Clinical Psychology Review* 33 (2013): 846–61.

Dennett, Daniel, and Gregg Caruso. "Just Deserts." *Aeon*, October 4, 2018. https://aeon.co/essays/on-free-will-daniel-dennett-and-gregg-caruso-go-head-to-head. Accessed November 22, 2018.

Dennis, M. "Looking Backward: Woodrow Wilson, the New South, and the Question of Race." *American Nineteenth Century History* 3 (2002): 77–104.

Desmarais, Sarah L., Andrea Gibas, and Tonia L. Nicholls. "Beyond Violence against Women: Gender Inclusiveness in Domestic Violence Research, Policy, and Practice." In *Violent Crime: Clinical and Social Implications.* Edited by Christopher J. Ferguson, 184–206. Thousand Oaks, CA: Sage Publications, 2010.

Diab, Lutfy N. "A Study of Intragroup and Intergroup Relations among Experimentally Produced Small Groups." *Genetic Psychology Monographs* 82 (1970): 49–82.

Diamond, Jared. *Guns, Germs and Steel: A Short History of Everybody for the Last 13,000 Years.* London: Vintage, 1997.

Diamond, Milton. "Sexual Identity, Monozygotic Twins Reared in Discordant Sex Roles and a BBC Follow-Up." *Archives of Sexual Behavior* 11 (1982): 181–86.

Dio. *Roman History.* www.loebclassics.com/view/LCL083/1917/volume.xml.

Douglas, Kevin, Laura Guy, and Stephen Hart. "Psychosis as a Risk Factor for Violence to Others: A Meta-Analysis." *Psychological Bulletin* 135 (2009): 679–706.

Doyen, Stéphane, Olivier Klein, Cora-Lise Pichon, and Axel Cleeremans. "Behavioral Priming: It's All in the Mind, but Whose Mind?" *PLoS ONE* 7 (2012). https://journals.plos.org/plosone/article?id=10.1371/journal.pone.0029081#pone.0029081.s001. Accessed November 24, 2018.

Drescher, Jack. "Queer Diagnoses Revisited: The Past and Future of Homosexuality and Gender Diagnoses in *DSM* and *ICD*." *International Review of Psychiatry* 27 (2015): 386–95.

Dube, Oeindrila, and S. P. Harish. *Queens.* NBER Working Paper No. 23337. April 2017. www.nber.org/papers/w23337.pdf. Accessed November 25, 2018.

Elliot, J. H. *Imperial Spain 1469–1716.* New York: Penguin: 2002.

Erickson, Mary. "Rethinking Oedipus: An Evolutionary Perspective of Incest Avoidance." *American Journal of Psychiatry* 150 (1993): 411–16.

Everitt, Anthony. *The Rise of Rome.* New York: Random House, 2013.

Faber, David. *Munich, 1938.* New York: Simon & Schuster, 2009.

Faria, Miguel. "Violence, Mental Illness, and the Brain—A Brief History of Psychosurgery: Part 1—From Trephination to Lobotomy." *Surgical Neurology International* 4 (2013): www.ncbi.nlm.nih.gov/pmc/articles/PMC3640229/. Accessed October 13, 2018.

Farr, Evelyn. *I Love You Madly: Marie-Antoinette and Count Fersen: The Secret Letters.* London: Peter Owen, 2016.

Farrow, Ronan. "From Aggressive Overtures to Sexual Assault: Harvey Weinstein's Accusers Tell Their Stories." *New Yorker*, October 10, 2017. www.newyorker.com/news/news-desk/from-aggressive-overtures-to-sexual-assault-harvey-weinsteins-accusers-tell-their-stories. Accessed February 3, 2019.

Fazel, S., and M. Grann. "The Population Impact of Severe Mental Illness on Violent Crime." *American Journal of Psychiatry* 163 (2006): 1397–1403.

Ferguson, Christopher J. "The Devil Wears Stata: Thin-Ideal Media's Minimal Contribution to Our Understanding of Body Dissatisfaction and Eating Disorders." *Archives of Scientific Psychology* 6 (2018): 70–79.

———. "How 'Toxic Masculinity' Is Hurting Boys." *Houston Chronicle*, March 26, 2018.

———. "Do Angry Birds Make for Angry Children? A Meta-Analysis of Video Game Influences on Children's and Adolescents' Aggression, Mental Health, Prosocial Behavior, and Academic Performance." *Perspectives on Psychological Science* 10 (2015): 646–66.

———. "Video Games and Youth Violence: A Prospective Analysis in Adolescents." *Journal of Youth and Adolescence* 40 (2011): 377–91.

———. "Genetic Contributions to Antisocial Personality and Behavior: A Meta-Analytic Review from an Evolutionary Perspective." *Journal of Social Psychology* 150 (2010): 160–80.

Ferguson, Christopher J., Mark Coulson, and Jane Barnett. "Psychological Profiles of School Shooters: Positive Directions and One Big Wrong Turn." *Journal of Police Crisis Negotiations* 11(2011): 141–58.

Ferguson, Christopher J., and Richard D. Hartley. "The Pleasure Is Momentary . . . the Expense Damnable? The Influence of Pornography on Rape and Sexual Assault." *Aggression and Violent Behavior* 14 (2009): 323–29.

Ferguson, Christopher J., and D. Cricket Meehan. "An Analysis of Females Convicted of Sex Crimes in the State of Florida." *Journal of Child Sexual Abuse: Research, Treatment, & Program Innovations for Victims, Survivors, & Offenders* 14 (2005): 75–89.

First, Michael B. "The Importance of Developmental Field Trials in the Revision of Psychiatric Classifications." *The Lancet Psychiatry* 3 (2016): 579–84.

Flores, Andrew, Jody Herman, Gary Gates, and Taylor Brown. *How Many Adults Identify as Transgender in the United States?* Los Angeles, CA: Williams Institute, 2016.

Fogg, Ryan, and Stephen A. Boorjian. "The Sexual Dysfunction of Louis XVI: A Consequence of International Politics, Anatomy, or Naïveté?" *BJU International* 106 (2010): 457–59.

Forcen, Fernando Espi, and Carlos Espi Forcen. "The Practice of Holy Fasting in the Late Middle Ages: A Psychiatric Approach." *Journal of Nervous and Mental Disease* 203 (2015): 650–53.

Frances, Allen. "The British Psychological Society Condemns *DSM-5*." *Psychology Today*, July 26, 2011. www.psychiatrictimes.com/dsm-5/british-psychological-society-condemns-dsm-5. Accessed March 16, 2019.

Fraser, Antonia. *Marie Antoinette: The Journey.* New York: Anchor Books, 2001.

Freedom House. *Freedom in the World: Democracy in Crisis.* 2018. https://freedomhouse.org/report/freedom-world/freedom-world-2018. Accessed September 24, 2018.

French, Lawrence. "Victimization of the Mentally Ill: An Unintended Consequence of Deinstitutionalization." *Social Work* (November–December 1987): 502–5.

Friedman, Susan Hatters, and Renée Sorrentino. "Postpartum Psychosis, Infanticide, and Insanity—Implications for Forensic Psychiatry." *Journal of the American Academy of Psychiatry and the Law* 40 (2012): 326–32.

Fukuyama, Francis. *The End of History and the Last Man*. New York: Free Press, 2006.

Furnham, Adrian, Steven C. Richards, and Delroy L. Paulhus. "The Dark Triad of Personality: A 10 Year Review." *Social and Personality Psychology Compass* 7 (2013): 199–216.

Galassi, Francesco M., Nicole Bender, Michael E. Habicht, Emanuele Armocida, Fabrizio Toscano, David A. Menassa, and Matteo Cerri. "St. Catherine of Siena (1347–1380 AD): One of the Earliest Historic Cases of Altered Gustatory Perception in Anorexia Mirabilis." *Neurological Sciences* (forthcoming).

Galligan, Patrick T. *Report on Certain Matters Related to Karla Homolka*. https:// drive.google.com/file/d/0B3ORC8Ev2VnnaDg5LWVWVjJzUGM/view. Accessed November 25, 2018.

Gesquiere, Laurence, Niki Learn, M. Carolina Simao, Patrick O. Onyango, Susan C. Alberts, and Jeanne Altmann. "Life at the Top: Rank and Stress in Wild Male Baboons." *Science* 333 (2011): 357–60.

Gilbert, Robert E. "Ronald Reagan's Presidency: The Impact of an Alcoholic Parent." *Political Psychology* 29 (2008): 737–65.

Gilligan, James. "The Last Mental Health Hospital." *Psychiatric Quarterly* 72 (2001): 45–61.

Globe and Mail. "Homolka's Psychiatric Report Released." *Globe and Mail*, June 5, 2005. www.theglobeandmail.com/news/national/homolkas-psychiatric-report-released/article20422606/. Accessed November 25, 2018.

Goodall, Jane. "Life and Death at Gombe." *National Geographic* 155 (1979): 595–621.

———. "Infant-Killing and Cannibalism in Free-Living Chimpanzees." *Folia Primatologica* 28 (1977): 259–82.

Goodwin, Jason. *Lords of the Horizons*. New York: Henry Holt, 1998.

Gottschalk, Martin, and Lee Ellis. "Evolutionary and Genetic Explanations of Violent Crime." In *Violent Crime: Clinical and Social Implications*. Edited by Christopher J. Ferguson, 57–74. Thousand Oaks, CA: Sage Publications, 2010.

Gray, Peter. "Why Zimbardo's Prison Experiment Isn't in My Textbook." *Psychology Today* 2013. www.psychologytoday.com/us/blog/freedom-learn/201310/why-zimbardo-s-prison-experiment-isn-t-in-my-textbook. Accessed October 15, 2018.

Gray, Richard. "Psychopathy and Will to Power: Ted Bundy and Dennis Rader." In *Serial Killers: Being and Killing.* Edited by S. Waller, 191–205. New York: Wiley-Blackwell, 2010.

Green, Peter. *Armada from Athens: The Failure of the Sicilian Expedition, 415–413.* London: Holder and Stoughton, 1970.

Greenberg, Gary. *The Book of Woe.* New York: Blue Rider Press, 2013.

Hadlow, Janice. *A Royal Experiment: The Private Life of King George III.* New York: Henry Holt, 2014.

Hampikian, Greg, Emily West, and Olga Askelrod. "The Genetics of Innocence: Analysis of 194 U.S. DNA Exonerations." *Annual Review of Genomics and Human Genetics* 12 (2011): 97–120.

Hare, Robert. *Without Conscience: The Disturbing World of the Psychopath among Us.* New York: Guilford Press, 1999.

Hayes, Christal. "'I Was Angry and I Sent It': Another Kavanaugh Accuser Referred to FBI after Recanting." *USA Today*, November 2, 2018. www.usatoday.com/story/news/politics/2018/11/02/brett-kavanaugh-accuser-referred-fbi-doj-investigation/1863210002/. Accessed February 8, 2018.

Henderson, Michael D., Sunshine Hillygus, and Trevor Tompson. "'Sour Grapes' or Rational Voting? Voter Decision Making among Thwarted Primary Voters in 2008." *Public Opinion Quarterly* 74 (2010): 499–529.

Herodian. *History of the Roman Empire since the Death of Marcus Aurelius.*

Hersh, Seymour M. "The Iran-Contra Committees: Did They Protect Reagan?" *New York Times*, April 29, 1990. www.nytimes.com/1990/04/29/magazine/the-iran-contra-committees-did-they-protect-reagan.html?pagewanted=all&src=pm. Accessed February 24, 2019.

Hess, Nicole, Courtney Helfrecht, Edward Hagen, Aaron Sell, and Barry Hewlett. "Interpersonal Aggression among Aka Hunter-Gatherers of the Central African Republic: Assessing the Effects of Sex, Strength, and Anger." *Human Nature* 21 (2010): 330–54.

Heston, Leonard, and Renate Heston. *The Medical Casebook of Adolf Hitler.* Briarcliff Manor, NY: Stein & Day, 1979.

Hickey, Eric. *Serial Murderers and Their Victims.* New York: Cengage, 2015.

Hill, Andreas, Niels Habermann, Wolfgang Berner, and Peer Briken. "Sexual Sadism and Sadistic Personality Disorder in Sexual Homicide." *Journal of Personality Disorders* 20, no. 6 (2006): 671–84.

Himmelmann, Lars. "From Barber to Surgeon—the Process of Professionalization." *Svensk Medicinhistorisk Tidskrift* 11 (2007): 69–87.

Hirano, Shigeo, James M. Snyder Jr., and Michael M. Ting. "Distributive Politics with Primaries." *Journal of Politics* 71 (2009): 1467–80.

Hobbes, Thomas. *Leviathan.* 1651.

Hoggart, Aja. "An Author Canceled Her Own YA Novel over Accusations of Racism. But Is It Really Anti-Black?" *Slate*, January 31, 2019. https://slate.com/culture/2019/01/blood-heir-ya-book-twitter-controversy.html. Accessed April 1, 2019.

Hollander, Matthew M., and Jason Turowetz. "Normalizing Trust: Participants' Immediately Post-Hoc Explanations of Behaviour in Milgram's 'Obedience' Experiments." *British Journal of Social Psychology* 56 (2017): 655–74.

Holley, David. "Japanese Guru: A Youthful Bully's Quest for Power." *Los Angeles Times*, March 27, 1995. http://articles.latimes.com/1995-03-27/news/mn-47649_1_japanese-guru. Accessed December 23, 2018.

Humphreys, Joy D., James R. Clopton, and Darcy A. Reich. "Disordered Eating Behavior and Obsessive Compulsive Symptoms in College Students: Cognitive and Affective Similarities." *Eating Disorders: The Journal of Treatment & Prevention* 15 (2007): 247–59.

Hunt, S. B. "Dr. Cartwright on 'Drapetomania.'" *Buffalo Medical Journal* 10 (1855): 438–42. https://books.google.com/books?id=coBYAAAAMAAJ&pg=PA438#v=onepage&q&f=false. Accessed March 2, 2019.

Inspectors General of the Intelligence Community, Central Intelligence Agency, Department of Justice and Department of Homeland Security. *Unclassified Summary of Information Handling and Sharing Prior to the April 15, 2013 Boston Marathon Bombings*. Washington, DC: Office of Inspectors General, 2014. https://oig.justice.gov/reports/2014/s1404.pdf. Accessed December 26, 2018.

Isaacson, Walter. *Steve Jobs*. New York: Simon and Schuster, 2011.

Johnson, Carolyn. "Elizabeth Holmes, Founder of Blood-Testing Company Theranos, Indicted on Wire Fraud Charges." *Washington Post*, June 15, 2018. www.washingtonpost.com/business/economy/elizabeth-holmes-founder-of-blood-testing-company-theranos-indicted-on-wire-fraud-federal-authorities-announce/2018/06/15/8779f538-70df-11e8-bd50-b80389a4e569_story.html?utm_term=.d49a72ece5bf. Accessed February 2, 2019.

Johnson, Dominic, and Jesse Bering. "Hand of God, Mind of Man: Punishment and Cognition in the Evolution of Cooperation." *Evolutionary Psychology* 4 (2006): 219–33.

Kagan, Donald. *The Outbreak of the Peloponnesian War*. Ithaca, NY: Cornell University Press, 1969.

Kahan, Dan M., Asheley Landrum, Katie Carpenter, Laura Helft, and Kathleen Hall Jamieson. "Science Curiosity and Political Information Processing." *Political Psychology* 38 (2017): 179–99.

Kalinaki, Daniel. "Entebbe Raid Humiliated Amin, Nearly Caused East African War." *Daily Nation*, July 3, 2016. www.nation.co.ke/news/Entebbe-raid-em

barrassed-Amin—nearly-caused-East-African-war/1056-3277804-1327oaiz/
index.html. Accessed September 24, 2018.

Kamarack, Elaine, Alexander Podkul, and Nick Zeppos. *Political Polarization and Voters in the 2016 Congressional Primaries*. Brookings Center for Effective Public Management. 2017. www.brookings.edu/wp-content/uploads/2017/01/primaries-paper-ii.pdf. Accessed March 27, 2019.

Kantor, Jodi, and David Streitfeld. "Inside Amazon: Wrestling Big Ideas in a Bruising Workplace." *New York Times*, August 16, 2015. www.nytimes.com/2015/08/16/technology/inside-amazon-wrestling-big-ideas-in-a-bruising-workplace.html?_r=0. Accessed February 2, 2019.

Kaufman, Michael. "Idi Amin, Murderous and Erratic Ruler of Uganda in the 70s Dies in Exile." *New York Times*, August 17, 2003. www.nytimes.com/2003/08/17/world/idi-amin-murderous-and-erratic-ruler-of-uganda-in-the-70-s-dies-in-exile.html. Accessed September 24, 2018.

King, Michael B., and Gillian Mezey. "Eating Behaviour of Male Racing Jockeys." *Psychological Medicine* 17 (1987): 249–53.

Kirkpatrick, Lee A. "Toward an Evolutionary Psychology of Religion and Personality." *Journal of Personality* 67 (1999): 921–52.

Knight, Leslie. "Enough with the Male-Bashing." *Forbes*, April 26, 2011. www.forbes.com/2011/04/26/enough-with-the-male-bashing.html#58b005ed6e5c. Accessed February 3, 2019.

Knight Foundation. *Free Expression on Campus: A Survey of U.S. College Students and U.S. Adults.* 2016. www.knightfoundation.org/media/uploads/publication_pdfs/FreeSpeech_campus.pdf. Accessed April 14, 2019.

Kohut, Tania. "Convicted Killer Karla Homolka Volunteers at Her Children's Montreal School: Reports." *Global News*, May 31, 2017. https://globalnews.ca/news/3491735/karla-homolka-school-montreal/. Accessed November 25, 2018.

Kohut, Taylor, Jodie L. Baer, and Brendan Watts. "Is Pornography Really about 'Making Hate to Women'? Pornography Users Hold More Gender Egalitarian Attitudes than Nonusers in a Representative American Sample." *Journal of Sex Research* 53 (2016): 1–11.

Kramer, Heinrich, and Sprenger Jacob. *Malleus Maleficarum*. 1487.

Kranish, Michael, and Marc Fisher. *Trump Revealed: An American Journey of Ambition, Ego, Money, and Power*. New York: Scribner, 2016.

Kroll, J., and B. Bachrach. "Sin and Mental Illness in the Middle Ages." *Psychological Medicine* 14 (1984): 507–14.

Kürti, László. "The Symbolic Construction of the Monstrous: The Elizabeth Bathory Story." *Journal of Ethnology and Folklore Research* 46, no. 1 (2009): 133–59.

Lachenmeier, Dirk W., David Nathan-Maister, Theodore A. Breaux, Eva-Maria Sohnius, Kerstin Schoeberl, and Thomas Kuballa. "Chemical Composition of Vintage Preban Absinthe with Special Reference to Thujone, Fenchone, Pinocamphone, Methanol, Copper, and Antimony Concentrations." *Journal of Agriculture and Food Chemistry* 56 (2008): 3073–3081.

Landgrave, Michelangelo, and Alex Nowrasteh. *Incarcerated Immigrants in 2016: Their Numbers, Demographics, and Countries of Origin.* The Cato Institute. 2018. www.cato.org/publications/immigration-research-policy-brief/their -numbers-demographics-countries-origin. Accessed April 1, 2019.

Langer, Walter. *The Mind of Adolf Hitler: The Secret Wartime Report.* New York: New American Library, 1972.

Lankford, Adam. "A Comparative Analysis of Suicide Terrorists and Rampage, Workplace, and School Shooters in the United States from 1990 to 2010." *Homicide Studies: An Interdisciplinary & International Journal* 17 (2013): 255–74.

Lee Brandy, X. *The Dangerous Case of Donald Trump: 27 Psychiatrists and Mental Health Experts Assess a President.* New York: Thomas Dunne Books, 2017.

León-Carrión, José, and Francisco Javier Chacartegui-Ramos. "Brain Injuries and Violent Crime." In *Violent Crime: Clinical and Social Implications.* Edited by Christopher J. Ferguson, 99–118. Thousand Oaks, CA: Sage, 2010.

Letzter, Rafi. "Scientists Are Furious after a Famous Psychologist Accused Her Peers of 'Methodological Terrorism.'" *Business Insider UK.* http://uk.businessinsider .com/susan-fiske-methodological-terrorism-2016-9?r=US&IR=T. Accessed November 24, 2018.

Lever, Evelyne. *Marie Antoinette: The Last Queen of France.* New York: St. Martin's Griffon, 2000.

Lifton, Robert Jay. "Aum Shinrikyo: The Threshold Crossed." *Journal of Aggression, Maltreatment & Trauma* 9 (2004): 57–66.

Light, Michael T., and Ty Miller. "Does Undocumented Immigration Increase Violent Crime?" *Criminology* 56 (2018): 370–401.

Lilienfeld, Scott O., Joshua D. Miller, and Donald R. Lynam. "The Goldwater Rule: Perspectives from, and Implications for, Psychological Science." *Perspectives on Psychological Science* 13, no. 1 (January 2018): 3–27.

Lim, Louisa. "Who Murdered China's Emperor 100 Years Ago?" NPR, November 14, 2008. www.npr.org/templates/story/story.php?storyId=96993694. Accessed February 13, 2019.

Linz, Daniel, Edward Donnerstein, and Steven Penrod. "The Findings and Recommendations of the Attorney General's Commission on Pornography: Do the Psychological 'Facts' Fit the Political Fury?" *American Psychologist* 42 (1987): 946–53.

Liu, Jia, Lu-ning Wang, and Jin-zhou Tian. "Recognition of Dementia in Early China." *Neurobiology of Aging* 33 (2012): 2948.e11-2948.e13.

Livy. *The History of Rome.* http://mcadams.posc.mu.edu/txt/ah/Livy/.

Lockie, Alex. "Conclusive Proof That It Is Trump's Policy to Separate Children from Their Families at the Border." *Business Insider*, June 18, 2018. www.busi nessinsider.com/trump-administration-policy-separating-children-border -cbp-dhs-2018-6. Accessed April 3, 2019.

Lofchie, Michael. "The Uganda Coup: Class Action by the Military." *Journal of Modern African Studies* 10 (1972): 19–35.

Loftus, Elizabeth. "Memory Faults and Fixes." *Issues in Science and Technology* 18 (2002): 41–50.

Lower, Wendy. *Hitler's Furies: German Women in the Nazi Killing Fields.* New York: Houghton Mifflin Harcourt, 2013.

Luo, Liqun. "Is There a Sensitive Period in Human Incest Avoidance?" *Evolutionary Psychology* 9 (2011): 285–95.

Macalpine, Ida, and Richard Hunter. "The 'Insanity' of King George III: A Classic Case of Porphyria." *British Medical Journal* 1 (1966): 65–71.

Maraz, Aniko, Róbert Urbán, Mark Damian Griffiths, and Zsolt Demetrovics. 2015. "An Empirical Investigation of Dance Addiction." *PLoS ONE* 10 (2015). http://journals.plos.org/plosone/article?id=10.1371/journal.pone.0125988. Accessed October 5, 2018.

Martin, Phillip. "Is the Waltham Triple Murder Investigation at a Dead End?" WGBH, April 12, 2018. www.wgbh.org/news/2018/04/12/news/waltham -triple-murder-investigation-dead-end. Accessed December 26, 2018.

Massachusetts Emergency Management Agency. *After Action Report for the Response to the 2013 Boston Marathon Bombings.* December 2014. www.mass .gov/files/documents/2016/09/uz/after-action-report-for-the-response-to-the -2013-boston-marathon-bombings.pdf. Accessed December 26, 2018.

Massie, Robert K. *Dreadnought.* New York: Random House, 1991.

McCall, Grant, and Nancy Shields. "Examining the Evidence from Small-Scale Societies and Early Prehistory and Implications for Modern Theories of Aggression and Violence. *Aggression and Violent Behavior* 13 (2008): 1–9.

McComb, Karen, Lucy Baker, and Cynthia Moss. "African Elephants Show High Levels of Interest in the Skulls and Ivory of Their Own Species." *Biology Letters* 2 (2006): 26–28.

McGillivray, Anne. "'A Moral Vacuity in Her Which Is Difficult If Not Impossible to Explain': Law, Psychiatry and the Remaking of Karla Homolka." *International Journal of the Legal Profession* 5 (1998): 255–88.

McGovern, George. *Grassroots: The Autobiography of George McGovern.* New York: Random House, 1977.

McKee, Ann, Robert Cantu, Christopher Nowinkski, E. Tessa Hedley-Whyte, Brandon E. Gavett, Andrew E. Budson, Veronica E. Santini, Hyo-Soon Lee, Caroline A. Kubilus, and Robert A. Stern. "Chronic Traumatic Encephalopathy in Athletes: Progressive Tauopathy Following Repetitive Head Injury." *Journal of Neuropathology and Experimental Neurology* 68 (2009): 709–35.

McMillan, Ian. "Insight into Bedlam: One Hospital's History." *Journal of Psychosocial Nursing and Mental Health Services* 35 (1997): 28–34.

Milgram, Stanley. "Behavioral Study of Obedience." *Journal of Abnormal and Social Psychology* 67 (1963): 371–78.

Miller, J., and W. Schwartz. "Brain Signals Do Not Demonstrate Unconscious Decision Making: An Interpretation Based on Graded Conscious Awareness." *Consciousness and Cognition* 24 (2014): 12–21.

Moes, Elizabeth. "Ted Bundy: A Case of Schizoid Necrophilia." *Melanie Klein & Object Relations* 9 (1991): 54–72.

Morrell, Kit. "Cato and the Courts in 54 B.C." *Classical Quarterly* 64 (2014): 669–81.

Morris, Ian. *Why the West Rules—For Now: The Patterns of History, and What They Reveal about the Future.* New York: Farrar, Straus and Giroux, 2010.

News Media, Public Education and Public Policy Committee. *An Official Division 46 Statement on the WHO Proposal to Include Gaming Related Disorders in ICD-11.* 2018. https://div46amplifier.com/2018/06/21/an-official-division -46-statement-on-the-who-proposal-to-include-gaming-related-disorders-in -icd-11/. Accessed October 5, 2018.

Newton-Fisher, Nicholas E. "Hierarchy and Social Status in Budongo Chimpanzees." *Primates* 45 (2004): 81–87.

Ng, Felicity. "The Interface between Religion and Psychosis." *Australasian Psychiatry* 15 (2007): 62–66.

Nishida, T. "Alpha Status and Agonistic Alliance in Wild Chimpanzees (Pan Troglodytes Schweinfurthii)." *Primates* 24 (1983): 318–36.

Norenzayan, Ara, and Azim F. Shariff. "The Origin and Evolution of Religious Prosociality." *Science* 322 (2008): 58–62.

Norenzayan, Ara, Azim F. Shariff, Will M. Gervais, Aiyana K. Willard, Rita A. McNamara, Edward Slingerland, and Joseph Henrich. "The Cultural Evolution of Prosocial Religions." *Behavioral and Brain Sciences* 39 (December 2014).

O'Farrell, John. *An Utterly Impartial History of Britain.* London: Transworld Publishers, 2007.

O'Neill, Ann. "Boston Marathon Bomber Dzhokhar Tsarnaev Sentenced to Death." CNN, May 15, 2015. www.cnn.com/2015/05/15/us/boston-bomb ing-tsarnaev-sentence/index.html. Accessed December 26, 2018.

Olson, Kyle B. "Aum Shinrikyo: Once and Future Threat?" *Emerging Infectuous Diseases* 4 (1999): 513–16. www.ncbi.nlm.nih.gov/pmc/articles/PMC2627754/ pdf/10458955.pdf Accessed December 24, 2018.

Open Science Collaboration. "Estimating the Reproducibility of Psychological Science." *Science* 349 (2015): 1–8.

Orben, Amy, and Andrew Przybylski. "The Association between Adolescent Well-Being and Digital Technology Use." *Nature: Human Behavior* 3 (2019): 173–82.

Panetta, Grace. "Sen. Dianne Feinstein Denies withholding Christine Blasey Ford's Allegations against Brett Kavanaugh for Political Reasons." *Business Insider*, September 27, 2018. www.businessinsider.com/dianne-feinstein-refutes-accusations-she-withheld-ford-allegations-political-ploy-2018-9. Accessed February 6, 2019.

Pappas, Stephanie. "Bill Cosby Deposition: What Is Somnophilia?" *LiveScience*. www.livescience.com/51562-what-is-somnophilia.html. Accessed February 3, 2019.

Parton, Drew M., and Michael R. Ent. "Vulnerable Narcissism Predicts Greater Spiteful Punishment of a Third-Party Transgressor." *Journal of Research in Personality* 76 (2018): 150–53.

Pearson, Patricia. *When She Was Bad*. New York: Penguin, 1997.

Perry, Gina. *Behind the Shock Machine: The Untold Story of the Notorious Milgram Psychology Experiments*. New York: The New Press, 2012.

Peters, Timothy, and Allan Beveridge. "The Madness of King George III: A Psychiatric Re-Assessment." *History of Psychiatry* 21 (2010): 20–37.

Philo. *On the Embassy to Gaius*. www.earlychristianwritings.com/yonge/book40.html.

Pies, Ronald. "How the *DSM-5* Got Grief, Bereavement Right." PsychCentral. 2013. https://psychcentral.com/blog/how-the-dsm-5-got-grief-bereavement-right/. Accessed October 5, 2018.

Pinker, Steven. *Enlightenment Now: The Case for Reason, Science, Humanism and Progress*. New York: Viking, 2018.

Pinker, Steven. *The Better Angels of Our Nature: Why Violence Has Declined*. New York: Viking, 2011.

Pitts, William L. "Davidians and Branch Davidians." Handbook of Texas Online. Texas State Historical Association. 2010. https://tshaonline.org/handbook/online/articles/ird01. Accessed December 22, 2018.

Pleshakov, Constantine. *Stalin's Folly: The Tragic First Ten Days of WWII on the Eastern Front*. New York: Houghton Mifflin, 2005.

Plutarch. *The Age of Alexander*. New York: Penguin Classics, 2012.

Plutarch. *Lives*. https://oll.libertyfund.org/pages/plutarch-s-parallel-lives.

Pow, Joni Lee, Alan Baumeister, Mike Hawkins, Alex S. Cohen, and James C. Garand. "Deinstitutionalization of American Public Hospitals for the Mentally Ill before and after the Introduction of Antipsychotic Medications." *Harvard Review of Psychiatry* 23 (2015): 176–87.

Prum, Richard. *The Evolution of Beauty: How Darwin's Forgotten Theory of Mate Choice Shapes the Animal World—and Us.* New York: Doubleday, 2017.

Puente, Maria. "Asia Argento Shock: Could #MeToo Be Damaged by Statutory Rape Allegation against Her?" *USA Today*, August 20, 2018. www.usatoday .com/story/life/people/2018/08/20/metoo-damaged-rape-allegation-against -leader-asia-argento/1042473002/. Accessed February 7, 2019.

Quintanilla, Beatriz. "Witchcraft or Mental Illness?" *Psychiatric Times*, June 21, 2010. www.psychiatrictimes.com/schizoaffective/witchcraft-or-mental-illness. Accessed October 14, 2018.

Raevskiy, Alexander E. "Psychological Aspects of the Aum Shinrikyo Affair." *Psychology in Russia: State of the Art* 7 (2014): 34–39.

Reader, Ian. "Scholarship, Aum Shinrikyô, and Academic Integrity." *Nova Religio* 3 (2000): 368–82.

Reavis, Dick. *Ashes of Waco: An Investigation.* Syracuse, NY: Syracuse University Press, 1998.

Reicher, Stephen S., and Alexander Haslam. "Rethinking the Psychology of Tyranny: The BBC Prison Study." *British Journal of Social Psychology* 45 (2006): 1–40.

Rentoumi, Vassiliki, Timothy Peters, Jonathan Conlin, and Peter Garrard. "The Acute Mania of King George III: A Computational Linguistic Analysis." *PLoS ONE* 12 (2017). www.ncbi.nlm.nih.gov/pmc/articles/PMC5362044/. Accessed December 13, 2018.

Rhee, Soo, and Irwin D. Waldman. "Genetic and Environmental Influences on Antisocial Behavior: A Meta-Analysis of Twin and Adoption Studies." *Psychological Bulletin* 128 (2002): 490–529.

Ricciuto, Daniel. "Anton Mesmer and Mesmerization: Past and Present." *Historical Review* 83 (2005): 135–37.

Roback, A. "Graeco-Roman Psychiatry." In *History of Psychology and Psychiatry*, 202–11. Secaucus, NJ: Citadel Press, 1961.

Roberts, Albert, and Linda Kurtz. "Historical Perspectives on the Care and Treatment of the Mentally Ill." *Journal of Sociology and Social Welfare* 14 (1987): 75–94.

Robbins, Brent. *The Medicalized Body and Anesthetic Culture.* New York: Palgrave Macmillan, 2018.

Robinson, Wendy Gale. "Heaven's Gate: The End?" *Journal of Computer-Mediated Communication* 3 (1997). https://academic.oup.com/jcmc/article/ 3/3/JCMC334/4584381. Accessed December 21, 2018.

Rodriguez, S. Fernando, Theodore R. Curry, and Gang Lee. "Gender Differences in Criminal Sentencing: Do Effects Vary across Violent, Property, and Drug Offenses?" *Social Science Quarterly* 87 (2006): 318–39.

Rogers, Guy. *Alexander: The Ambiguity of Greatness*. New York: Random House, 2005.

Rogerson, Barnaby. *The Last Crusaders*. New York: Overlook, 2009.

Rogin, Michael. "Politics, Emotion, and the Wallace Vote." *British Journal of Sociology* 20 (1969): 27–49.

Roselli, C. "Neurobiology of Gender Identity and Sexual Orientation." *Journal of Neuroendocrinology* 30 (2018): 1–8.

Rosenau, William. "Aum Shinrikyo's Biological Weapons Program: Why Did It Fail?" *Studies in Conflict & Terrorism* 24 (2001): 289–301.

Rosenhan, David. "On Being Sane in Insane Places." *Science* 179 (1973): 250–58.

Rothenberg, Albert. "Eating Disorder as a Modern Obsessive-Compulsive Syndrome." *Psychiatry: Interpersonal and Biological Processes* 49 (1986): 45–53.

Rule, Ann. *The Stranger Beside Me*. New York: Pocket Books, 2008.

Ruttenberg, Jim. "A Long-Delayed Reckoning of the Cost of Silence on Abuse." *New York Times*, October 22, 2017. https://www.nytimes.com/2017/10/22/business/media/a-long-delayed-reckoning-of-the-cost-of-silence-on-abuse.html. Accessed February 3, 2019.

Rychlak, Joseph F. "In Search and Proof of Human Beings, Not Machines." *Journal of Personality Assessment* 85 (2005): 239–56.

Shenk, Joshua. "Lincoln's Great Depression." *Atlantic Monthly*, October 2005. www.theatlantic.com/magazine/archive/2005/10/lincoln-apos-s-great-depression/4247/#.

Sherif, Muzafer. "Superordinate Goals in the Reduction of Intergroup Conflict." In *Intergroup Relations: Essential Readings*. Edited by Michael A. Hogg and Dominic Abrams, 64–70. New York: Psychology Press, 2001.

Shimmack, Uli. "Auditing Social Psychology Textbooks: Hitler Had High Self-Esteem." *Replicability Index*. 2018. https://replicationindex.wordpress.com/2018/12/28/socpsytextbookch2self/?fbclid=IwAR3R8FOoFZRggEdaoAWqcI7g73OK6HptlHXIbcGDIArG_xmTTQDagAQrN10. Accessed December 26, 2018.

Shirley, Craig. *Last Act: The Final Years and Emerging Legacy of Ronald Reagan*. Nashville, TN: Nelson Books, 2015.

Sibbett, Ruth A., Tom C. Russ, Alison Pattie, John M. Starr, and Ian J. Deary. "Does Incipient Dementia Explain Normal Cognitive Decline Determinants? Lothian Birth Cohort 1921." *Psychology and Aging* 33 (2018): 674–84.

Sides, John, Chris Tausanovich, and Christopher Warshaw. "On the Representativeness of Primary Electorates." *British Journal of Political Science* (forthcoming).

Simonton, Dean Keith. "Mad King George: The Impact of Personal and Political Stress on Mental and Physical Health." *Journal of Personality* 66 (1998): 443–66.

Snopes.com. "Are Bert and Ernie Gay?" www.snopes.com/fact-check/open
-sesame/. Accessed April 14, 2019.

South, Susan C., Robert F. Krueger, Gun Peggy Knudsen, Eivind Ystrom,
Nikolai Czajkowski, Steven H. Aggen, Michael C. Neale, Nathan A. Gil-
lespie, Kenneth S. Kendler, and Ted Reichborn-Kjennerud. "A Population
Based Twin Study of *DSM–5* Maladaptive Personality Domains." *Personality
Disorders: Theory, Research, and Treatment* 8 (2017): 366–75.

Spillius, Alex. "Ronald Reagan Had Alzheimer's 'While in White House' His
Son Claims." *Telegraph*, January 16, 2011. www.telegraph.co.uk/news/world
news/us-politics/8262924/Ronald-Reagan-had-Alzheimers-while-in-White
-House-his-son-claims.html. Accessed February 25, 2019.

Spitzer, Robert L., and Joseph L. Fleiss. 1974. "A Re-Analysis of the Reliability
of Psychiatric Diagnosis." *British Journal of Psychiatry* 125 (1974): 341–47.

State's Attorney for the Judicial District of Danbury. *Report of the State's Attorney for
the Judicial District of Danbury on the Shootings at Sandy Hook Elementary School
and 36 Yogananda Street, Newtown, Connecticut on December 14, 2012.* Danbury,
CT: Office of the State's Attorney Judicial District of Danbury, 2013.

Staub, Ervin. *The Roots of Evil.* Cambridge: Cambridge University Press, 1992.

Steinert, Christiane, Thomas Munder, Sven Rabung, Jürgen Hoyer, and Falk
Leichsenring. "Psychodynamic Therapy: As Efficacious as Other Empirically
Supported Treatments? A Meta-Analysis Testing Equivalence of Outcomes."
American Journal of Psychiatry 174 (2017): 943–53.

Stride, P., and K. Lopes Floro. "Henry VIII, McLeod Syndrome and Jacquetta's
Curse." *Journal of the Royal College of Physicians, Edinburg* 43 (2013): 353–60.

Suetonius. *The Life of Caligula.* https://facultystaff.richmond.edu/~wstevens/
history331texts/caligula.html.

Suetonius. *The Lives of the Twelve Caesars.* www.perseus.tufts.edu/hopper/text?d
oc=Perseus:text:1999.02.0132.

Sukkar, Isabella, Madeleine Gagan, and Warren Kealy-Bateman. "The 14th
Century Religious Women Margery Kempe and Catherine of Siena Can Still
Teach Us Lessons about Eating Disorders Today." *Journal of Eating Disorders*
5 (July 2017). https://jeatdisord.biomedcentral.com/articles/10.1186/s40337
-017-0151-5. Accessed December 18, 2018.

Sullivan, Andrew. "When Racism Is Fit to Print." *New York Magazine*, August
2018. http://nymag.com/intelligencer/2018/08/sarah-jeong-new-york-times
-anti-white-racism.html. Accessed April 1, 2019.

Sullivan, Lawrence. "No Longer the Messiah: US Federal Law Enforcement
Views of Religion in Connection with the 1993 Siege of Mount Carmel near
Waco, Texas." *Numen* 43 (1996): 213–34.

Swaab, Dick, and E. Fliers. "A Sexually Dimorphic Nucleus in the Human Brain." *Science* 228 (1985): 1112–15.

Swaab, Dick, and Alicia Garcia-Falgueras. "Sexual Differentiation of the Human Brain in Relation to Gender Identity and Sexual Orientation." *Functional Neurology* 24 (2009): 17–28.

Szádeczky-Kardoss, Irma. "The Bloody Countess: An Examination of the Life and Trial of Erzsébet Báthory." *Life and Science*, September 2005. https://notesonhungary.wordpress.com/2014/05/31/the-bloody-countess/. Accessed September 25, 2018.

Szasz, Thomas S. "The Myth of Mental Illness." *American Psychologist* 15 (1960): 113–18.

Tattersall, Ian. "Once We Were Not Alone." *Scientific American*, January 2000. www.ucd.ie/artspgs/langevo/earlyhominids.pdf. Accessed December 15, 2018.

Taylor, Nicholas H. "Popular Opposition to Caligula in Jewish Palestine." *Journal for the Study of Judaism* 32 (2001): 54–70.

Terrizzi, John A. "Is Religion an Evolutionarily Evoked Disease-Avoidance Strategy?" *Religion, Brain & Behavior* 7 (2017): 328–30.

Thornhill, Randy, and Craig T. Palmer. *A Natural History of Rape: Biological Bases of Sexual Coercion.* Cambridge, MA: MIT Press, 2000.

Thucydides. *The Complete Writings of Thucydides.* Translated by R. Crawley. New York: Random House, 1934.

Toppo, Greg. "Time to Dismiss the Stanford Prison Experiment?" *Inside Higher Ed*, June 20, 2018. www.insidehighered.com/news/2018/06/20/new-stanford-prison-experiment-revelations-question-findings. Accessed October 15, 2018.

Trump, Donald J., and Tony Schwartz. *The Art of the Deal.* New York: Random House, 1987.

Tuchman, Barbara. *The Guns of August.* New York: Random House, 1994.

———. *March of Folly.* New York: Random House, 1985.

Uche, Chibiuke. "The British Government, Idi Amin and the Expulsion of British Asians from Uganda." *Interventions: International Journal of Postcolonial Studies* 19 (2017): 818–36.

Ullman, Richard. "Human Rights and Economic Power: The United States Versus Idi Amin." *Foreign Affairs*, April 1978. www.foreignaffairs.com/articles/uganda/1978-04-01/human-rights-and-economic-power-united-states-versus-idi-amin. Accessed September 24, 2018.

U.S. Department of Justice. *Report to the Deputy Attorney General on the Events at Waco, Texas.* Washington, DC: US Department of Justice, 1993. www.justice.gov/archives/publications/waco/report-deputy-attorney-general-events-waco-texas. Accessed December 22, 2018.

U.S. Government Accountability Office. *Countering Violent Extremism*. Washington, DC: United States Government Accountability Office, 2017. www.gao.gov/assets/690/683984.pdf. Accessed December 26, 2018.

Valinsky, Jordan. "Laurene Powell Jobs Pushes Back on Her Stepdaughter's Memoir." CNN, August 28, 2018. https://money.cnn.com/2018/08/28/technology/laurene-powell-jobs-statement/index.html. Accessed February 2, 2019.

Vinding, Mikkel C., Mads Jensen, and Morten Overgaard. "Distinct Electrophysiological Potentials for Intention in Action and Prior Intention for Action." *Cortex: A Journal Devoted to the Study of the Nervous System and Behavior* 50 (2014): 86–99.

de Waal, Frans. "Aggression as a Well-Integrated Part of Primate Social Relationships: A Critique of the Seville Statement on Violence." In *Aggression and Peacefulness in Humans and Other Primates*. Edited by James Silverberg and J. Patrick Gray, 37–56. New York: Oxford University Press, 1992.

Wakefield, Edward. "Plan of an Asylum for Lunatics." *The Philanthropist* 2 (1812): 226–29.

Wakefield, Jess. "Wonderful Tonight: How Old Is Eric Clapton, What Happened to His Son, What Are the 'Tears in Heaven' Singer's Biggest Songs and Who Is His Wife?" *Sun* June 30, 2018. www.thesun.co.uk/tvandshowbiz/6657776/eric-clapton-son-hit-songs-wife/. Accessed October 6, 2018.

Waldman, Katy. "'Small Fry,' Reviewed: Lisa Brennan-Jobs's Mesmerizing, Discomfiting Memoir." *New Yorker*, September 6, 2018. www.newyorker.com/books/page-turner/small-fry-reviewed-lisa-brennan-jobss-mesmerizing-discomfiting-memoir. Accessed February 2, 2019.

Washburn, Anthony N., and Linda J. Skitka. "Science Denial across the Political Divide: Liberals and Conservatives Are Similarly Motivated to Deny Attitude-Inconsistent Science." *Social Psychological and Personality Science* (forthcoming).

Washington Post Staff. "Full Text: Donald Trump Announces a Presidential Bid." June 16, 2015. www.washingtonpost.com/news/post-politics/wp/2015/06/16/full-text-donald-trump-announces-a-presidential-bid/?utm_term=.e8b9aaee886f. Accessed April 1, 2019.

Weinstein, Yana, Marci E. J. Gleason, and Thomas F. Oltmanns. "Borderline but Not Antisocial Personality Disorder Symptoms Are Related to Self-Reported Partner Aggression in Late Middle-Age." *Journal of Abnormal Psychology* 121 (2012): 692–98.

Wetzel, Eunike, Anna Brown, Patrick L. Hill, Joanne M. Chung, Richard W. Robins, and Brent W. Roberts. "The Narcissism Epidemic Is Dead; Long Live the Narcissism Epidemic." *Psychological Science* 28 (2017): 1833–47.

Whitaker, Robert. *Mad in America*. Philadelphia: Basic Books, 2002.

White, Matthew. *Atrocities: The 100 Deadliest Episodes in Human History.* New York: W. W. Norton, 2012.

Wilson, Douglas. *Honor's Voice: The Transformation of Abraham Lincoln.* New York: Vintage, 1999.

Winterling, Aloys. *Caligula: A Biography.* Oakland: University of California Press, 2009.

Wright, Laura. "Syntactic Structure of Witnesses' Narratives from the 16th-Century Court Minute Books of the Royal Hospitals of Bridewell and Bedlam." *Neuphilologische Mitteilungen* 96 (1995): 93–105.

Xenophon. *Hellenica.* www.perseus.tufts.edu/hopper/text?doc=Xen.%20Hell.

Yetzer, Andrea M., Tom Pyszczynski, and Jeff Greenberg. "A Stairway to Heaven: A Terror Management Theory Perspective on Morality." In *Atlas of Moral Psychology.* Edited by Kurt Gray and Jesse Graham, 241–51. New York: Guilford Press, 2018.

Young, Cathy. "Feminists Treat Men Badly. It's Bad for Feminism." *Washington Post*, June 30, 2016. www.washingtonpost.com/posteverything/wp/2016/06/30/feminists-treat-men-badly-its-bad-for-feminism/?utm_term=.4e730c10da1e. Accessed February 3, 2019.

Zimbardo, Philip. *The Lucifer Effect: Understanding How Good People Turn Evil.* New York: Random House, 2007.

INDEX